Wörterbuch der Pädagogik
Englisch / Deutsch

© Wolfgang Dohrmann 2007

6., vollständig überarbeitete und ergänzte Auflage 2007

Redaktionelle Mitarbeit: Ann Robertson B.Sc., Dr. phil.
Umschlaggestaltung: Aischa Dohrmann,
aischad@web.de
Druck: Druckerei Bode GmbH, 04808 Wurzen

dohrmannVerlag.berlin
für europäische und interkulturelle Pädagogik
Ringstr. 78
12205 Berlin
www.dohrmann-verlag.de
Tel: 030 / 833 64 41
Fax: 030 / 80 40 98 90
e-mail: info@dohrmann-verlag.de
ISBN 978-3-9809179-4-0

Holland + Josenhans GmbH & Co.
Postfach 10 23 52
70019 Stuttgart
www.holland-josenhans.de
Tel: 0711 / 614 39 20
Fax: 0711 / 614 39 22
e-mail: verlag@huj.03.net

ISBN 978-3-7782-5848-4

Wolfgang Dohrmann

Wörterbuch der Pädagogik
Teil I: Englisch - Deutsch
Teil II: Deutsch - Englisch

Dictionary of Education
Part I: English – German
Part II: German – English

dohrmannVerlag.berlin
Verlag Holland + Josenhans

Vorwort zur 6. Auflage

Liebe Leserin, lieber Leser!

Die vorliegende 6. Auflage wurde nicht nur wiederum gründlich überarbeitet und aktualisiert, sondern erhielt auch einen Facelift, der gleichzeitig den Beginn einer neuen Epoche für dieses Buch markiert: In den Bereichen Vertrieb und Marketing arbeiten wir mit dem Stuttgarter Schulbuchverlag **Holland + Josenhans** zusammen, einem renommierten Fachbuchverlag, der an den meisten deutschen Berufs- und Berufsfachschulen bekannt ist. Die Redaktion und die inhaltliche Verantwortung verbleiben jedoch beim Autor und beim **dohrmannVerlag**.

Das vorliegende Wörterbuch richtet sich an Studierende der Fachrichtung Sozialpädagogik, an Lehrerinnen und Lehrer sowie an Praktikerinnen und Praktiker, die in einen fachlichen Austausch mit Interessierten aus anderen Ländern treten möchten. Die Benutzung dieses Wörterbuchs setzt Grundkenntnisse im Englischen voraus und ersetzt nicht ein allgemeines Wörterbuch. Es erleichtert jedoch die Suche nach fachsprachlichen Entsprechungen, da aus den zahlreichen Bedeutungen eines Begriffs der jeweils anderen Sprache gezielt solche in dieses Glossar aufgenommen wurden, die in einem pädagogischen Zusammenhang relevant sind. Dazu ein Beispiel, gleich von der ersten Seite „Englisch-Deutsch": Schul- und Großwörterbücher listen für *acceptance* vier bis sechs unterschiedliche Bedeutungen aus ganz unterschiedlichen Fachgebieten auf, darunter „Wirtschaft", „Rechtsprechung" und „Zoologie"; das vorliegende Nachschlagewerk beschränkt sich mit *Billigung, Anerkennung* auf zwei Bedeutungen, die im pädagogischen Kontext relevant sind, und fügt als Beispiel für eine häufige Zusammensetzung *peer acceptance, Anerkennung durch Gleichaltrige* hinzu.
Ein zweiter Schwerpunkt sind Fachbegriffe aus der Pädagogik oder verwandten Disziplinen, die sich nicht in allgemeinen Wörterbüchern finden; ein Beispiel dafür von der ersten Seite „Deutsch-Englisch" ist der *Ablösungsprozess (psych): detachment process*.
Ein dritter Schwerpunkt sind Wendungen, die aufgrund unterschiedlicher sozialer Systeme eigentlich nicht übersetzbar sind. Beispiel: Ein Berufsbild, das der deutschen *Erzieherin* entspricht, gibt es in keinem europäischen Land. Hier ist also eine kurze Erläuterung notwendig. Und zu guter Letzt: Die Sprachentwicklung gerade in der englischen Sprache verläuft so rasant, dass zahlreiche Begriffe aus dem US-Sprachgebrauch wie *to mainstream* oder *motherese* wie auch aus dem Umfeld der britischen *Early Excellence Centres*, wie *story time, key worker, containment scheme*, noch gar nicht in deutschen Wörterbüchern angekommen sind.
Über Kritik und Anregungen freut sich auch weiterhin...

Wolfgang Dohrmann

Abkürzungen

Brit	Englischer Sprachgebrauch bzw. Institution / Einrichtung im Vereinigten Königreich
US	US-amerikanischer Sprachgebrauch bzw. Institution / Einrichtung in den USA
Engl }	
Scot }	Einrichtungen / Institutionen in den jeweiligen Teilen
Wales }	des Vereinigten Königreichs
N.I. }	
Irl.	Institution / Einrichtung in Irland
D	Institution / Einrichtung in Deutschland
v	Verb
adj	Adjektiv
pl	Mehrzahl
Abk	Abkürzung
m	maskulin
f	feminin
n	neutrum
fig	figürlich, im übertragenen Sinne
i.w.S.	im weiteren Sinne
coll	umgangssprachlich
sl	Slang
F	familiärer Sprachgebrauch
rel	religiöser Gebrauch
psych	psychologischer Gebrauch
päd	pädagogischer Gebrauch
soz	soziologischer Gebrauch
jur	juristischer Gebrauch
®	Eigenname
[...]	Aussprachehinweis
>	vgl. auch Eintrag zu folgendem Stichwort
~	ersetzt das ganze Stichwort
|	zusammen mit ~ : das Stichwort wird nur bis hier ersetzt

Anmerkung:
Mit einem Bindestrich verbundene Wörter werden in der alphabetischen Ordnung wie ein Wort behandelt, also *school trip* vor *school-age*.

A

A level (Brit) Abitur, Hochschulreife; **take one's ~s** das Abitur machen (Abkürzung für **Advanced level**; gewöhnlich muss man in mehreren Fächern seine **A levels** machen, um zum Studium zugelassen zu werden, daher meist Plural)

abandon (v) verlassen, im Stich lassen, (Kinder) aussetzen; **~ed child** ausgesetztes Kind

aberrant behaviour abweichendes Verhalten

ability Können, Fähigkeit, Intelligenz, Begabung

ability grouping Leistungsdifferenzierung

able, be ~ to do sth. etwas können

able-bodied people Nicht-Behinderte

abolish (v) abschaffen

abortion Abtreibung, Früh- oder Fehlgeburt; **legal ~** Schwangerschaftsabbruch

abscond (v) durchbrennen, abhauen

absence without leave unerlaubtes Fernbleiben

absentee der/die Abwesende

absent-minded geistesabwesend

abundance Überfluss

abuse (v) missbrauchen; **sexually ~** sexuell missbrauchen

abuse Missbrauch; **alcohol ~** Alkoholmissbrauch

abuse solvents Lösemittel missbrauchen; schnüffeln

abused and abandoned children misshandelte und vernachlässigte *(i.w.S. verlassene)* Kinder

acceleration *(psych)* Akzeleration

academic (adj) akademisch; **~ work** wissenschaftliche, „theoretische" im Gegensatz zu „praktischer Arbeit"

accept somebody for a job/school jmd. eine Einstellungszusage geben/in die Schule aufnehmen

acceptance Billigung, Anerkennung; **peer ~** Anerkennung durch Gleichaltrige

accessible (adj) zugänglich, erreichbar

acculturation Akkulturation, Kulturaneignung, kulturelle Anpassung

ache Schmerz; (v) schmerzen, weh tun

achieve (v) vollbringen, schaffen, leisten, zustande bringen, ausführen

achieved role erworbene Rolle

achievement (große) Leistung, Errungenschaft

achievement oriented leistungsorientiert

achievement test Leistungstest

acquaintance der/die Bekannte; Vertrautheit

acquire (v) (*Wissen etc.*) erwerben; sich erw. aneignen; erreichen

acquired erworben, anerzogen, angewöhnt

acquisition of language Spracherwerb

act out (something) (v) etwas ausleben, ausagieren, nachspielen; ~ **a story** eine Geschichte nachspielen

action committee Bürgerinitiative, Aktionskomitee

action pattern Handlungsmuster

active discovery learning entdeckendes Lernen

activity Aktivität, Beschäftigung

activity and adventure holiday Aktiv-Ferien

adapt (v) sich anpassen, adaptieren, sich an etwas gewöhnen

adaptability Anpassungsfähigkeit; **social** ~ soziales Anpassungsvermögen, Eingewöhnung

adaptation Anpassung; **social** ~ soziale Anpassung

adapted | housing, ~ accommodation (Brit) behindertengerechte Wohnung

adaptive behaviour angepasstes Verhalten

ADD (attention deficit disorder) Aufmerksamkeits-Defizit-Syndrom

addict der/die Süchtige; **be addicted** süchtig sein

ADHD (attention deficit hyperactivity disorder) Aufmerksamkeits-Defizit- und Hyperaktivitäts-Syndrom

adjust (v) angleichen, (sich) anpassen

adjustment Anpassung, Eingewöhnung

administer (v) verwalten

admission test Zugangstest

adolescence Adoleszenz, die Zeit des Erwachsenwerdens,

Jugend

adolescent der/die Heranwachsende

adopt (v) adoptieren, annehmen

adopted child Adoptivkind

adoption agency Adoptionsstelle, -Büro

adoption counselling Adoptionsberatung

adoption procedures and implementation Adoptionsvermittlung

adoptive parents Adoptiveltern

adult der/die Erwachsene

adult (adj) erwachsen, reif

adult education Erwachsenenbildung, Andragogik

adult education centre Volkshochschule

adult styles of engagement; adult engagement styles Arten der Beteiligung von Erwachsenen (*meist* an der Erziehung von Kindern)

adult vocational education berufliche Erwachsenenbildung

adulthood Erwachsenenalter

advance (v) fördern, voranbringen

advanced skills teacher (Brit) Aufstiegsposition für > *classroom teacher* im Elementar- oder Primarbereich

advanced technical college Fachhochschule

advanced training Fortbildung

adventure education Abenteuerpädagogik

adventure playground Abenteuerspielplatz

adventure pursuits Erlebnispädagogik

adventure society Erlebnisgesellschaft

advice Rat (-schlag)

advice and guidance Beratung und Anleitung

advise (v) beraten

adviser, advisor Berater

advisory (adj) beratend

advisory | board, ~ committee Beirat, Gut-achterkommission

advisory body, ~ council Beirat

advocacy *(päd)* Interessenvertretung, Sachwalterschaft, Fürsprache

advocacy group Lobby

affect (v) betreffen, **that does not ~ me** das betrifft mich nicht, geht mich nichts an

affection Liebe, Zuneigung (**for, towards** zu)

affectionate (adj) liebevoll, zärtlich

affective education gefühlsbetonte Erziehung
affective objectives affektive Lernziele
affirmation (positive) Bestätigung
affluence Fülle, Überfluss; **demoralization by ~** Wohlstandsverwahrlosung
affluent (adj) reichlich, wohlhabend; **~ society** Wohlstandsgesellschaft
afford (v) sich etwas leisten, *(Zeit)* erübrigen
afraid Angst haben, **be ~ to do sth.** Angst davor haben, etwas zu tun
after care Nachsorge (z.B. bei Heimerziehung)
afternoon session Nachmittagsbetreuung
after-school | club (ASC), ~ care, ~provision, ~ facilities Nachmittagsbetreuung für Schulkinder; Hort, Kinderhort (D)
age Alter; **the boys' ~s are 2, 4 and 5** die Jungen sind ... Jahre alt; **be six years of ~** sechs Jahre alt sein; **come of ~** volljährig, mündig werden; **under ~** minderjährig; **children ~d between 3 and 5** Kinder im Alter von 3 bis 5 Jahren

age appropriate group altershomogene Gruppe
age band Altersspanne
age bracket Altersgruppe; **the 0 – 3 ~** die Gruppe der 0– bis 3-Jährigen
age distribution Altersgliederung
age limit Altersgrenze
aged (adj) bejahrt, betagt; ...jährig, im Alter von...; **children ~ 2 – 5** Kinder im Alter von 2 – 5 Jahren
age-grade placement altersgemäße Einstufung
age-group Altersgruppe; **traditional ~** altershomogene Gruppe
age-integrated alle Altersstufen umfassend
age-integrated centres altersübergreifende Kitas
agency Geschäftsstelle, Agentur, Träger; *(päd)* Wirkung; **statutory and voluntary agencies** öffentliche und freie Träger
agency responsible for a sector of work Träger
agenda Tagesordnung
age-range Altersspannweite
aggravate (v) verschlechtern, verschlimmern
aggression Aggression, Angriff

aggressive (adj) angriffslustig, aggressiv

aggro (Brit. sl.) Zoff, Krawall; **they are looking for ~** sie suchen Streit

aging Altern, Alterung

agree (v) einverstanden sein

agreement Übereinstimmung, Übereinkunft, Abkommen, Vertrag

aim Ziel

alien Ausländer, Außerirdischer; (adj) fremd, ausländisch

alienate (v) befremden; **feel ~d from society** sich der Gesellschaft entfremdet fühlen; **culturally ~d** soziokulturell benachteiligt

alienated (adj) (gesellschaftlich) unangepasst

alienation Entfremdung

alimony Unterhaltszahlung

all-day school Ganztagsschule

all-through comprehensive school Gesamtschule mit Oberstufe

allocate (v) zuordnen, zuteilen; bewilligen *(z.B. Finanzmittel)*

allowance Zuteilung, Zuschuss, Beihilfe, Taschengeld

alternative | life style, ~ movements Alternativbewegung

amateur theatre Laientheater

ambiguity Zweideutigkeit, Mehrdeutigkeit, Unklarheit

ambiguity tolerance Ambiguitätstoleranz

ambivalence Ambivalenz, Doppelwertigkeit, Zwiespältigkeit

amenity centre Freizeitzentrum

amnesia Amnesie, Gedächtnisverlust

anal stage anale Phase

ancillary | worker, ~ staff Hilfspersonal

ancillary rooms Nebenräume

anger Zorn, Wut; **filled with ~** wütend sein

Anglican Anglikaner; (adj) anglikanisch **Anglican Church, Church of England (C. of E.)** Staatskirche in England

angry (adj) böse, zornig; **be ~ with / at somebody** mit / auf jemand böse sein, sich über jmd. ärgern

animated (adj) *(Unterhaltung, Gebärde)* lebhaft

annoyed (adj) ärgerlich

antenatal (adj) Schwangerschafts-, Schwangeren-; vorgeburtlich

anthroposophy Anthroposophie

antiauthoritarian playgroup Kinderladen (D)

antiauthoritarian upbringing antiautoritäre Erziehung

anti-bias education Erziehung gegen Vorurteile und Rassismus; vorurteilsbewusste Erziehung

anti-illiteracy programme Alphabetisierung

antic Mätzchen, Possen

anxiety Angst, Sorge; **stranger ~** Fremdeln, Angst vor Fremden

anxious (adj) besorgt

aphasia Sprachverlust

appalling (adj) entsetzlich, schrecklich

application Bewerbung; Anwendung, Antrag

application form Antragsformular, Antrag, Bewerbungsformular

application-oriented pedagogic research anwendungsorientierte Erziehungsforschung

applied (adj) anwendungsorientiert; **~ social research** angewandte Sozialforschung

appraisal Bewertung, Beurteilung

appreciate (v) würdigen, etw. schätzen

apprehensions Befürchtungen

apprehensive (adj) besorgt, ängstlich; **to be ~ about** vor etwas Angst haben

approach Ansatz, Annäherung, Betrachtungsweise, Versuch, Methode

appropriate (adj) angemessen

appropriate risks angemessene Risiken

approved (adj) anerkannt *(rechtlich, behördlich etc.)*

April Fool Aprilscherz; **to play an ~ on** jemanden in den April schicken

April Fool's Day der erste April

aptitude Neigung, Begabung, Eignung; **linguistic ~** Sprachbegabung; **learning ~** Lernfähigkeit; **social ~** soziale Anpassungsfähigkeit

aptitude test Eignungsprüfung

arbitrate (v) vermitteln, schlichten

area Bereich

area of learning Lernbereich

area youth office Bezirksjugendamt

argue (v) streiten, diskutieren
argument Begründung; *auch*: Auseinandersetzung
arithmetic Rechnen; **mental ~** Kopfrechnen
art education Kunsterziehung
artefacts Gegenstände, Objekte (die in irgendeiner Weise bearbeitet sind)
articulated services verbundene Angebote, Dienste
arts and humanities Kunst und geisteswissenschaftliche Fächer in Oberschule und Universität
arts teacher Kunsterzieher(in), Kunstlehrer(in)
aspiration Bestreben, Ambition; **educational ~s** Bildungsansprüche
assembly Versammlung, Morgenandacht *(z.B. in der Schule in GB)*; **~ is taken by a member of staff** die Morgenandacht wird von einem Lehrer / einer Lehrerin gehalten
assertion Behauptung; **self ~** Selbstbewusstsein, Geltendmachen seiner Rechte, Durchsetzungsvermögen
assertive (adj) zur Geltung kommend, positiv
assertiveness Selbstbewusstsein, Selbstachtung
assessment Leistungsbeurteilung, Einschätzung
assignment *(päd)* Aufgabe, Arbeit
assignment plan Arbeitsplan
assimilate (v) angleichen
assimilatory schemata *(psych)* Assimilationsschemata
assistant teacher (*eigentlich: foreign language assistant*) muttersprachlicher Lehrer im Fremdsprachenunterricht (mst. in Ausbildung)
assisted living betreutes Wohnen
assisted-living community Gemeinschaft von Menschen, die betreut wohnen
assume (v) annehmen, voraussetzen, unterstellen; **~ a role** eine Rolle übernehmen
Asylo Gutschein für Asylbewerber zum Einkauf von Nahrungsmitteln
asylum Asyl; **political ~** politisches Asyl; **apply for ~** Asyl beantragen
asylum seeker Asylbewerber
attachment *(päd)* Bindung, Zugehörigkeit; **the concept of ~** der Bindungsbegriff, der Begriff der Zugehörigkeit

attachment person Bezugsperson

attainment Erreichung, Leistung

attend (v) anwesend sein, teilnehmen an, begleiten, besuchen

attendance Anwesenheit; (Brit) *(jur)* Freizeitarrest; **regular ~ at school** regelmäßiger Schulbesuch

attendance centre (Brit) Jugendarrestanstalt *(in der Freizeitarrest verbüßt wird)*

attendant Begleiter(in), Aufseher(in)

attention Aufmerksamkeit, Beachtung; **pay ~ to** Beachtung schenken

attention deficient hyper-activity disorder, attention deficit disorder Aufmerksamkeitsdefizitsyndrom (ADS)

attention span Konzentrationsvermögen

attentive (adj) aufmerksam

attentiveness Aufmerksamkeit

attitude Einstellung, Haltung; **parental ~** elterliche Einstellung

audacity Kühnheit, Waghalsigkeit

audible (adj) hörbar, vernehmlich

auditory (adj) das Gehör betreffend

authoritarian leadership autoritärer Erziehungsstil

authorities *(mst. pl)* Behörde(n), Obrigkeit

authority Amt, Behörde, z.B. **local education ~ (LEA)** (Brit) örtliches Schul-/ Bildungsamt, Amt für Volksbildung

authority guardianship Amtspflegschaft, Amtsvormundschaft

authorization Genehmigung, Erlaubnis, Bevollmächtigung

autism Autismus

autonomy Autonomie, Selbstständigkeit

auxiliary Hilfs-, Zusatz-, (in Zusammensetzungen); **~ worker** Zusatzkraft (mit verkürzter Ausbildung)

average Durchschnitt, **on ~** im Durchschnitt, durchschnittlich; **above / below ~** über / unter dem Durchschnitt

average family Durchschnittsfamilie

aversion Aversion, Vermeidung, Abneigung

aversive stimulus unange-

nehmer Reiz
avid *(adj)* begeistert, passioniert
avoidance Vermeidung
avoidance behaviour Vermeidungsverhalten
awaken *(meist passiv)* **to be ~ed by** geweckt werden von
award Auszeichnung, Berufsbezeichnung, Titel
aware; **be ~** sich bewusst sein, wissen
awareness Bewusstsein, Kenntnis; **environmental ~** Umweltbewusstsein
awkward *(adj)* ungeschickt, unbeholfen, linkisch, tölpelhaft

B

babble (v) stammeln, plappern, schwatzen
babbling stage Lallstadium *(bei Babys)*
baby Baby, Säugling; **have a ~ / be going to have a ~** ein Kind bekommen
baby (and toddler) nest Tagesbetreuung für 0-3-Jährige *(etwa: Krippe in D.)*
baby blues postnatale Depression
baby bottle Trinkflasche
baby buggy (Brit) Buggy, Sportwagen
baby care Säuglingspflege
baby carriage (US) Kinderwagen
baby talk Babysprache
baby tooth Milchzahn
baby walker Laufstuhl
baby's changing table Wickeltisch
baby's dummy Schnuller
Babygro ® Strampler
babyhood Säuglingsalter
babyish kindisch
baby-minder (Brit) Tagesmutter
babysit (v) babysitten
bachelor erster akademischer Grad, berufsqualifizierend, zumeist nach 3 bis 4 Jahren, z.B. **BA, BEd**
Bachelor of Education (BEd) berufsqualifizierender Abschluss zum **teacher** (*nursery and primary education* bzw. *preschool and primary education*) auf Hochschulniveau nach meist 4-jährigem Studium

back shift Spätschicht, Spätdienst
backward (adj) langsam, schwerfällig, zurückhaltend, *(in der Entwicklung)* zurückgeblieben
bad (adj) ungezogen, böse, **use ~ language** Kraftausdrücke benutzen
bag lady Stadtstreicherin
balance beam Balancierbalken
balanced (adj) ausgewogen, ausgeglichen
ball alley Kugelbahn
ban (v) verbieten, **he was ~ned from playing** er erhielt Spielverbot; **to lift a ban** ein Verbot aufheben
Band-Aid ® (US) Heftpflaster
bank holidays (Brit) gesetzliche Feiertage
baptism Taufe
baptize (v) taufen
bar | graph, ~ chart Säulen-, Stabdiagramm
bare necessities Grundbedürfnisse
baric sense (judging weight) *(Montessori)* barischer Sinn (Beurteilung des Gewichts);
baric sense tablet Gewichtsbrettchen
barrier-free environment Barrieren-freie Umwelt
basal pedagogy basale Pädagogik
bashing körperliche Misshandlung
basic (adj) grundlegend, elementar, Grund...
basic and extension courses Grund- und Leistungskurse
basic assumptions Grundannahmen
basic belief Grundüberzeugung
basic family Kernfamilie
basic idea Grundidee
basic knowledge Grundwissen
basic mistrust Grundmisstrauen
basic necessities Lebensgrundlagen
basic needs Grundbedürfnisse
basic principles Grundprinzipien
basic requirement Grundvoraussetzung
basic skills Grundfähigkeiten, Basisfähigkeiten
basic training Grundausbildung
basic trust Urvertrauen
basics ABC, Basiswissen
batter (v) auf jemanden einschlagen, übel zurichten, misshandeln

battered | baby, ~child, ~wife misshandeltes Kind, (Ehe-)Frau

battered wives' shelter Frauenhaus

becoming (päd) Sich-Entwickeln

BEd > Bachelor of Education

bed-sitter Ein-Zimmer-Wohnung, möbliertes Zimmer

bedtime story Gutenachtgeschichte

bed-wetting Bettnässen

befriender Person des Vertrauens

behaviour Verhalten, Benehmen; **deviant** ~ abweichendes Verhalten; **innate** ~ angeborenes Verhalten; **maladjusted** ~ unangepasstes Verhalten

behaviour observation Verhaltensbeobachtung

behaviour pattern Verhaltensmuster

behavioural | disorder, ~ disturbance Verhaltensstörung

behavioural therapy Verhaltenstherapie

being (päd) So-Sein

being active (päd) Handeln

being in touch with oneself Kontakt zu sich selbst haben, sich selbst spüren

belly Bauch, Magen, Unterleib

belly-ache Bauchweh

belly-button Bauchnabel

belonging (päd) Zugehörigkeit

beneficial to the environment umweltfreundlich

benefit Zuwendung, *(soziale)* Leistung; **family, housing, maternity** ~ Kinder-, Wohn-, Mutterschaftsgeld; **sickness, unemployment** ~ Kranken-, Arbeitslosengeld; **social security** ~ Sozialhilfe; **to be on ~(s)** von Sozialhilfe / staatl. Leistungen leben

better off *(finanziell)* besser gestellt

bias Tendenz, Voreingenommenheit; **anti-bias education** Erziehung gegen Vorurteile und Rassismus; **bias awareness education** vorurteilsbewusste Erziehung

biased (adj) voreingenommen

bib Lätzchen

bilingual (adj) zweisprachig

bilingual education zweisprachige Erziehung

bilingualism Zweisprachigkeit

biodegradable biologisch abbaubar

biographical method biographische Methode
biological paternity leibliche Vaterschaft
birth Geburt; **give ~** entbinden; **give ~ to** gebären, zur Welt bringen; **she gave ~ prematurely** sie hatte eine Frühgeburt; **from** *oder* **since ~** von Geburt an
birth certificate Geburtsurkunde
birth control Geburtenregelung, -beschränkung
birth injury Geburtsschaden
birth mark Muttermal
birth rate Geburtenziffer
bite-size course Schnupperkurs
blackboard Schultafel, Wandtafel
blame (v) verantwortlich machen **(for** für)
blended family Stieffamilie, Patchwork-Familie
blindfolded mit verbundenen Augen
block of flats Wohnblock
blueprint, natural ~ natürlicher Bauplan
board game Brettspiel
board of managers Verwaltungsrat
board of trustees Kuratorium
boarding child Heimkind, Pflegekind
boarding out Fremdunterbringung (von Kindern)
boarding school Internat, Heimschule
bodies responsible for the statutory youth services Träger der öffentlichen Jugendhilfe
bodily functions Körperfunktionen
body Körper; *(soz, jur)* Körperschaft, Gesellschaft
body awareness Körper-bewusstsein
body corporate under public law Körperschaft des öffentlichen Rechts
body responsible for schools Schulträger
bond (v) Bindungen herstellen
bonding Bindung; *(psych)* Bonding, Mutter-Kind-Bindung
bone of contention Zankapfel
bonfire Freudenfeuer; **B~ Night** (Brit) (Abend des) **Guy Fawkes' Day** (5. November)
borderline case *(psych)* Grenzfall, Borderline-Fall
borstal (Brit) *(veraltet)* Jugendstrafanstalt
bottle bank Altglascontainer

bottle brush Flaschenbürste
bottle heater Flaschenwärmer
bottle-fed mit der Flasche gefüttert
bottle-fed child Flaschenkind
bottle-feed (v) mit der Flasche aufziehen, aus der Flasche ernähren
bounce (v) springen, hüpfen; ~ **the ball back** den Ball zurückwerfen
boundaries Grenzen
bowling alley Kugelbahn
Boxing Day (Brit) der zweite Weihnachtstag
brain injury Hirnschädigung
breaking the voice Stimmbruch
breast-fed child Stillkind
breast-feed (v) stillen
breech | birth, ~ delivery Steißgeburt
breech presentation Steißlage
brief description Kurzbeschreibung
bright (adj) hell, glänzend, *fig.* „hell", gescheit, klug; **a ~ child** (überdurchschnittlich) begabtes Kind
brilliant (adj) hochbegabt
bring up (v) aufziehen, erziehen; *auch:* etwas zur Sprache bringen

British Sign Language (BSL) Gebärdensprache für Gehörlose
broaden the mind den Horizont erweitern
broken home zerrüttete, gestörte Familienverhältnisse
broken marriage zerrüttete Ehe
BSL > British Sign Language
BTEC National Diploma (Business and Technology Education Council) (Brit) *etwa*: Fachhochschulreifeprüfung
buggy Kinderwagen
building corner Bauecke
bulimia Bulimie
bully (v) drangsalieren, tyrannisieren, schikanieren, einschüchtern, „mobben"
burdens of the past Altlasten
buried knowledge verschüttetes Wissen
burn-out Motivationserschöpfung, Ausgebranntsein
burp (F) Rülpser, „Bäuerchen"; (v) aufstoßen, „ein Bäuerchen machen"
butt (F) Po

C

C. of E. > Church of England

c.v. > curriculum vitae

caesarean | delivery, ~ birth Kaiserschnittgeburt; **~ section** Kaiserschnitt

cane (Rohr)Stock; **get the ~** eine Tracht Prügel bekommen, (mit dem Stock) schlagen

capability Fähigkeit

capable (adj) imstande sein, fähig sein

cardboard Pappe, Pappkarton

cardgame Kartenspiel

care Pflege, Betreuung, Fürsorge, Obhut; **early childhood ~** frühkindliche Betreuung / Pflege; **take ~** sich bemühen; in Acht nehmen; **sick people need special ~** kranke Menschen brauchen besondere Fürsorge; **be in ~** in Pflege sein; **take ~ of somebody** auf jmd. aufpassen

care (v) **for somebody** sich um jmd. kümmern; **well ~ed for** gut versorgt

care and control *(jur)* Personensorge

care and custody of a person *(jur)* Personensorge; **person who exercises the right of care and custody** Personensorgeberechtigte/r

care assistant (Brit) Pflegeassistent

career Karriere, Laufbahn

careers guidance counsellor; careers officer Berufsberater(in)

care-giver Betreuer(in), Pflegekraft, *auch:* Bezugsperson

care in the community Betreutes Leben im Wohnumfeld

care-order Sorgerechtsanordnung, Heimeinweisung (Fürsorgeerziehung); gerichtliche Übertragung der Elternrechte auf das Jugendamt (Brit)

care worker (Heim-)Erzieher(in)

carer Betreuer(in)

carry out (v) durchführen

case Fall, Patient

case history Vorgeschichte, Krankengeschichte, Anamnese

case report Fallbericht

case study Fallstudie, Einzel-

fallanalyse
case work Einzelfallhilfe; (auf den Einzelfall bezogene) Sozialarbeit
case worker (Einzelfälle betreuender) Sozialarbeiter
cash benefit Geldleistung
casual labour Gelegenheitsarbeit
catchment area Einzugsgebiet
cater (v) (Bedürfnisse) berücksichtigen; sich um (Speisen und Getränke) kümmern
celebrate (v) feiern, ehren, würdigen; *i.w.S.* respektieren, anerkennen; **to celebrate children** Kinder wertschätzen
celebration Feier
centre for school-age children (Kinder-) Hort (D)
centre of gravity Schwerpunkt
centre-based settings zentrale Einrichtungen mit unterschiedlichen Angeboten
cerebral palsy Cerebralparese, Gehirnlähmung
certificate Zeugnis, Attest, Bescheinigung
certificate of (good) conduct Führungszeugnis
certificate of attendance Teilnahmebescheinigung
certify (v) bescheinigen, bestätigen; **this is to ~ that...** hiermit wird bescheinigt *oder* bestätigt, dass...
chalk and talk Frontal-unterricht
challenge (v) herausfordern, anzweifeln, in Frage stellen, (Aufmerksamkeit) fordern
challenging behaviour herausforderndes, provozierendes Verhalten
change a baby dem Baby neue Windeln anlegen
character Wesensart, Persönlichkeitsmuster
character development Charakterentwicklung
charitable (adj) wohltätig, gemeinnützig, karitativ
charity Nächstenliebe; wohltätige Organisation, gemeinnützige Einrichtung
chart Schaubild, Diagramm, Tabelle; **circular ~** Kreis-, Tortendiagramm
chatter (v) schwatzen
chatterbox Quasselstrippe, Plappermäulchen
cheeky (adj) frech
chew one's finger-nails an den Fingernägeln kauen
chicken pox Windpocken
child Kind (*pl:* **children**);

an only ~ ein Einzelkind; **illegitimate** ~ uneheliches Kind; **young** ~ Kleinkind; **be a good** ~ ! sei artig!

child abuse Kindesmisshandlung

child allowance Kinderfreibetrag

child and adolescent psychotherapy Kinder- und Jugendpsychotherapie

child and youth welfare Jugendhilfe

child benefit (Brit) Kindergeld, Erziehungsgeld, Kinderzulage

child guidance Erziehungsberatung, Jugendpsychiatrie, heilpädagogische Betreuung

child guidance centre Kinderberatungszentrum

child guidance clinic Erziehungsberatungsstelle (mit Therapie)

child initiated vom Kind ausgehend

child labour Kinderarbeit

child maintenance (Brit) private Unterhaltszahlung für Kinder

child molester Kinderschänder

child neglect Kindesvernachlässigung

child prodigy Wunderkind

child protection Schutz des Kindes

child raising allowance Erziehungsgeld

child raising leave Erziehungsurlaub

child rearing *(veraltet)* Kindererziehung

child rearing leave (US) Erziehungsurlaub

child study Verhaltensbeobachtung bei Kindern

child support Unterhalt; Alimente

Child Tax Credit (CTC) (Brit) steuerliche Beihilfe für Familien mit Kindern, wird mit Formular CTC1 beantragt

child welfare Jugendhilfe

child welfare department (US) örtliches *oder* staatliches Jugendamt

child worker Jugendfürsorger(in), Jugendpfleger(in)

child's play *(fig)* ein Kinderspiel

childbearing *(Kind)* gebären

child-bed Kinder-, Wochenbett

childbirth Geburt; ~ **preparation** Geburtsvorbereitung

childcare Kinderbetreuung, Kinderpflege; *social services department:* Kinder-, Jugendfürsorge

childcare allowance staatlicher Zuschuss für die häusliche Kindererziehung

childcare assistant Kinderpflege-Assistent

childcare center (US) Kindertagesstätte, die den Sozialbehörden untersteht, für Kinder von unter einem Jahr bis zum Schulalter

childcare centre Kindertagesstätte

childcare leave Erziehungsurlaub

childcare subsidy öffentliche Finanzierung von Kinderbetreuung und Erziehung

childcare tax credit (Brit) steuerfinanzierter Zuschuss zu den Kinderbetreuungskosten bedürftiger Familien

childcare worker Kinderpfleger(in); Assistenzkraft in der Vorschule neben dem > *classroom teacher*, Erziehungsfachkraft

child-centred kindzentriert

child-centred curriculum von Schülern und Lehrern gemeinsam festgelegter Lehrplan

child-centred education Pädagogik vom Kinde aus; nicht-direktive Erziehung

child-directed educational approach Kind-orientierter pädagogischer Ansatz

childhood Kindheit; **from** *or* **since** ~ schon als Kind; **second** ~ zweite Kindheit *(Senilität)*

childish (adj) kindlich, kindisch

childlore überlieferte Kinderverse, -sprüche

childminder Tagesmutter

childminding Kinderbetreuung; Tagespflege

childproof (adj) kindersicher

Children and Young Persons Act (Brit) Gesetz, den Schutz und die Rechte junger Menschen betreffend

children exemption (US) (Steuer-) Freibetrag für Kinder

children's allowance Kindergeld

children's centre (Brit) Kinder- und Familienzentrum

children's home Kinderheim

children's nurse Kinderpflegerin

children's planning meeting Kinderkonferenz

children's rights movement Bewegung zur Wahrung der Rechte der Kinder

child-teacher ratio Kind-Erzieher-Verhältnis, Gruppenstärke, Erzieherschlüssel

christen (v) taufen

christening Taufe

Christian name Taufname; > first name

Christmas Day erster Weihnachtsfeiertag; **~ Eve** Heiligabend (**Boxing Day** (Brit) Zweiter Weihnachtsfeiertag)

chuffed (adj) (Brit, coll.) hocherfreut

chuffedness stolze Zufriedenheit, das "geschafft!"-Gefühl

Church of England (C.of E.) Englische Staatskirche

Church of Scotland Schottische Kirche

church voluntary community service diakonischer Jugendeinsatz

church-run (adj) kirchlich geführt

circle time Morgenkreis, Kreisgespräch

circular Erlass, Rundschreiben

circular reaction Zirkulärreaktion

Citizens Advice Bureau (CAB) (Brit) Bürgerberatungsstelle

civic centre Behördenzentrum

civic education Staatsbürgerkunde, Gemeinschaftskunde

civil marriage standesamtliche Trauung

civil rights Bürgerrechte

civil servant (Brit) Angestellte/r der Zentralregierung in London; i.w.S. auch: Beamter, Beamtin; Angestellte/r im öffentlichen Dienst

Civil Service öffentlicher Dienst

civil service employee Angestellte/r im öffentlichen Dienst

clapping game Spiel mit Händeklatschen

class size Klassengröße

classes on infant care Säuglingspflegekurse

classroom, inclusive Integrationsklasse, integrative Klasse

classroom teacher qualifizierte(r) Lehrer(in) ohne Beförderungsamt

cleaning rota Putzplan

client Klient

client-centered counselling Gesprächsführung

climbing equipment Klettergestell
climbing frame Klettergerüst
climbing rope Kletterseil
cloakroom Garderobenraum
close down (v) schließen *(abwickeln)*
cloze test *(päd)* Lückentest
clumsy (adj) schwerfällig, unbeholfen, tollpatschig
cluster Anhäufung, Bündel; *(psych)* Gruppe hoch korrelierender (Persönlichkeits-) Merkmale; *(soz)* Klumpen
clutter (v) hastig sprechen, poltern, heraussprudeln, vollstopfen
clutter Unordnung, Wirrwarr
coaching Nachhilfe
code of practice Ausführungsvorschrift, Handbuch
coeducation Koedukation
cognition Erkenntnis, Erkenntnisvermögen, Wahrnehmung
cognitive (adj) kognitiv, Erkenntnis...
cognitive competencies, ~ capacities kognitive Fähigkeiten
cognitive development kognitive Entwicklung
cognitive objectives kognitive Lernziele

cohabitation Zusammenleben, eheähnliche Gemeinschaft
cohabiting couple unverheiratet zusammenlebendes Paar
collaborative task Gemeinschaftsaufgabe
colleague Kollegin / Kollege
collect (v) jemanden abholen (z.B. Kind von der Kita)
college (Brit) College, unabhängiger Teil innerhalb einer Universität; höhere Lehranstalt, Institut, Akademie, Fach(hoch)schule; (US) Hochschule, die BA und MA verleihen kann
go to ~ (US) studieren
college for educators Fachschule / Fachakademie für Sozialpädagogik (D)
college of education Pädagogische Hochschule
college of further education Kolleg, Fortbildungseinrichtung, in der u.a. Berufsschulunterricht stattfindet (>NVQ; >GNVQ; >NNEB)
colour tablets *(Montessori)* Farbenplättchen, Farbtäfelchen
comfort (v) jemanden trösten
commitment Verpflichtung, Bindung

common curriculum Pflicht- und Wahlfächer

common law marriage ehe-ähnliche Gemeinschaft

common sense knowledge Alltagswissen

commonalities Gemeinsamkeiten

communal living Wohngemeinschaft

communal living with social worker support betreute Wohngemeinschaft

community Gemeinwesen, Öffentlichkeit; *(rel)* Gemeinde

community action group Bürgerinitiative

community association Nachbarschaftsverein

community care Nachbarschaftshilfe; gemeindenahe Betreuung *(d.h. nicht in Heimen, Anstalten)*

community care centre Sozialstation

community centre Gemeindezentrum

community development Gemeinde-, Stadtentwicklung

community education niedrigschwellige Bildungsangebote für Erwachsene (schulisch, beruflich); (Scot) Gemeinwesenarbeit

community education services (Scot) regionale Erziehungs- und Bildungsbehörden

community home (Brit) Erziehungsheim

community of learners Gemeinschaft Lernender

community project Beschäftigungsprogramm

community regeneration Stadterneuerung; Verbesserung des Wohnumfeldes

community relations Beziehung zwischen den Bevölkerungsgruppen

community service (Brit) *(freiwilliger oder als Strafe auferlegter)* sozialer Dienst

community work Gemeinwesenarbeit

comparative (adj) vergleichend

compassionate (adj) mitfühlend

compensate for (v) etwas ausgleichen, kompensieren

compensatory education zusätzliche und / oder spezielle Unterrichtsangebote für benachteiligte Kinder, kompensatorische Erziehung

competence model Kompetenzmodell (welches von

den Fähigkeiten statt von den Schwächen/Defiziten des Kindes ausgeht) > *deficit model*

competencies, upgrade ~ Kompetenzen erweitern

complementary (adj) ergänzend; **an establishment ~ to life at home** eine familienergänzende Einrichtung

complexity Komplexität

complex and severe learning difficulty Mehrfachbeeinträchtigung

compliance Einwilligung

compliance with rules Einhalten der Vorschriften, Regeln

comply (v) einwilligen, s. fügen

comply with a law beachten eines Gesetzes

composure Körperhaltung; *auch:* inneres Gleichgewicht

comprehension Verständnis

comprehensive (adj) umfassend

comprehensive school Gesamtschule

comprehensive university Gesamthochschule

compulsion Zwang

compulsive (adj) zwangsmäßig

compulsory education allgemeine Schulpflicht

compulsory non-military national service Zivildienst (D); **person on ~** Zivildienstleistender *("Zivi")* (D)

compulsory school age gesetzliches Einschulungsalter; **to become of ~** das gesetzliche Einschulungsalter erreichen

compulsory subjects Pflichtfächer

computaholic Computerfreak

concept Vorstellung, Idee, Begriff; *auch:* Plan, Entwurf, Konzept; **the ~ of attachment** der Bindungsbegriff; **the ~ of containment** der Begriff des Umschlossenseins, Aufgehobenseins

concept formation Begriffsbildung

conception Plan, Konzeption, Entwurf; *auch:* Empfängnis

concomitant effect Begleiterscheinung, **~ learning** inzidentes Lernen (> incidental learning)

concussion of the brain Gehirnerschütterung

condition Bedingung

conditioned (adj) *(psych)* bedingt, konditioniert

conditioning therapy *(psych)* Verhaltenstherapie
confer (v) ; **to ~ with somebody** sich mit jemandem beraten
confidence Vertrauen, Selbstvertrauen
confident (adj) zuversichtlich, selbstbewusst
confidential (adj) vertraulich
confirm (v) bestätigen
conflict avoidance Konfliktvermeidung
conflict evasion Konfliktvermeidung
connecting (päd) Verbundenheit
connection schema das Verhaltensmuster der „Verbindung"
conscience Gewissen
conscientious objector Wehrdienstverweigerer *(aus Gewissensgründen)* (D)
conscious (adj) bewusst
consciousness Bewusstsein
conscription Einberufung, Wehrpflicht
consent (v) zustimmen; **age of ~** (Ehe-) Mündigkeit
conservation Naturschutz
conservationist Naturschützer
consistency (adj) Beständigkeit

constipation Verstopfung
constraint Zwang
consultant Gutachter, Spezialist
contact list Adressenliste
contact person Ansprechpartner/in
contact time die Zeit, die eine Erzieherin mit dem Kind verbringt
contagious disease ansteckende Krankheit
containment Umschlossensein, Aufgehobensein,
containment scheme das Verhaltensmuster des Umschließens, Einfüllens
contemporaries Gleichaltrige
content analysis Inhaltsangabe
contextual approach Situationsansatz
contiguity Berührung, Nähe, Nachbarschaft
contingency Möglichkeit, Zufall
contraception Empfängnisverhütung
contract of employment Dienstvertrag
contribute (v) beisteuern
contributing (päd) Mitwirkung
contribution Beitrag
Convention on the Rights of

the Child Übereinkommen über die Rechte des Kindes (Vereinte Nationen, 1989)
convey (v) mitteilen, ausdrücken
cooperation Mitarbeit
cooperative (adj) kooperativ, mitarbeitsbereit
cooperative (society) Genossenschaft
core aims and objectives zentrale Zielsetzung
core and radial schema das Verhaltensmuster von „Nabe und Speichen"
core Kern, Herz, Mark; ~ **curriculum** Pflichtfächer; ~ **knowledge** Grundwissen; ~ **principles** Grundprinzipien
corporal punishment körperliche Bestrafung
cot Kinderbett
council Rat, Ratsversammlung; **local** ~ Gemeinderat; **city/town**~ Stadtrat
council estate Wohnviertel mit Sozialwohnungen
council flat Sozialwohnung
council housing (Brit) sozialer Wohnungsbau
council tenant Mieter einer Sozialwohnung
counselling Beratung; **educational** ~ Erziehungsberatung; **group** ~ Gruppenberatung; **individual** ~ Einzelberatung; **parent** ~ Elternberatung; **vocational** ~ Berufsberatung
counselling in child care Mütterberatung
counselling services Beratungsdienste
counselling students in training Praktikantenberatung
counsellor Berater / Beraterin
counting frame Rechenrahmen
country of origin Herkunftsland
course (of instruction) Lehrgang
cover (v) *(fig)* abdecken, behandeln; **the meeting should ~ the following aspects** die folgenden Aspekte sollten in dem Treffen besprochen / behandelt werden
coverage rate Anteil; **what is the ~ for children in day nurseries?** wie hoch ist der Anteil der Kinder in Krippen?; **universal coverage** hundertprozentige Abdeckung
cradle Wiege
craft Fertigkeit, Geschicklichkeit, Kunst
craft classes Werkunterricht

craft shop Werkraum
craft teacher Werklehrer/in
crash (*sl*) schlafen **the boy's welcome to ~ with us any time** der Junge kann jederzeit gerne bei uns schlafen
crawl (v) krabbeln, kriechen, schleichen
crawler Krabbelkind
crayon Buntstift; **wax ~** Wachsmalstift
creative corner Spielecke für künstlerische Aktivitäten
creative development Entwicklung der kreativen Fähigkeiten
creativity Kreativität
crèche Krippe; Gelegenheitsbetreuung, z.B. Kinderbetreuung bei Veranstaltungen sowie für betriebliche Einrichtungen
credit Anerkennung, Ansehen; **to her ~, she is managing to reflect on her work** man muss es ihr anrechnen, dass sie es schafft, über ihre Arbeit nachzudenken
creeping on hands and feet Vierfüßer-Gang
crib Kinderbettchen, Gitterbett
cross-cultural (adj) inter-kulturell
cross-disciplinary learning fachübergreifendes Lernen
cross-section (*repräsentativer*) Querschnitt
crowd Menge
cube Würfel
cuddle (v) schmusen, hätscheln
cuddly toy Kuscheltier
cultural diversity kulturelle Vielfalt
culturally alienated soziokulturell benachteiligt / randständig
current practice die aktuelle Praxis
currently (adj) gegenwärtig, zur Zeit
curriculum Lehrplan
curriculum design Lehrplangestaltung
curriculum vitae (C.V.) Lebenslauf
custodial care Beaufsichtigung und Pflege (des Kindes)
custodial parent sorgeberechtigter Elternteil
custodial rights Sorgerecht; **person having ~** Sorgeberechtigter
custodian (*jur*) Betreuer/in
custody Obhut, Sorgerecht; **joint ~** gemeinsames Sorgerecht; **full ~** alleiniges Sorgerecht; **be in ~ of somebo-**

dy unter jmds. Obhut; **the mother was given (the) ~ of the children** die Mutter erhielt das Sorgerecht für die Kinder; **right of ~** Sorgerecht; **withdrawal of (the right of) ~** Sorgerechtsentzug

cutback Kürzung, Senkung *(von Mitteln, Leistungen)*; **~ in the social welfare system** Sozialabbau

cute (adj) süß, niedlich

cuts Kürzungen *(finanzieller Art)*

cycle Turnus; **on a 3-week ~** im 3-Wochen-Turnus

cycle way Fahrradweg

cylinder inset *(Montessori)* Einsatzzylinder

D

dab *(schema)* Klecks, Tupfer

daft (adj) (F) verrückt, blöd, bekloppt

daily allowance Tagegeld, Pflegesatz

daily rota Tagesplan

day care Tagespflege

day care center (US) > child care center

day care centre (for children and young people) Kindertagesstätte (Kita), Tageseinrichtung für Kinder im Vorschulalter, z.T. auch im Schulalter

day care establishment for children Tageseinrichtung für Kinder

day care institution Tageseinrichtung für Kinder

day care mother Tagesmutter

day nursery Tageseinrichtung für Kinder bis 4 Jahre

day unit Tageseinrichtung

daily schedule Tagesablauf

DDA > Disability Discrimination Act

deaf (adj) gehörlos, taub; **the ~** die Gehörlosen

deaf and dumb (F) taubstumm

deaf person Gehörlose(r)

deafening (adj) ohrenbetäubend

deaf-mute (adj) *(veraltet)* taubstumm

decentration Dezentrierung

defamation Diffamierung

defect *(veraltet)* Mangel, Fehler, Defekt; **speech ~**

Sprachschädigung; **physical** ~ Körperbehinderung

defective child *(veraltet)* geistig (intellektuell) zurückgebliebenes Kind

defence mechanism (psych) Abwehrmechanismus

defensiveness Abwehrhaltung, Überempfindlichkeit (gegenüber Kritik)

defiance Trotz

deficiency Unzulänglichkeit

deficit model Defizitmodell in der Erziehungswissenschaft > *competence model*

degree (akad.) Grad

degree course Studiengang an einer Hochschule (der zu einem akad. Abschluss führt)

deinstitutionalization Herausnahme aus institutioneller Unterbringung (Heim, Anstalt)

delicate (adj) zart, fein, empfindlich, schwächlich

delicate child Risikokind

delinquency Kriminalität, Straffälligkeit

delinquent Straftäter

deliver (v) entbinden, zur Welt bringen

delivery room Kreißsaal

delousing Entlausung

demand Bedarf, Nachfrage

denominational school Bekenntnisschule

dentition Zahnung *(bei Kindern)*

Department for Education and Employment (DfEE) (Brit) Ministerium für Bildung und Arbeit, zuständig für einen Teil der vorschulischen Erziehungseinrichtungen

Department for Education and Skills (Brit) Ministerium für Bildung und Ausbildung

Department of Education (Brit) Bildungsministerium in Nordirland

Department of Education (DOE) (US) Erziehungsministerium

Department of Education and Science (DES) (Brit) Ministerium für Erziehung und Wissenschaft

Department of Health and Human Services (DHHS) (US) Ministerium für Gesundheit und Soziales

dependency Abhängigkeit

dependent (adj) abhängig

dependent child abhängiges Kind

deploy (v) (Mitarbeiter) einsetzen, einplanen

deprivation *(Liebes- etc.)* Entzug, Verlust, Entbehrung, Mangel, Deprivation

deprive (v) jemandem etwas vorenthalten, entziehen; (i.w.S.) jemanden berauben

deprived (adj) unterprivilegiert, sozial benachteiligt

deprived child an Liebesentzug, Zuwendungsmangel leidendes Kind

deprived minority entrechtete Minderheit

deprived persons benachteiligte, unterprivilegierte Personen

desire Begehren, Wunsch, Verlangen

desire for education Bildungsdrang

desire to change Leidensdruck

desk officer Sachbearbeiter(in)

destitute (adj) verwahrlost

destitution Verwahrlosung, äußerste Verarmung

detached youth work mobile Jugendarbeit

detachment process *(psych)* Ablösungsprozess

detain (v) festhalten, in Haft halten

detention (Brit) *(jur)* kurzzeitige Freiheitsstrafe für Jugendliche; Nachsitzen *(in der Schule)*

detention centre (Brit) Jugendstrafanstalt für Kurzzeitstrafen

determination Entschlossenheit

determine (v) entscheiden, feststellen, bestimmen, ermitteln, beschließen

develop (v) (sich) entwickeln, (Muskeln etc.) bilden, (Fähigkeiten) entfalten, (Gedanken, Plan) ausarbeiten

development Entwicklung, Bildung, Wachstum; **mental** ~ geistige Entwicklung

development delay Entwicklungsverzögerung

development plan Entwicklungsplan, Arbeitsplan

developmental age Entwicklungsalter

developmental disorder Entwicklungsstörung

developmental levels Entwicklungsstufen

developmental lines Entwicklungslinien

developmental progress Entwicklungsfortschritt

developmental psychology Entwicklungspsychologie

developmental stage Entwicklungsstufe

developmental tasks Entwicklungsaufgaben

developmentally appropriate entwicklungsmäßig angemessen

deviant behaviour abweichendes Verhalten, Verhaltensauffälligkeit

deviation Devianz

devolution (Brit) Dezentralisierung *(insbesondere Übertragung von Rechten an schottische, walisische, nordirische Behörden)*

diaper (US) Windel; **put on / change a baby's** ~ Baby wickeln / Windeln wechseln

diaper rash Wundsein *(beim Säugling)*

diary Tagebuch, Terminkalender

dice game Würfelspiel

didactic (adj) didaktisch, lehrhaft, belehrend

didactic toys lehrreiches, didaktisches Spielzeug

diet Nahrung, Ernährung; **vegetable** ~ vegetarische Ernährung; **be on a** ~ auf Diät gesetzt sein

dietary requirements Diät-, Essensvorschriften

differently abled people (US) *(politisch korrekt für)* behinderte Menschen

differentiation by ability Leistungsdifferenzierung

dignity Würde

dinner Hauptmahlzeit, *(warmes)* Mittag- oder Abendessen; **after** ~ nach dem Essen

direct teaching Frontalunterricht

disability Beeinträchtigung, Leistungsminderung, Körperbehinderung; Unvermögen; **learning** ~ Lernbehinderung

Disability Discrimination Act (DDA) (Brit) Gesetz zur Gleichstellung von Behinderten

disability rights movement Behindertenrechtsbewegung

disability studies (US) Studien zur Behinderung *(interdisziplinärer Studiengang unter Einschluss der Pädagogik)*

disabled (adj) (körperlich oder geistig) behindert

disabled person Behinderte(r); **integration of** ~s Rehabilitation Behinderter

disablement Behinderung

disadvantage Nachteil, Schaden

disadvantaged (adj) benachteiligt

disadvantaged group benachteiligte Gruppe

discipline Schulung, Erziehung, Disziplin; **well ~d** (wohl)diszipliniert; **badly ~d** undiszipliniert

discretion Umsicht, Besonnenheit; Verfügungsfreiheit; **age** (*od.* **years) of ~** Strafmündigkeit; Gutdünken; **at (your) ~** nach (Ihrem) Belieben

discretionary (adj) nach eigenem Ermessen

discriminate (v) (scharf) unterscheiden; **~ between** unterschiedlich behandeln; **~ against s.o.** j-n benachteiligen oder diskriminieren; **~ in favour of s.o.** j-n begünstigen oder bevorzugen

discrimination unterschiedliche Behandlung, Diskriminierung; **~ against (in favour of) someone** Benachteiligung (Begünstigung) einer Person

discriminatory practice diskriminierende Praxis

disdain Hochmut, Verachtung

disease Krankheit, „Laster"; **contagious ~** ansteckende Krankheit

disinfest (v) von Ungeziefer befreien, entlausen

dismal (adj) bedrückend, trostlos, furchtbar

disorder Störung, Krankheit; **speech ~** Sprachstörung

disparity Ungleichheit

display (v) ausstellen; aushängen

display Auslage, Ausstellung; frei zugängliches Spielzeug / Material im Gruppenraum

disposable nappy Einmalwindel aus Papier

disruptive child schwer erziehbares Kind

disseminate (v) (Ideen) verbreiten

dissemination Verbreitung

distance learning Fernunterricht

distract (v) ablenken

distracted (adj) abgelenkt, zerstreut

distress Schmerz, Kummer, Hilfsbedürftigkeit, akute Not

disturbance Störung

diversity Vielfalt, Heterogenität, Verschiedenheit

divorce (Ehe)Scheidung; **obtain a ~** geschieden werden; **seek a ~** auf Scheidung klagen; (v) scheiden

divorcee Geschiedene(r)

doctor's certificate ärztliches Attest

do-gooder (F) Weltverbesserer; Gutmensch

dole milde Gabe; **be** (*od.* **go**) **on the dole** arbeitslos sein

doll *(Spielzeug-)*Puppe; **~'s house** Puppenstube, -haus; **~'s pram** Puppenwagen; **~'s face** *(fig)* Puppengesicht

doll's corner Puppenecke, Spielecke

dolly *(Kindersprache)* Puppe

domestic (adj) häuslich, Haushalts-, Familien-

domestic | economy, ~ science Hauswirtschaftslehre

domestic affairs häusliche Angelegenheiten (*auch:* innere Angelegenheiten / Innenpolitik)

domestic life Familienleben

domestic play area Wohnbereich, Wohnecke im Gruppenraum

domestic rights Rechte einer Frau als Hausfrau

domestic violence Gewalt in der Familie

dormitory Schlafsaal

dough (play-dough) Teig; Knetmasse

Down's Syndrome Down-Syndrom

draft (v) entwerfen, abfassen eines Entwurfs

draft Entwurf, Konzept, Erstfassung

drama Schauspiel, auch als Unterrichtsfach; **~ group** Laienspielgruppe

draw (v) ziehen, zuziehen; zeichnen, malen; ein Los ziehen, losen; **~ up** einen Plan machen, entwerfen, ausarbeiten

drawing Zeichnung, Skizze; **~ block** Zeichenblock; **~ pin** Reißzwecke

drawstring Kordel an Kleidungsstücken

drill Drill, Exerzieren, strenge Schulung

drive *(psych)* Trieb, Antrieb

drop off (v) *(z.B. Kind in die Kita)* bringen; jemanden absetzen

drop-in centre Jugendcafé, Teestube

drop-in facility offenes Angebot

drop-out Aussteiger(in); **school ~** Schulabbrecher(in)

drug Medikament, Droge

drug abuse Drogenmissbrauch, Arzneimittelmissbrauch

drug addict Drogensüchtige(r)

drug counselling Drogenberatung

drug dependency Drogenabhängigkeit

drug withdrawal Drogenentzug

dry-nurse Säuglingsschwester *(veraltet)*

dual citizenship doppelte Staatsbürgerschaft

duty Pflicht; **~ to give assistance** Fürsorgepflicht; **~ to maintain confidentiality** Schweigepflicht; **~ of supervision (parental)** Aufsichtspflicht (der Eltern)

duty rota Dienstplan

dyad Dyade, Paarverhältnis

dyslexia Legasthenie, Lese-Rechtschreib-Schwäche

E

early bonding Primärbeziehung

early childhood Kleinkindalter

early childhood development frühkindliche Entwicklung

early childhood education Kleinkindpädagogik, frühkindliche Erziehung

early childhood institutions vorschulische Erziehungseinrichtungen

early childhood special education Frühförderung für lernbehinderte Kinder

early childhood worker / educator Erzieher(in) im vorschulischen Bereich

early education childcare worker (Brit) Synonym für > *nursery nurse*

Early Excellence Centre (EEC) (Brit) („Zentrum ausgezeichneter Früherziehung": Seit Anfang der 90er Jahre; geplant sind etwa 300 Einrichtungen in GB) Tageseinrichtungen, die sowohl in der vorschulischen Erziehung wie in der Eltern- und Familienarbeit neue Wege beschreiten; seit 2003 ersetzt durch > *children's centres*

Early Head Start Program (US) Programm zur Unterstützung werdender Mütter und junger Familien aus

einkommensschwachen Schichten *(seit 1994)*
early infancy Säuglingsalter
early shift Frühdienst, Frühschicht
early years education Früherziehung
early years setting Einrichtung der Früherziehung; *i.w.S.* Kinder-Tageseinrichtung
eating disorder Essstörung
ECEC (Early Childhood Education and Care) frühkindliche Erziehung und Betreuung
ecological (adj) ökologisch, Umwelt...
ecologically | harmful umweltfeindlich; ~ **beneficial** umweltfreundlich
ecology Ökologie
ecology-minded (adj) umweltbewusst
eco-sensitive (adj) umweltbewusst
ecosystem Ökosystem
educare Erziehung verbunden mit Pflege
educate (v) erziehen, unterrichten, ausbilden
educated (adj) gebildet
education Erziehung, (Aus-) Bildung, Bildungsstand, Schulwesen, Ausbildungsgang, Pädagogik, Erziehungswissenschaft; **compulsory** ~ allgemeine Schulpflicht; **elementary** ~ Volks-, Grundschulbildung; Volksschulwesen; **general** ~ Allgemeinbildung; **health** ~ Gesundheitserziehung; **preschool** ~ Vorschulerziehung; **primary** ~ Grundschulerziehung; **remedial** ~ Heilerziehung, Heilpädagogik; **secondary** ~ Erziehungsabschnitt für 12 – 17-Jährige; **special** ~ **class** Sonderklasse für (lern)behinderte Schüler(innen), **vocational** ~ Berufsausbildung
education act Schulgesetz
education of leisure Freizeiterziehung, Freizeitpädagogik
education system Bildungswesen
educational (adj) erzieherisch, Erziehungs-, pädagogisch, Unterrichts-
educational adviser *etwa:* Kita-Berater
educational career Bildungsgang
educational counselling Erziehungsberatung

educational counsellor Ausbildungsberater

educational court orders (jur) Erziehungsmaßregeln

educational endeavours pädagogische Bemühungen

educational leave Bildungsurlaub

educational level Bildungsniveau

educational measures Erziehungsmaßnahmen

educational methods Erziehungsmittel

educational misery Bildungsnotstand

educational psychologist Schulpsychologe / Schulpsychologin

educational psychology Schulpsychologie

educational reform movement reformpädagogische Bewegung

educational toys pädagogisch wertvolles Spielzeug

educationist, educationalist Erziehungswissenschaftler, Pädagoge

educationally subnormal child (ESN) lernbehindertes Kind

educative (adj) erzieherisch, Erziehungs-, bildend, Bildungs-

educator Erzieherin, Erzieher; Pädagoge, Erziehungswissenschaftler. Dieser Begriff ist im Englischen zur Bezeichnung von Berufen in der Kinder- und Jugendhilfe noch wenig gebräuchlich, statt dessen gibt es eine Vielzahl von Berufsbezeichnungen für das jeweilige Tätigkeitsfeld entsprechend der unterschiedlichen Ausbildungsgänge.

edutainment bildende Unterhaltung

EEC > Early Excellence Centre

e-generation Internetgeneration, Computergeneration

ego *(psych)* Ich, Ego; Selbstbewusstsein

egoism Egoismus

elderly, the Senioren, ältere Menschen

elementary education Volks- Grundschulbildung; Volksschulwesen

elementary family Kernfamilie

elementary school Grundschule

eligibility test Eignungstest

eligible (adj) berechtigt, geeignet

embedded context Milieu, in

welches jemand eingebettet ist

emotional dependency emotionale Bindung, Abhängigkeit

emotional well-being emotionales Wohlbefinden

emotionally disturbed emotional, psychisch, seelisch gestört

empathy Einfühlungsvermögen, Empathie

employ (v) beschäftigen, einstellen

employee Arbeitnehmer

employer Arbeitgeber

employment | agency, ~ bureau Stellenvermittlung; **~ and training programmes** Beschäftigungs- und Ausbildungsprogramme; **~ service agency** Arbeitsamt

empower (v) stärken, unterstützen

empowerment Stärkung; Unterstützung (bes. sozialer Minderheiten)

empty nest Familie, deren Kinder ausgezogen sind; **~ syndrome** Gefühl der Verlassenheit, wenn die Kinder ausgezogen sind

enable (v) jmd. befähigen, etw. ermöglichen

enabler Pfleger(in), Betreuer(in)

enacted social institution soziale Einrichtung

enactive mode darstellende Methode

enclosed play space eingezäuntes Spielgelände

enclosure *(schema)* Ein-, Umgrenzung, Umhegung

enclosure schema das Verhaltensmuster „einzäunen, umgeben"

encounter Begegnung

encourage (v) ermuntern, unterstützen, fördern

encouraging (adj) ermutigend, vielversprechend

end Resultat, Zweck

engaged (adj) vertieft; **deeply ~** mit voller Aufmerksamkeit bei einer Sache sein

enhance (v) verbessern, unterstützen

enhancing school performance schulische Leistungen verbessern

enjoyment Vergnügen; **~ without restraints** Vergnügen ohne Beschränkungen

enrol (v) sich anmelden, einschreiben

enrolment Anmeldung

enrolment fee Anmeldegebühr

enrolment form Anmeldeformular

ensuring readiness to learn and readiness for school die Bereitschaft zum Lernen sicherstellen und die Schulreife gewährleisten

entitlement Berechtigung

entrance examination Aufnahmeprüfung

entrance qualification for... Eingangsvoraussetzung (z.B. für Schulbesuch, Ausbildung)

entry requirement Zugangsvoraussetzung

entry unemployment Jugendarbeitslosigkeit

envelop (v) einwickeln, verhüllen

envelopment Hülle, Umhüllung

envelopment scheme das Verhaltensmuster der „Umhüllung"

environment Umwelt, Umgebung, Milieu; **warm, supportive** ~ anregende, unterstützende Umgebung

environment laboratory Umweltlabor

environmental awareness Umweltbewusstsein

environmental education Umwelterziehung

environmental factors örtliche, räumliche Gegebenheiten

environmental influences Umwelteinflüsse

environmental pollution Umweltverschmutzung

environmental protection Umweltschutz

environmentalist Umweltschützer

equal opportunities Chancengleichheit

Equal Opportunities Commission (Brit) Amt für Gleichstellung

equal protection clause Gleichheitsgrundsatz

equal rights for women Gleichberechtigung der Frau

equal treatment Gleichbehandlung

equality of rights Gleichberechtigung

equally entitled (adj) gleichberechtigt

equitable (adj) gerecht

escape conditioning negative Verstärkung

ESN > educationally sub-normal child

essential (adj) wesentlich, erforderlich; **~ly** im Wesentlichen, eigentlich, in der

Hauptsache
establish (v) einrichten
establish relationships Beziehungen herstellen
establishment Einrichtung, Anstalt
establishment without fixed membership offene Einrichtung
esteem Wertschätzung, Achtung
ethnic German children Aussiedlerkinder
ethnic joke Witz auf Kosten einer ethnischen Minderheit
ethos Leitgedanke, Philosophie, Ethos
European Baccalaureate Europäisches Abitur
European Union (EU) Europäische Union (EU)
evaluate (v) auswerten, bewerten
evaluation Auswertung, Bewertung; **self-~** Selbstbewertung, Selbsteinschätzung
even-handed (adj) gerecht; **she is ~ with all the children** sie behandelt alle Kinder gleichberechtigt
evening | classes, ~ school Abendschule, Fortbildungskurs; Zweiter Bildungsweg
evidence of having a positive attitude eine positive Einstellung war vorhanden
examination Prüfung, Untersuchung, Examen
examination paper Prüfungsarbeit, -aufgabe
examine (v) prüfen, untersuchen
exceptional child Sonderkind, von der Norm abweichendes Kind
exclude (v) ausgrenzen
exclusion Ausschluss, Ausgrenzung
exempt (v) befreien, ausnehmen
exercise book Schulheft
exercise therapy Bewegungstherapie
expectations of... Erwartungen an...
expenditure cut Ausgabenkürzung
expenses Kosten, Ausgaben
experience (Lebens)Praxis, (praktische) Erfahrung, Fach-, Sachkenntnis; **previous ~** Vorkenntnisse
experienced (adj) erfahren, fachkundig
experiential (adj) empirisch; ~ **knowledge** praktische Erfahrung; *(päd)* ~ **learning** Lernen durch systematische Beobachtung und praktische

Erfahrung; ~ **arena** Erfahrungsfeld
explanation Erklärung
exploratory activities forschendes Handeln
exploratory trip Erkundung (Exkursion)
exposure (Kindes-) Aussetzung; Ausgesetztsein; **to suffer from** ~ an Unterkühlung leiden
expressing (päd) Sich-Ausdrücken
extended family Mehrgenerationen-Familie, Großfamilie
extended hours erweiterte Öffnungszeiten
extended nursery and primary schools erweiterte Einrichtung von Kindergarten und Grundschule (Initiative der brit. Regierung in den 90er Jahren)
extended-age centre altersübergreifende Tageseinrichtung
external observer nicht teilnehmender Beobachter
extrafamilial care außerfamiliäre Kinderbetreuung
extrafamilial influences außerfamiliäre Einflüsse

F

face-to-face contact direkter persönlicher Kontakt
facial expression Gesichtsausdruck, Mimik
facilitate (v) erleichtern
facilitator Vermittler(in), Moderator(in)
facility Einrichtung, Institution
fact of experience Erfahrungstatsache
factual books Sachbücher
facultative subject Wahlfach
faculty Fähigkeit, Vermögen; Gabe, Talent
faculty of hearing Hörvermögen
faculty of speech Sprach-vermögen
fail (v) (*in einer Prüfung*) durchfallen; ~ **in** in (*einem Fach*) durchfallen; jemanden durchfallen lassen
fail ein „nicht bestanden"; **he got a ~ in English** er ist in Englisch durchgefallen
failure Durchfallen (in der Prüfung); Versager, (F) „Niete"
fairy Fee, Elfe

fairy tale Märchen
fairyland Feen-, Märchenland
familiar (adj) vertraut, bekannt, gewohnt; **to be ~** vertraut sein mit
familiarization Eingewöhnung
familiarization visit Besuch zum Kennenlernen
family Familie; Geschlecht; Sippe; Verwandtschaft; **a ~ of four** eine vierköpfige Familie; **start a ~** eine Familie gründen; **to be ~** zur Familie gehören; **to be (like) one of the ~** (praktisch) zur Familie gehören
family advice centre Familienberatungsstelle
family aide Familienhelfer(in)
family allowance (Brit) *(veraltet)* Kindergeld
family benefit Kindergeld
family care familiäre, elterliche Pflege
family centre (Brit) Tageseinrichtung für Kinder und Eltern („Familienzentrum")
family counselling Familienberatung
family credit (Brit) Kindergeld *(bes. zur Unterstützung von finanzschwachen Familien)*
family daycare Tagespflegestelle; Familientagespflege; **~r** Tagesmutter
family doctor Hausarzt / Hausärztin
family dysfunction (psych) Familienstörung
family name Familienname
family oriented policy familienorientierte Politik
family placement Familienunterbringung
Family Planning Association (Brit) Stiftung, die bei Schwangerschaftsproblemen berät und hilft sowie Kliniken betreibt
family reunion Familienzusammenführung
family support measures familienunterstützende Maßnahmen
family ties Familienbindung
family values der Wertbegriff der Familie, die Werte von Ehe und Familie
family worker *(at a nursery)* Erzieher(in), der/die für ein Kind und Eltern zuständig ist
fantasy Vorstellung, Hirngespinst, Einbildung; **a world of ~** eine Traumwelt

far senses Fernsinne
fastening Verschluss *(bei Kleidungsstücken)*
father-absent family vaterlose Familie
fatherhood Vaterschaft
father-in-law Schwiegervater
fatherless (adj) vaterlos
F.E. > further education
fear Furcht, Angst
feature Gesichtszug, Merkmal, Charakteristikum
fee Gebühr, Beitrag; **school ~** Schulgeld
feed (v) Nahrung zuführen, füttern; **(at the breast)** *einen Säugling* stillen
feeding bottle Saugflasche, Milchflasche
feel confident zuversichtlich sein
feeling of inferiority Minderwertigkeitsgefühl; **~ of superiority** Überlegenheitsgefühl
feeling of self-worth Selbstwertgefühl
fee-paying (adj) gebührenpflichtig
feisty lebhaft, quirlig
fellowship Stipendium
felt-tip pen Filzschreiber
female weiblich; **a ~ student** eine Studentin

female education Frauenbildung
feral child in Tiergesellschaft aufgewachsenes, wildes Kind, z.B. Wolfskind
fertility Fruchtbarkeit
fertility clinic Klinik zur Behandlung zeugungsunfähiger Paare
fertility rate Geburtenrate
fetus, foetus Fötus, Leibesfrucht
fidget Unruhe, Zappelei; „Zappelphilipp"; (v) herumzappeln
fidgety nervös, zappelig
field trip Ausflug, Exkursion
field of interest Interessengebiet
fight over fundamental issues Prinzipienstreit
file Akte; Datei; **~ keeping** Aktenführung
file (v) zu den Akten nehmen
filial (adj) kindisch, Kindes..., Sohnes..., Tochter...
filiation Kindschaftsverhältnis
final examination Abschlussprüfung
final-year class Abschlussklasse
financial approval, e.g. of a grant Bewilligung, z.B. eines Zuschusses

fine Geldstrafe
fine motor development feinmotorische Entwicklung
fine motor (muscle) skills Feinmotorik
finger Finger; **first, second, third ~** Zeige-, Mittel-, Ringfinger **fourth** *(od.* **little)** kleiner Finger; **keep one's fingers crossed for s.o.** j-m den Daumen drücken; **five ~ exercise** *(fig)* Kinderspiel
finger spelling Fingerzeichensprache, Gehörlosensprache, Gebärdensprache
fingerpaint Fingerfarbe; (v) mit Fingerfarbe malen
fingertip Fingerspitze
fire drill Feuerschutzübung
first contact Anlaufstelle
first language acquisition Erstspracherwerb
first language Muttersprache
first name Vorname
first school Grundschule
fit of rage Rappel, Wutanfall
flat rate Pauschale, festgesetzter Beitrag
flatmate Mitbewohner
flogging Tracht Prügel, Prügelstrafe
flooding Reizüberflutung
floor exercises Bodenturnen

flow of information Informationsfluss
fluent (adj) flüssig, geläufig
focused intervention zielgerichtete Intervention, Unterstützung
foetus > fetus
folktale Volksmärchen
folkways Brauch, Brauchtum
follow rota den Dienstplan befolgen; *(vom Dienstplan vorgesehene)* Routine-Tätigkeiten durchführen
follow-my-leader Kinderspiel, bei dem jede Aktion des Anführers nachgemacht werden muss
follow-up control Erfolgskontrolle
follow-up study Anschlussstudie
forceps delivery Zangengeburt
foreign born im Ausland geboren
foreign language acquisition Fremdsprachenerwerb
foreign worker ausländische(r) Arbeitnehmer(in)
foreigner Ausländer
form (Schul)Klasse
form teacher Klassenlehrer
formation Bildung, Entstehung
formative (adj) prägend; ~

years prägende, entscheidende Jahre

formula Milchpulver für Babys; adaptierte Babynahrung

foster (v) *(Kind)* aufziehen, in Pflege haben oder geben; fördern

foster child (parents, father, mother etc.) Pflegekind, - Eltern, - Vater, - Mutter etc.

found (v) gründen *(Vergangenheit: founded)*

foundation Stiftung; **charitable** ~ gemeinnützige Stiftung

foundation stage Elementarbereich, 3 bis 5 Jahre

foundation subject Pflichtfach, - Gegenstand

foundling Findling, Findelkind; ~ **hospital** Findelhaus

fraternal twins zweieiige Zwillinge

free choice activity Freiarbeit

free interchange Durchlässigkeit (fig)

free flow play „free flow play", vertieftes, frei fließendes, selbstvergessenes Spiel

free of charge beitragsfrei

free play Freispiel

free provision of teaching materials Lernmittelfreiheit

free work Freiarbeit

freedom principle das Prinzip Freiheit

freelance (adj) freischaffend, freiberuflich

freelancer Freiberufler; freier Mitarbeiter

frequency Häufigkeit

freshman Student im 1. Semester

Freudian slip Freudsche Fehlleistung

fringe Rand, Randbezirk; **on the ~s of society** am Rand der Gesellschaft; **the ~** die Alternativszene

fringe benefit Zusatzleistung zum Gehalt

fringe group Randgruppe

front office Sekretariat, Empfang

full age, of ~ mündig, volljährig

full sister leibliche Schwester

full-day schooling Ganztags-Schulwesen

full-time (adj) hauptberuflich (tätig), ganztags; **she works ~** sie arbeitet ganztags

full-time care Ganztagsbetreuung

full-time job Ganztagsstellung

full-time training school, full-time vocational school

Berufsfachschule (D)
full-time worker hauptamtliche(r) Mitarbeiter(in)
full-timer ganztägig Beschäftigte(r)
fully-fledged (adj) voll entwickelt
fundamental skills Grundfähigkeiten
funded education (öffentlich) finanzierte Erziehungseinrichtungen
funding Finanzierung
funding arrangements die Art der Finanzierung
funding problems Finanzierungsprobleme
fund-raising Geld-, Mittelbeschaffung, Spenden einsammeln
funnies *(pl)* (F) Comic strips, Witzseite
further education Fortbildung, Weiterbildung, tertiäres Bildungssystem; > **college of** ~
further reading Literaturhinweise
further training Fortbildung, Weiterbildung

G

gaga (adj) *(coll)* plemplem, vertrottelt
game Spiel, Sport; **games** (Brit) (Schul-) Sport; **board** ~ Brettspiel
game of skill Geschicklichkeitsspiel
games teacher (Brit) Sportlehrer/in
GCE > General Certificate of Education
GCSE > General Certificate of Secondary Education
gender soziales Geschlecht; grammatisches Geschlecht, Genus
gender identity Geschlechtsidentität
gender mainstreaming Förderung der Chancengleichheit für Frauen und Männer
gender stereotypes Geschlechtsrollenklischees
gender studies interdisziplinäre Studien zur Gleichstellung von Frauen und Männern in der Gesellschaft
gendering Prozess der Ausbildung einer geschlechtsspezifischen Identität

General Certificate of Education (GCE) (Brit) *(etwa)* Mittlere Reife (D)

General Certificate of Secondary Education (GCSE) (Brit) *früher* **O-level (Ordinary level)**, erste Prüfung, die Schüler im Alter von 16 Jahren in England, Wales und Nordirland ablegen. Sie wird in einem bis (meist) sieben oder acht Fächern abgelegt. In Schottland > Standard Grade (Scottish Certificate of Education)

general education Allgemeinbildung

general knowledge Allgemeinwissen

General National Vocational Qualification (Brit) Schulische Kurse und Abschlussprüfungen in berufsorientierten Fächern, wird an Fachschulen und Schulen erworben

general practitioner (GP) (Brit) Arzt / Ärztin für Allgemeinmedizin, praktischer Arzt / Ärztin; Hausarzt / Hausärztin

generation gap Generationsunterschied, Generationenkonflikt

generational cycle Generationszyklus

genetic heredity Anlage

genital stage genitale Phase

German measles Röteln

gestures Gesten, Handbewegungen

gift Geschenk, Begabung

gifted child (hoch)begabtes Kind

gifts and occupations *(päd)* *(Fröbel)* Spielgaben

give birth (v) gebären

GNVQ > General National Vocational Qualification

going through *(schema, päd.)* Hindurchgehen, Durchschreiten

good practice hohe Qualität

gooey (adj) klebrig, pampig

GP > general practitioner

grade (Schul-)Klasse; **skipping** ~ Klasse(n) überspringen

grade (v) **to ~ sb./sth.** jdn./ etwas benoten

grade school (US) Grundschule

grading system Notensystem (Brit); Noten (**marks**) reichen von A (sehr gut) bis G

graduate Hochschulabsolvent(in), Inhaber(in) eines akad. Grades; **high-school** ~ (US) Schulabsolvent(in),

Abiturient(in); (adj) (US) staatlich geprüft, Diplom..., z.B. ~ **nurse** staatl. gepr. Krankenschwester

graduate school Studienangebote für Graduierte, i.w.S. die höheren Fachsemester

grammar school (Brit) Gymnasium; (US) Grundschule

grannie, granny (F) Oma

grant Stipendium, (Ausbildungs-) Beihilfe, Zuschuss; **education** ~ Ausbildungsförderung; **recipient of a** ~ Zuwendungsempfänger

grant (v) bewilligen

grant custody of a child ein Kind zusprechen (bei der Scheidung)

grant-aid Förderung; **application for** ~ Förderungsantrag

grasp (v) greifen

grasp(ing) reflex Greifreflex *(bei Babys)*

grassroots Basis

great-grandchild Urenkel(in)

great-grandmother Urgroßmutter

great-great-grandfather Ururgroßvater

grid *(schema)* Gitter, Raster

gross motor development grobmotorische Entwicklung

grounded, to be ~ Stubenarrest haben

grounding Basis-, Grundlagenwissen; **give someone a thorough** ~ **in language and number work** jemandem eine gute Grundlage im sprachlichen Bereich und im Rechnen geben

group circle time Gruppenkreis

group counselling Gruppenberatung

group dynamics Gruppendynamik

group escort Gruppenbetreuer(in)

group interaction Gruppenverhalten

group leader Gruppenerzieher(in)

group pedagogics Gruppenpädagogik

group size Gruppengröße

group work Gruppenarbeit

grouped according to age altergemäße Eingruppierung

grow (v) wachsen; **haven't you grown!** bist du aber gewachsen!

grow apart (v) sich auseinander leben

grow into (v); **to** ~ **sth.** sich in etwas eingewöhnen

grow out (v); **to ~ of sth.** aus etwas hinauswachsen, für etwas schon zu alt sein; **our daughter's ~n out of dolls** unsere Tochter ist aus dem Puppenalter heraus

grow together (v) zusammenwachsen, gemeinsam (auf-) wachsen

grow up (v) erwachsen werden; **to ~ on sth.** mit etwas aufwachsen

growing pains Wachstumsschmerzen

grown (adj) erwachsen, ausgewachsen

grown-up Erwachsener; (adj) erwachsen

growth spurt Wachstumsschub

guardian Vormund; **local authority ~** Amtsvormund

guardianship Vormundschaft, Pflegschaft

guardianship court Vormundschaftsgericht

guidance Führung, (An-) Leitung, Hilfestellung, Richtlinie; **child ~ (clinic)** Erziehungsberatung, Jugendpsychiatrie, heilpädagogische Betreuung

guidance counselor Psychologe zur Beratung Jugendlicher

guidance instructor Anleiter(in) während der praktischen Ausbildung

guidelines Richtlinien

guilt Schuld

gym *Abk. f.* **gymnasium** Turnhalle

gym-shoes Turnschuhe

H

half sister Halbschwester

half time halbe Arbeitszeit; (adj) Halbtags...

half-term (Brit) kurze Schulferien in der Mitte eines Trimesters (**term**)

half-wit *(coll)* Trottel, Depp

hall Aula

hall of residence Studentenheim

Hallowe'en Abend vor Allerheiligen

hammock Hängematte

handicap Behinderung *(heute oft abwertend benutzt)*; Nachteil; **mental / physical ~** geistige / körperliche Behinderung; **learning ~** Lern-

behinderung; **the ~ped** die Behinderten
handicapped (adj) behindert
handicapped children behinderte Kinder
handicapped people Behinderte
handicraft Handarbeit, handwerklich
handicraft class Bastelkurs
handicrafts table Basteltisch
handout Arbeitsbogen, Infomaterial
hands on (to do sth. ~) (zum) Anfassen, Anpacken, „Vormachen"
hands on approach interventionistischer Ansatz; Handlungsorientierung
hands on experience praktische Erfahrung
haven *(fig)* (sicherer) Hafen, Zufluchtsort, Asyl
H.E. > Higher Education
head Leiter(in)
head lice Kopfläuse
head of department Fachbereichsleiter(in)
head of school Schulleiter(in)
Head Start (US) > Early Head Start Program
headmaster *(veraltet)* Schulleiter
headmistress *(veraltet)* Schulleiterin

headteacher Leiter(in) einer Schule oder eines Kindergartens
health authority Gesundheitsamt
health care Gesundheitsfürsorge
health certificate ärztliches Attest, Gesundheitszeugnis
health education Gesundheitserziehung, -Aufklärung, -Lehre
health guidance Gesundheitsberatung
health insurance Krankenversicherung; **~ company** Krankenkasse
Health Service (Brit) staatlicher Gesundheitsdienst
health visitor Krankenpfleger(in) oder Krankenschwester an einer Sozialstation; Mitarbeiter(in) des Gesundheitsamtes
hearing Gehör; **to be hard of** ~ schwerhörig sein
hearing aid Hörgerät
hearing defect Hörbehinderung
hearing impaired hörgeschädigt
hearing impairment Hörschädigung
hearing loss Hörverlust

heaven Himmel(reich), Paradies

helper syndrome Helfersyndrom

helpline Notruf, telefonischer Beratungsdienst

hereditary (adj) erblich, angeboren

heuristic play materials Tastmaterialien; Spielmaterialien, die das Forschen und Suchen anregen

hidden curriculum heimlicher Lehrplan

hide-and-seek Versteckspiel; **to play** ~ Verstecken spielen

hideaway Versteck, Zuflucht

hiding place Versteck

high school (US) Highschool, Oberschule, Sekundarstufe

highchair Hochstühlchen für Kinder

higher education Hochschulausbildung

Higher National Certificate (HNC) (Brit) Fachhochschulzertifikat

Higher National Diploma (HND) (Brit) Fachhochschuldiplom

Highers, Higher Grade *(scot)* schottische Hochschulreife; **to take one's Highers** (Scot) sein Abitur machen

highly gifted hochbegabt

high-risk group Risikogruppe

high-risk pregnancy Risikoschwangerschaft

hold on festhalten

holding Halt geben; **the concept of** ~ der Begriff des Halt-Gebens

holiday schemes for children and young people Kinder- und Jugenderholung

holiday(s) (Brit) Urlaub, Ferien, Feiertag; **school** ~s Schulferien; **to spend one's** ~s **in** seine Ferien in ... verbringen

holistic (adj) ganzheitlich

holistic approach ganzheitlicher Ansatz

holistic learning ganzheitliches Lernen

holistic pedagogics ganzheitliche Pädagogik

home Zuhause, Heim; **to leave** ~ ausziehen; **to set up** ~ sich eine Wohnung einrichten; **come from a broken** ~ aus einem kaputten Zuhause kommen; **old people's** ~ Altenheim; **parental** ~ Elternhaus

home birth Hausgeburt

home corner Spielecke (im Gruppenraum)

home economics Hauswirtschaftslehre

home for the elderly Altenpflegeheim

home help Hauspfleger(in)

home help service (Brit) Hauspflegedienst für Behinderte

home language zu Hause gesprochene Sprache

home play area Wohnbereich, Wohnecke im Gruppenraum

homeless (adj) obdachlos; **the ~** (pl) die Obdachlosen; **~ness** Obdachlosigkeit

homemaker Hausfrau, Hausmütterchen

homework Hausaufgaben

horseplay (v) toben, Unfug anstellen

hospice Hospiz

hospital Krankenhaus; **children's ~** Kinderkrankenhaus; **maternity ~** Geburtsklinik

hospitalism Hospitalismus

hospitality Gastfreundschaft

hospitalization Krankenhauseinweisung, -Aufenthalt

host Gastgeber(in)

host family Gastfamilie

hostile (adj) feindselig, abgeneigt, ungünstig

hourly paid | employee, ~ job Angestellte(r) oder Job auf Stundenlohnbasis

house Haus, Klassengruppe; *(Zusammenfassung von Klassen in britischen Schulen, abgeleitet von den verschiedenen „Wohnhäusern" in Internaten)*; **keep ~** den Haushalt führen; **set up ~** einen eigenen Hausstand gründen; **to move ~** umziehen

house for battered women Frauenhaus

house group Abteilung, Wohneinheit in britischen Internaten

house husband Hausmann

housing allowance Mietbeihilfe

housing benefit (Brit) Wohngeld

housing estate Wohnsiedlung

housing project Sozialwohnungen

hug, to ~ somebody (v) jemanden umarmen

human, human being Mensch

human dignity Menschenwürde

humanities, the *(pl)* Geisteswissenschaften

humiliate (v) jemanden erniedrigen, demütigen

humiliated (adj) gedemütigt
hyperactive (adj) hyperaktiv
hypersensitive (adj) überempfindlich

I

ice skate Schlittschuh
iconic mode abbildende Methode
id *(psych)* Es
ID bracelet *(bei Babys:)* Namensband
identical twins eineiige Zwillinge
identificatory learning Imitationslernen
identity Identität, Übereinstimmung; **~ of interest** Interessengleichheit
IEP > Individual Education Plan
ill (adj) krank; **to be ~ with a cold** eine Erkältung haben; **to fall ~** krank werden
illegitimate child nicht ehelich geborenes Kind

illiteracy Analphabetentum
illiterate Analphabet; (adj) des Lesens und Schreibens nicht kundig; *i.w.S.* ungebildet
illness Krankheit
image Abbild, genaues Ebenbild, Leitbild; **spitting ~** das exakte Ebenbild; **she's the spitting image of her mother** sie ist ihrer Mutter wie aus dem Gesicht geschnitten
imagination Vorstellungskraft, Fantasie, Einbildungskraft
imaginative play area Spielgebiet für Rollenspiele innerhalb eines Gruppenraums
imagine (v) sich etwas vorstellen
imagining Fantasieren
imitative learning Imitationslernen
immature (adj) unreif, kindisch
immersion Eintauchen; *(päd)* Zweitspracherwerb, in dem ausschließlich die Zielsprache verwendet wird
immigrant family Einwandererfamilie
immigration laws Einwanderungsgesetze
impaired (adj) beeinträchtigt

impaired | hearing, ~ vision Hör-, Sehbehinderung

impairment Schädigung, Behinderung; **hearing ~** Hörschaden; **dual sensory ~** Schädigung des Sehens und Hörens; **motor ~** Schädigung der Motorik

impartial (adj) unparteiisch

impediment Behinderung; **speech ~** Sprachfehler

implement (v) etwas in die Tat umsetzen; realisieren

implementation Anwendung, Umsetzung (in die Praxis)

implicate (v) folgern

implicit understanding stillschweigende Übereinkunft

impoverishment Verarmung, Verelendung

imprinting Prägung

impromptu (adj) spontan

improve (v) verbessern

improvised game Stegreifspiel

improvement Verbesserung, Fortschritt

inability Unfähigkeit

inadequate (adj) nicht ausreichend, unangemessen

inalienable rights unveräußerliche Rechte

inborn (adj) angeboren

incidental learning beiläufiges, unbeabsichtigtes Lernen

include (v) integrieren

inclusion Inklusion - gemeinsame Erziehung von Behinderten und Nicht-Behinderten

inclusion coordinator Inklusionsberater

inclusion in preschool vorschulische Inklusion

inclusive (adj) inklusiv

inclusive classroom setting inklusiver Klassenverband

inclusive education inklusiver Unterricht

inclusive nursery Inklusionskindergarten

inclusive teacher Inklusionslehrer(in)

income Einkommen, Verdienst; **people on low ~s** Menschen mit niedrigem Einkommen

income support Sozialhilfe, Hilfe zum Lebensunterhalt

incompatible (adj) unvereinbar

inconsistency Unstimmigkeit, Widersprüchlichkeit

inconsistent (adj) inkonsequent, widersprüchlich

increase Zunahme, Wachstum

incubator Brutkasten *(für Babys)*

incurable (adj) unheilbar

indecent assault sexueller Übergriff

indecent exposure exhibitionistische Handlungen

independent living selbstbestimmtes Leben

independent school (Brit) Schule in freier Trägerschaft, z.B. konfessionelle Schule, die Schulgeld verlangt; > maintained school

independent sector (Brit) der Bereich der privaten oder freien Schulen; > maintained sector

index finger Zeigefinger

indifferent (adj) gleichgültig

individual counselling Einzelberatung

Individual Education Plan (IEP) persönlicher Bildungsplan, individueller Entwicklungsplan

individualisation Individualisierung

individuation Vereinzelung

indoor (adj) Innen...; **to do ~ activities with the children** mit den Kindern im Haus spielen

indoor pool Hallenschwimmbad

indoor sport Hallensport

induce (v) verursachen, herbeiführen

induce labour die Wehen einleiten

induction conference Einführungsveranstaltung

induction course Einführungskurs

induction period Einführungsphase

induction report Einführungsbericht

ineducable schwer erziehbar, lernbehindert

inequality Ungleichheit; **social ~** soziale Ungleichheit

inequity Ungerechtigkeit

inertia Trägheit

infancy früheste Kindheit; **in ~** im Kleinkindalter

infant Säugling; Kleinkind; Kind im Kindergartenalter; **newborn ~** Neugeborenes

infant and nursery school Grundschule mit Kindergarten

infant care Säuglingspflege

infant class erste Grundschulklasse

infant mortality Säuglingssterblichkeit

infant pedagogics Kleinstkindpädagogik

infant prodigy Wunderkind

infant school (GB) erste Jahre der Grundschule (4–11 Jahre)

infant teacher Grundschullehrer(in)
infantile paralysis Kinderlähmung
inferiority complex Minderwertigkeitskomplex
infertility Unfruchtbarkeit; **male** ~ Zeugungsunfähigkeit
infertility clinic Klinik zur Behandlung zeugungsunfähiger Paare
infirmary Krankenstation, Schulklinik
inflammation Entzündung
influence Einfluss
in-group Insidergruppe, angesagte Clique, Eigengruppe
inhibit (v) hemmen, jemanden hindern
inhibited (adj) gehemmt, verklemmt
inhibition Verbot, Hemmung
in-home childcare service häuslicher Kinderbetreuungsdienst
in-house training hausinterne Fortbildung
initial | phase; ~ **stage** Anfangs-/ Einführungsphase
initial reading scheme Erstleselehrgang
initial training Erstausbildung

initial vocational training *(berufliche)* Erstausbildung
injury Verletzung, Schaden; **birth** ~ Geburtsschaden; **brain** ~ Hirnschädigung
in-laws „angeheiratete Verwandtschaft", Schwiegereltern, Schwiegerkinder und Schwager
innate (adj) angeboren, von Natur aus
innate behaviour angeborenes Verhalten
inner peace innere Ruhe
inoculation Schutzimpfung
in-patient Patient in stationärer, klinischer Behandlung
insane (adj) geisteskrank
insatiable curiosity unstillbare Neugier
in-service training berufsbegleitende Weiterbildung
inset *(Montessori)* Einsatzfigur
inspector of schools, school inspector (Brit) Schulrat
institution Einrichtung, Institution, Heim, Anstalt
institutional care Anstaltsfürsorge
institutionalize (v) in ein Heim einweisen
institutionalized (adj) unselbstständig; **to be** ~ unter Hospitalismus leiden; durch

Heimaufenthalt unselbstständig sein

instruct (v) belehren, bilden, unterrichten, anweisen

instructor Lehrer(in), Dozent(in), Ausbilder(in); **driving ~** Fahrlehrer(in)

intake Aufnahme, Aufnahmequote, Zulassungszahl; **~ of food** Nahrungsaufnahme; **~ of children** Anzahl der aufgenommenen Kinder

integrated day offener Lerntag (Aufhebung des Stundenplans)

integrated teaching fächerübergreifender Unterricht

integration Eingliederung (von Ausländern, Behinderten)

integration of disabled persons Rehabilitation Behinderter

integrative group Integrationsgruppe für behinderte und nicht behinderte Kinder

integrative teacher Integrationslehrer(in)

intellectual work geistige Arbeit

interaction Wechselwirkung, Interaktion; **non-verbal ~** nonverbale Interaktion

interdenominational (adj) interkonfessionell

interdependence gegenseitige Abhängigkeit, Wechselwirkung, Interdependenz

interdisciplinary co-operation interdisziplinäre Zusammenarbeit

interest area (im Gruppen-, Klassenraum) Spielbereich

interim examination Zwischenprüfung

interim report Zwischenbericht

intermediate school certificate *etwa:* Realschulabschluss

intern (US) Praktikant(in)

internal inhibition innere Hemmung

internalisation Internalisierung

internship (US) Praktikum

interpersonal contact zwischenmenschlicher Kontakt

interplay Wechselspiel, wechselseitige Beziehung

intersections *(schema)* Einmündungen

intervention Eingreifen, Intervention; **focused ~** zielgerichtetes Eingreifen; **subtle ~** vorsichtiges Eingreifen

intolerance of ambiguity Intoleranz gegen Mehrdeutigkeit od. Unterschiedlichkeit

intrinsic (adj) immanent, innewohnend, intrinsisch, von innen kommend; ~ **part** wesentlicher Bestandteil

intrinsic motivation intrinsische Motivation

introductory | meeting; ~ dialogue Einführungstreffen

introspection Selbstbeobachtung

intrusive (adj) aufdringlich

invalid (adj) körperbehindert

invalid chair Rollstuhl

invalidity Ungültigkeit

inventory Fragebogen

investigate (v) untersuchen, erforschen

involuntary (adj) unfreiwillig, erzwungen; unabsichtlich; ~ **movement** unabsichtliche Bewegung

involvement Engagiertheit, Beteiligung, Betroffensein

irritation Ärger, Irritation

islandization (soz) Verinselung

item Gegenstand, Posten, Tagesordnungspunkt

J

jack-in-the-box Schachtelmännchen; **like a ~** wie ein Hampelmann

jackknife Taschenmesser

jack-o'-lantern (US) Kürbislaterne

jack-of-all-trades Alleskönner

jacks (US) Kinderspiel: man wirft einen Ball in die Luft und hebt vor dem Auffangen mit der selben Hand so viele Gegenstände wie möglich hoch

jaundice Gelbsucht

jaw-breaker Zungenbrecher; (US) steinharter Bonbon

jealousy Eifersucht, Neid

jello, Jell-O ® (US) Wackelpudding, Götterspeise

jigsaw Laubsäge

jigsaw puzzle Puzzlespiel

job Arbeit, Stelle;
full-time/part-time ~ volle/halbe Stelle; **steady ~** fester Arbeitsplatz;
to apply for a ~ sich um eine Stelle bewerben; **to get a ~** eine Stelle bekommen; **to give up a ~** eine Stelle

kündigen; **be out of a** ~ arbeitslos sein
job centre Arbeitsamt
job counsellor Arbeitsberater
job creation scheme Arbeitsbeschaffungsmaßnahme
job description Stellenbeschreibung
job release (Brit) vorzeitiger Ruhestand *(zur Schaffung neuer Arbeitsplätze)*
job satisfaction Zufriedenheit mit der Arbeitsstelle
job specification Arbeitsplatzbeschreibung
Job Seekers Allowance (Brit) Arbeitslosenunterstützung
join (v) mitmachen, beitreten; ~ **in** sich beteiligen, mitspielen; **to** ~ **in the game** sich am Spiel beteiligen
joint committee Vermittlungsausschuss
joint custody gemeinsames Sorgerecht
joint education gemeinsame Erziehung (von behinderten und nicht-behinderten Kindern)
joint efforts gemeinsame Anstrengungen
joint responsibility Mitverantwortung
joint vocational | training überbetriebliche Ausbildung; ~ **centre** überbetriebliche Ausbildungsstätte
jumping jack Hampelmann
jungle gym (US) Klettergerüst
junior college (US) Vorbereitungscollege mit den ersten 2 Studienjahren
junior high school (US) Oberschule 7. – 9. Klasse
junior school (Brit) 7. – 11. Lebensjahr der Grundschule
junkie Fixer
juvenile (adj) Jugend-, jugendlich
Juvenile Court (Brit) Jugendgericht
juvenile delinquency Jugendkriminalität
juvenile delinquent jugendlicher Straftäter

K

keen (adj) begeistert, leidenschaftlich, stark; ~ **desire** heftiges Verlangen; ~ **interest** lebhaftes Interesse; ~ **swimmer** begeisterter Schwimmer; **be** ~ **on** begeistert von; **he is** ~ **on dan-**

cing er ist ein begeisterter Tänzer
keep down (v) jemanden unterdrücken, klein halten
keep in (v) jemanden da behalten, (Schüler) nachsitzen lassen, nicht aus dem Haus lassen
keep off (v) wegbleiben, jemanden fern halten
keep together (v) zusammenbleiben, zusammenhalten
key competences Schlüsselfähigkeiten
key concept Schlüsselbegriff, -konzept, Leitbegriff
key elements Schlüsselelemente
key note Grundgedanke
key question Schlüsselfrage
key word Schlüsselbegriff
key-worker Bezugserzieher
kick out of school aus der Schule werfen
kid('s) stuff (US) Kinderkram
kiddie (F) Kindchen, Kleiner
kiddie kitchen Puppen-, Spielzeugküche
kidding; are you ~ ? machst du Witze? **just ~!** war nicht ernst gemeint! **no ~** im Ernst?
kin *(veraltet)*, **kinsfolk, kinship, kinsman / -woman** Verwandtschaft; Familie
kinesthesia Kinästhetik *(durch die Sinne wahrgenommene (Eigen-)Bewegung im Raum)*
kindergarten (Brit) Kindergarten, oft als private Einrichtung; (US) Vorschule
kindergarten | educator, ~teacher Erzieherin, Erzieher
knowledge Erkenntnis, Wissen, Kenntnisse
knowledge base Wissensbasis, Verständnis

L

labelling *(soz)* Etikettierung, Kennzeichnung
labelling approach *(soz)* Etikettierungsansatz
labour Wehen; **to be in ~** in den Wehen liegen; **to induce ~** die Wehen einleiten
labour pains Geburtswehen
labour ward Kreißsaal
language Sprache; **bad ~** Schimpfwörter; **native ~, first ~** Muttersprache; **second ~** Zweitsprache; **technical ~** Fachsprache

language acquisition Spracherwerb
language development Sprachentwicklung
language of origin Herkunftssprache
language proficiency Sprachfertigkeit
language skills Sprachkompetenz
large muscle skills Grobmotorik
last name Nachname, Familienname
latch-key child Schlüsselkind
late shift Spätdienst
latency period *(psych)* Latenzperiode
lateral trajectory *(schema)* seitlich verlaufende, gerade Linien
LEA (Brit) > Local Education Authority
leaflet (Hand-)Zettel, Flugblatt
leapfrog Bockspringen; **to play a game of** ~ Bockspringen spielen
learn (v) lernen; ~ **by heart** auswendig lernen; ~ **the hard way** auf die harte Tour lernen; ~ **by experience** aus Erfahrung lernen; ~ **by one's mistakes** aus seinen Fehlern lernen; ~ **something by rote**; **rote ~ing** etwas auswendig lernen, pauken
learned behaviour angelerntes Verhalten
learning aptitude Lernfähigkeit
learning by discovery entdeckendes Lernen
learning by trial and error Lernen durch Versuch und Irrtum
learning difficulties Lernschwierigkeiten; ~, **moderate (MLD)** moderate Lernschwierigkeiten; ~, **profound and multiple (PMLD)** schwerste Lernschwierigkeiten; ~, **severe (SLD)** schwere Lernschwierigkeiten; ~, **specific (SpLD)** spezifische Lernschwierigkeiten
learning disability Lernstörung, Lernbehinderung
learning from model Modelllernen
learning games Lernspiele
learning goal Lernziel
learning story Bildungs- und Lerngeschichte *(im pädagogischen Konzept von Margret Carr)*
learning support assistant Assistenzkraft für

Schüler(innen) mit sonderpädagogischem Förderbedarf, Lernförderer
learning support coordinator Koordinator/in für Lernförderung
least restrictive school placement am wenigsten einschränkende Beschulung
leave Erlaubnis; Urlaub; **absence without ~** unerlaubtes Fernbleiben; **maternity ~** Mutterschaftsurlaub; **sick ~** Genesungsurlaub; **annual ~** Jahresurlaub; **to be on ~** auf Urlaub sein
leave of absence Freistellung
leaving certificate Abgangszeugnis; *in Irland:* Hochschulzugangsberechtigung
left-handed person Linkshänder(in)
left-handedness Linkshändigkeit
leftie, lefty (F) Linkshänder(in)
legal | obligation, ~ requirement gesetzliche Verpflichtung / Erfordernis
legal abortion legaler Schwangerschaftsabbruch
legal advice centre (Brit) Rechtsberatungsstelle
legal capacity Geschäftsfähigkeit

legal custody (Brit) Sorgerecht
legal entitlement Rechtsanspruch
legal responsibility Rechtsfähigkeit, rechtliche Verantwortung, Schuldfähigkeit
legal responsibility to care Aufsichtspflicht
legitim(at)ize a child ein Kind rechtlich anerkennen
legitimacy Ehelichkeit (der Geburt)
leisure Muße
leisure | centre, ~ complex Freizeitzentrum
leisure activities Freizeitbeschäftigung
leisure provision Freizeitangebot
leisure society Freizeitgesellschaft
leisure time Freizeit
lenience, leniency Nachsicht, Milde
leotard Turnanzug
lesson (Unterrichts-)Stunde; Lektion; **take guitar ~s** Gitarrenunterricht nehmen
letter of excuse Entschuldigungsschreiben
letting go loslassen
level of development Entwicklungsstufe
level of education Bildungs-

niveau

liaise (v) mit jemandem zusammenarbeiten, Kontakt aufnehmen

life cycle Lebenszyklus

life skills lebenspraktische Fähigkeiten

linguistic aptitude Sprachbegabung

linguistic development sprachliche Entwicklung

link up (v) sich zusammenschließen

linked behaviour zusammengehörendes, verbundenes Verhalten

listless (adj) teilnahmslos, schlaff

literacy Lese- und Schreibkompetenz, Literalität **computer** ~ Computerkenntnisse, Computerkompetenz

literacy campaign Alphabetisierungskampagne

literacy level Quote der Menschen, die lesen und schreiben können

literacy skills Schreibkompetenz

literal (adj) wörtlich; ~ **translation** wörtliche Übersetzung

literate (adj) lesen und schreiben können; *(i.w.S.)* gebildet

live on welfare von der Wohlfahrt leben

local administration örtliche Verwaltung

local authority Gemeindeverwaltung, Bezirksamt

local authority guardian Amtsvormund

local authority nursery (Brit) Oberbegriff für Kinder-Tageseinrichtungen, die der jeweiligen Gemeindeverwaltung unterstellt sind

local council (Brit) Gemeinderat

Local Education Authority (LEA) (Brit) örtliches Schulamt, Amt für Volksbildung

local government officer (Brit) Angestellte(r) im öffentlichen Dienst einer Gemeinde oder Stadt

local health / welfare authority (Brit) örtliches Gesundheits- / Sozialamt

locker Schließfach; **lockable** ~ abschließbares Schließfach

lollipop | lady, ~ woman, ~ man (Brit) Schülerlotsin, Schülerlotse

lone parent Alleinerziehende(r)

lone-parent family Ein-Eltern-Familie

long-term memory Langzeitgedächtnis

look after (v) sich um jemanden / etwas kümmern, betreuen

look for (v) jemanden / etwas suchen

look forward (v) sich auf ... freuen

look out (v) aufpassen

loop Schleife

lower class Unterschicht

low-income family Familie mit geringem Einkommen

lunch Mittagessen; **what's for ~ ?** was gibt's zu Mittag?; **~ break** Mittagspause

lunchtime Mittagszeit; Mittagspause

lying-in *(veraltet)* Wochenbett

M

M.Ed > Master of Education

maiden name Mädchenname

main carer Bezugserzieher(in); Person, zu der das Kind die stärkste Beziehung hat

mainstream Regel..., *z.B.* ~ **childcare centre** Regelkita *im Gegensatz zur Sonder- oder Integrationskita*; ~ **school** Regelschule

mainstream class teacher (Irl) Lehrer(in) ohne Fächerspezialisierung im Primarbereich

mainstream somebody (v) jemanden integrieren

mainstreaming Integration von behinderten und nichtbehinderten Kindern in einer Regeleinrichtung > **gender mainstreaming**

maintain (v) Unterhalt leisten; **to ~ a family / a child** eine Familie / ein Kind unterhalten

maintained educational provision öffentlich finanzierte Bildungseinrichtungen

maintained school öffentlich finanzierte Schule; > **independent school**

maintained sector (Brit) der Bereich der öffentlich finanzierten Schulen; > **independent sector**

maintenance (payment) Unterhaltszahlung

maintenance assistance Unterhaltshilfe

maintenance order gericht-

liche Aufforderung, den Unterhaltsverpflichtungen nachzukommen
maintenance responsibility Unterhaltspflicht
majority Volljährigkeit, Mündigkeit; **age of** ~ Volljährigkeitsalter; **to reach one's** ~ volljährig werden
maladaption Fehlanpassung
maladjusted (adj) verhaltensauffällig, verhaltensgestört
maladjusted behaviour unangepasstes Verhalten
malady Krankheit, Leiden; **social** ~ gesellschaftliches Übel
maldevelopment Fehlentwicklung
male (adj) männlich
male nurse Krankenpfleger
male-dominated (adj) von Männern beherrscht
malleable materials formbare Materialien
malnourished (adj) unterernährt
malnutrition Unterernährung
malpractice Verstoß gegen Berufs- oder Standesethos
maltreatment Misshandlung
manageress, manager Leiter(in), z.B. einer Kita
mandatory grant gesetzliche Ausbildungsförderung
maniac Verrückter, Wahnsinniger, Irrer
manic depression manische Depression
manipulative stage Greifalter *(in der Säuglingsentwicklung)*
manual alphabet Gebärdensprache für Gehörlose
manual skills Handgeschicklichkeit
marginal group *(soz)* Randgruppe
marginal man Außenseiter der Gesellschaft
marginalization Ausgrenzung
marginalized children ausgegrenzte, benachteiligte Kinder, Angehörige von Minderheiten
marital status Familienstand
mark (Schul-)Note, Zensur; **to get bad / good** ~**s** schlechte / gute Noten erhalten
marked-time climbing Art des Treppensteigens, bei der beide Füße auf jede Stufe gesetzt werden
marker pen dicker Filzschreiber
marriage Heirat, Trauung; **an arranged** ~ eine arrangierte Ehe; **same-sex** ~

gleichgeschlechtliche Ehe; **state of ~** Ehestand

marriage certificate Trauschein, Heiratsurkunde

marriage guidance counsellor Eheberater

married name Ehename

Master of Education (M.Ed) (Brit) Magister der Erziehungswissenschaften (höherer akademischer Grad)

material Material; Stoff; Unterlagen

maternal (adj) mütterlich; **my ~ grandfather** mein Großvater mütterlicherseits

maternal employment Berufstätigkeit von Müttern

maternity Mutterschaft

maternity | allowance, ~ benefit (Brit) Mutterschaftsgeld

maternity | clothes, ~ dress Umstandskleid

maternity clinic Entbindungsklinik

maternity hospital Geburtsklinik

maternity leave Mutterschaftsurlaub

maternity pay (Brit) Lohnfortzahlung für Mütter

maternity protection betrieblicher Mutterschutz

matriarchy Matriarchat

matrimonial (adj) Ehe....; ehelich

matrimony Ehestand

maturation Reifung

mature (adj) erwachsen, reif

maturity Reife; **social ~** soziale Reife

meal time Essenszeit

meals on wheels (Brit) Essen auf Rädern; Lieferung warmer Mahlzeiten nach Hause

meaning Bedeutung; **the process of ~ making** etwas mit Bedeutung füllen

means test (Brit) bei der Beantragung von Sozialleistungen notwendiger Nachweis der Bedürftigkeit

measles Masern

media education Medienerziehung

mediate (v) vermitteln; **~ a settlement** eine Vereinbarung aushandeln

mediation committee Vermittlungsausschuss

mediation Vermittlung bei Konflikten, Mediation

medical certificate ärztliches Attest, Gesundheitszeugnis

meet the needs (v) Interessen wahren; Bedürfnissen entgegenkommen

memory Erinnerung, Gedächtnis

mental (adj) geistig, mental, psychisch, seelisch; (F) verrückt, übergeschnappt
mental cruelty seelische Grausamkeit
mental development geistige Entwicklung
mental disability psychische Störung, geistige Behinmderung
mental faculties Geisteskräfte
mental hospital Nervenklinik
mental retardation geistige Behinderung
mentally handicapped person geistig behinderte Person
merry-go-round Karussell
mess up (v) etwas verpfuschen, in Unordnung bringen; **messed up** verkorkst
messy activities Tätigkeiten, bei denen es schmutzig / klebrig / pampig werden kann
messy play Spiel mit Matsch und Pampe, Leim und Knete
metabolic disorder, ~ disease Stoffwechselkrankheit
metacognition Meta-Erkenntnis
middle name zweiter Vorname

middle school (US) Oberschule grade 6–8, ca. 12–15 Jahre
midwife Hebamme
midwifery Geburtshilfe
migrant Zuwander/er/in; **migrant worker** Wanderarbeiter(in), ausl. Arbeiter(in)
mild *(in Zusammenhang mit Behinderungen)* leicht
milk tooth Milchzahn
minimum age Mindestalter
minor Minderjährige(r); *(Universität)* Nebenfach
minority Minderheit, Minorität
minority group Minderheitsgruppe, Randgruppe
mirror (v) spiegeln *(auch fig.)*
misbehave (v) ungezogen sein
miscarriage Fehlgeburt
miscarry (v) eine Fehlgeburt haben
misfit Außenseiter, Eigenbrötler
mismatch Missverhältnis, Ungleichgewicht
mischief Unfug
mixed ability mit unterschiedlicher Leistungsfähigkeit, z.B. ~ **class** Schulklasse ohne Leistungsdifferen-

zierung im Gegensatz zum > *streaming*

mixed-age classes altersgemischte Gruppen

mixed-age grouping Altersmischung

mixed-age provision altersgemischte Angebote

mixture of languages Sprachenmischung

mobility Durchlässigkeit

model Vorbild

modelling Lernen am Modell, Modell-Lernen, Beobachtungslernen

modelling compound Modelliermasse

moderate (adj) angemessen, vernünftig; *(in Zusammenhang mit Behinderungen)* mäßig

moderation Mäßigung

moderator Vermittler, Diskussionsleiter, Prüfungsvorsitzender

molest (v) quälen, (sexuell) belästigen; schikanieren

molester lästiger Mensch, Peiniger(in); **child ~** Kinderschänder

monitor (v) dokumentieren, aufzeichnen; **~ing sheet** Dokumentations-, Erfassungsbogen

moral education Moralerziehung

morning session Vormittagsbetreuung

mother | land, ~ country Heimatland, Herkunftsland

mother tongue Muttersprache

Mother's Day (Brit) Muttertag

motherese mutterisch (die Art, wie eine Mutter mit ihrem Kind spricht) *(„Motherese plays a role in language development")*

motherhood Mutterschaft

mother-in-law Schwiegermutter

mother-to-be werdende Mutter

mother-toddler-group Mutter-Kind-Gruppe, Miniclub

motor ability motorische Fähigkeit

motor behaviour Motorik, motorisches Verhalten

motor impairment physische Einschränkung, Behinderung

mould (v) kneten, formen

move house (v) umziehen

moving up (päd) Versetzung

Ms *(no pl)* Anrede *(mündlich wie schriftlich)* für verheiratete ebenso wie unverheiratete Frauen

multi-cultural (adj) multikulturell

multi-ethnic society Vielvölkergesellschaft

multihandicap, multiple handicap Mehrfachbehinderung

multilingual mehrsprachig

multiple birth Mehrlingsgeburt

multiple deprivation mehrfache Benachteiligung (Arbeit, Bildung, Wohnung...)

multiplication table Einmaleins-Tafel

multi-racial society Vielvölkergesellschaft

multisensory educational approach multisensorischer pädagogischer Ansatz

municipal (adj) städtisch, kommunal

municipal authorities Stadtverwaltung, Behörde

municipality Gemeinde, Kommune, Bezirk, Stadt

musical sense musikalischer Sinn

mute (adj) stumm

mutual (adj) gegenseitig

mutual recognition of national professional qualifications gegenseitige Anerkennung nationaler Berufsabschlüsse

N

nanny Kindermädchen im Privathaushalt; Oma

nap Nickerchen; **take a ~** ein Nickerchen machen

nap time Schlafenszeit *(am Mittag)*

napkin Serviette

nappy (Brit) Windel; **cloth ~** Stoffwindel; **disposable ~** Wegwerfwindel aus Papier; **put on / change a baby's ~** Baby wickeln / Windeln wechseln

nappy liner Windeleinlage

nappy rash Wundsein unter der Windel, Windelausschlag

narrow age-band geringe Altersdifferenz

natal (adj) Geburts...; **~ period** der Geburtsvorgang

natality Geburtenziffer

National Council for Voluntary Organizations (Brit) Dachverband der freien Wohlfahrtsverbände

National Health Service (NHS) (Brit) staatlicher Gesundheitsdienst

National Insurance (Brit) Sozialversicherung; **~ con-**

tributions Sozialversicherungsbeiträge

National Nursery Examination Board (Brit) (NNEB) 2-jährige Ausbildung für die Altersgruppe der 0–5-Jährigen zur *Nursery Nurse*, schliesst ab mit *Certificate* oder *Diploma in Nursery Nursing*

National School (Irl) Primarschule

national service Wehrdienst

National Society for the Prevention of Cruelty to Children (NSPCC) (Brit) Nationaler Kinderschutzbund

National Union of Teachers (NUT) (Brit) Lehrer/innen-Gewerkschaft

National Vocational Qualification in Childcare and Education (NVQ) (Brit) meist berufsbegleitende Ausbildung auf mittlerem Niveau, führt auch zur Fachhochschulreife

native American amerikanische(r) Ureinwohner(in)

native language Muttersprache

native speaker Muttersprachler(in)

nativity play Krippenspiel

natural childbirth natürliche / sanfte Geburt

naturalization Einbürgerung

naturalize (v) einbürgern

nature and/or nurture Anlage und/oder Umwelt

nature conservation (Brit) Naturschutz

nature cure Naturheilverfahren

near senses Nahsinne

née (adj) geborene/r ...

need Bedürfnis, Notwendigkeit

needle work Handarbeiten

negative reinforcement negative Verstärkung

neglect (v) vernachlässigen; ~ed child vernachlässigtes, verwahrlostes Kind

neglectful (adj) nachlässig

negligence Vernachlässigung, Fahrlässigkeit; **gross** ~ grobe Fahrlässigkeit

neighbourhood nurseries Nachbarschafts-Kindergärten *(eine Initiative der brit. Regierung in den 90er Jahren)*

neonatal (adj) Neugeborenen-, ~ **unit** Neugeborenenstation

neonatal period Zeitraum bis zum Alter von einem Monat

neonate neugeborenes Kind (bis ein Monat)

nest Nest, Heim;
empty ~ Familie, deren Kinder ausgezogen sind;
empty ~ syndrome Gefühl der Verlassenheit, wenn die Kinder ausgezogen sind

newborn | baby, ~ infant neugeborenes Kind

newly qualified teacher (Brit) Lehrer(in) während der Einführungsphase (ähnlich dem/der Referendar(in) in D.)

next of kin nächste Angehörige

night school Abendschule

nightmare Alptraum

NNEB > *National Nursery Examination Board*

non-contact time Verfügungszeit; Vor- und Nachbereitungszeit; die Zeit, die Erzieherinnen für Team- und Elterngespräche haben (ohne Kinder)

non-contributory Beitragsfreiheit

non-custodial parent Elternteil, welches nicht das Sorgerecht hat

non-denominational nicht konfessionsgebunden

non-denominational school Gemeinschaftsschule

non-discrimination Gleichbehandlung

non-governmental organization (NGO) Nicht-Regierungs-Organisation

non-parental care außerfamiliäre Betreuung

non-participant observation nicht-teilnehmende Beobachtung

non-professional helping group Selbsthilfegruppe

non-profit organization gemeinnützige Organisation

non-profit status Gemeinnützigkeit

non-residents Besucher / Teilnehmer(innen), die nicht im Hause wohnen

non-segregation Nicht-Ausgrenzung

non-statutory nicht-staatlich, freiwillig

Northern Ireland Department of Education Erziehungsministerium von Nordirland

nosy (adj) (F) neugierig

notion Begriff, Vorstellung, Ahnung

noughts and crosses (Brit) Zeichenspiel für zwei Personen

nought to three years 0 bis 3 Jahre

nuclear family Kernfamilie
number work Rechnen, Umgang mit Zahlen
numeracy rechnerische Fähigkeiten
numeracy skills Rechenkompetenz
nurse (v) pflegen, heilen; ~ **a child** ein Kind stillen, auf dem Arm wiegen
nurse Kindermädchen, Krankenschwester; **male** ~ Krankenpfleger; **wet** ~ Säugamme *(veraltet)*
nursery (Brit) *kurz für* **nursery school** Kindergarten; Kinderzimmer
nursery class (Brit) Kindergarten, besonders an einer Schule
nursery nurse, nursery worker, nursery assistant (Brit) Kinderpfleger(in) mit 2-jähriger Ausbildung für die Altersgruppe 0 - 5, arbeitet als Hilfskraft (**auxiliary worker**) *in* **nursery school, nursery class, reception class** *oder als* Gruppenerzieherin im **family centre** oder in einer **local authority nursery,** auf der Kinderstation im Krankenhaus, im Privathaushalt als **nanny**. *Ausbildung:* National Nursery Examination Board (>NNEB) *oder* Council for Awards in Children's Care and Education (CACHE) *oder* > BTEC National Diploma in Caring Services oder > NVQ Level III in Nursing
nursery officer (Brit) Erzieher(in) in einer > **local authority nursery**
nursery rhyme Kinderlied, -vers
nursery school (Brit) Kindergarten; (US) Kindergarten für 2 – 5-jährige Kinder in einer > pre-school
nursery school teacher Erzieher(in) im Kindergarten; *eigentl. Titel in Brit:* **teacher (nursery and primary education** *bzw.* **preschool and primary education** *bzw.* **primary and secondary education)**; meist 4 Jahre Ausbildung auf Hochschulniveau, Abschluss **BEd (Bachelor of Education)** *oder* > **PGCE (Postgraduate Certificate in Education)**
nursery tale Ammenmärchen
nursery worker Mitarbeiter(in) in einer Kita; umgangssprachlich

synonym benutzt wie „Kita-Erzieher(in)" in D.
nursing home Pflegeheim (für alte Menschen); Entbindungsklinik
nursing mother stillende Mutter
nursing room Wickelraum *(z.B. im Kaufhaus)*
nurture (v) erziehen, hegen, kümmern um, jemanden oder etwas fördern
NVQ > National Vocational Qualification

O

O level > ordinary level
OAP > old age pensioner
obedient (adj) gehorsam, folgsam
obese (adj) fettleibig
obesity Fettleibigkeit
obey (v) gehorchen, folgen
object permanence Objektpermanenz
objection Einwand
objective Zielsetzung; **main** ~ Hauptziel
obligatory (adj) verpflichtend
observation Beobachtung; > participant ~; > non-participant ~; > specific ~; > random ~
observation sheet Beobachtungsbogen
observation visit Hospitation
observational learning Lernen durch Beobachtung
observe (v) beobachten
observe in action (v) hospitieren
observer Beobachter; > participant ~; > non-participant ~
obsession Zwangsvorstellung, Besessenheit
occupation Beruf, Beschäftigung; **favourite** ~ Lieblingsbeschäftigung
occupational disease Berufskrankheit
occupational therapy Beschäftigungstherapie
occupied (adj) beschäftigt
odd job Gelegenheitsarbeit
of age mündig
offender Straftäter(in); **first** ~ Ersttäter; **young** ~ jugendlicher Straftäter
offensive (adj) widerlich, ekelhaft
officer Beamter
official duties Dienstpflichten

official guardian Amtsvormund

Ofsted (Office for Standards in Education) (Brit) Unabhängige Organisation zur Sicherung von Qualitätsstandards in der (vor)schulischen Erziehung

OHP > overhead projector

old age pensioner (OAP) Rentner(in)

old people's home Altenheim

one-off payment Einmalzahlung (Abfindung, Beihilfe)

one-parent benefit (Brit) erhöhtes Kindergeld für allein Erziehende

one-parent family Einelternfamilie; **to grow up in a ~** von einem Elternteil aufgezogen werden

one-stop shop Einrichtung, die verschiedene Angebote zusammenfasst

one-to-one persönlich; **~ work** Einzelarbeit; **on a ~ basis** unter vier Augen; **~ situation** mit jemandem allein sein; **~ lessons** Einzelunterricht; **~ attention** Einzelbetreuung

only child Einzelkind

on-the-job-training Ausbildung am Arbeitsplatz

open activities for young people offene Jugendarbeit

open plan Großraum...; *in der Kita*: offene Arbeit, gruppenübergreifend

open plan office Großraumbüro

opening | hours, ~ times Öffnungszeiten

openness Offenheit

operational learning Verhaltensänderung aufgrund von Erfahrung, Erfahrungslernen

opinion Meinung

opinion | poll, ~ survey *(soz)* Meinungsumfrage

oppress (v) unterdrücken

oppression Unterdrückung

optional (adj) fakultativ, wahlfrei, freiwillig

oracy mündliche Ausdrucksfähigkeit

oral | interview, ~ questioning mündliche Befragung

oral examination mündliche Prüfung

oral stage orale Phase

oral test mündliche Prüfung

oral-sensory stage oral-sensorische Phase

ordinary level (O level) ehem. Schulabschluss in GB, entsprach etwa dem Realschulabschluss in D., heute ersetzt durch > **GCSE**

in England und > **Standard grade** in Schottland.
organic farming biologischer Anbau
organic vegetable Biogemüse
orientation in values Wertorientierung
orphan Waise
orphanage Waisenhaus
orthodontist Kieferorthopäde
outburst (emotionaler oder verbaler) Ausbruch
outcast Ausgestoßene(r), Geächtete(r)
outdoor area Außenbereich
outdoor pursuits Erlebnispädagogik
outdoors im Freien
out-group Außengruppe, Fremdgruppe
outing Ausflug; **class ~** Klassenausflug; **family ~** Familienausflug; **to go on an ~** einen Ausflug machen
out-of-school educational daycare facility Hort (D)
out-of-school | provision, ~ services pädagogisches Angebot für Schulkinder außerhalb der Schule
out-patient ambulante(r) Patient(in)
outragious (adj) empörend, schockierend, ungeheuerlich

outside play area Außenspielbereich; Freigelände
overall number Gesamtzahl
overanxious (adj) überängstlich
overdo (v) übertreiben
overestimate (v) überschätzen
overhead projector Tageslichtprojektor
overhear (v) zufällig mithören
overprotection übermäßige Beschützung
overprotective (adj) überbehütend
overt behaviour offenes Verhalten
overtime Überstunden; **to work ~** Überstunden machen
overwatched überbehütet
overwhelming (adj) überwältigend, unwiderstehlich
Oxfam (Oxford Committee for Famine Relief) Gemeinnützige Hilfsorganisation für bedürftige Menschen, bes. in der 3. Welt; **~ Shop** „Dritte Welt Laden"

P

pacifier Schnuller
pacify (v) beruhigen
paediatric nurse (Brit) Kinderkrankenschwester
paediatrician (Brit) Kinderarzt/ärztin
paediatrics (Brit) Kinderheilkunde
paid leave for new parent Erziehungsurlaub
pain-killer schmerzstillendes Mittel
pains (*pl*) Schmerzen (*auch seelisch*); Sorgen
paint box Malkasten
paint-brush Malpinsel
pajamas (US) Schlafanzug
pamper (v) jmd. verwöhnen
pampered (adj) verwöhnt
Pancake Day (Brit) Fastnachtsdienstag
pancake landing Bauchlandung
panel Gruppe, Team
pantomime (Brit) Laienspiel, Weihnachtsspiel, Pantomime
pap (F) Babybrei
paper tissue Papiertaschentuch
paper-and-pencil-work schriftliche Arbeiten
paper-chase (Brit) Schnitzeljagd
papier-mâché Pappmaschee
paramedical orientation gesundheitliche, pflegerische Orientierung
paramedically trained personnel Personal mit einer Ausbildung in den Gesundheitsberufen
parent Elternteil; ~s Eltern; **single ~** allein Erziehende(r)
parent counseling Elternberatung
parent participation Elternbeteiligung
parentage elterliche Sorge
parental (adj) Eltern-, elterlich
parental attitude elterliche Einstellung
parental consent Zustimmung der Eltern
parental contributions Elternbeiträge (finanzieller Art)
parental control / neglect Beaufsichtigung / Vernachlässigung durch die Eltern
parental family Abstammungs-, Herkunftsfamilie
parental home Elternhaus
parental leave Erziehungsur-

laub („Elternzeit" in D.)
parental rights and duties *(jur)* elterliche Sorge
parental rights elterliche Rechte
parent-child relation Eltern-Kind Beziehung
parenthood Elternschaft
parenting Pflege, Betreuung und Erziehung von Kindern; Kindererziehung
parentless (adj) elternlos; ~ **child** Waise
parent-managed centre Eltern-Initiativ-Kindertagesstätte; „Kinderladen"
parent-run von den Eltern betrieben
parents' action group Elterninitiative
parents' council Elternbeirat; Gesamtelternvertretung
parents' meeting Elternabend
parent-teacher organization (PTO) (US); **parent-teacher-association** (Brit) Eltern-Lehrer-Beirat an einer Schule
parish Pfarrgemeinde; Landgemeinde, Bezirk
partial-birth abortion Abtreibung im fortgeschrittenen Stadium der Schwangerschaft

partially disabled teilweise behindert
participant Teilnehmer(in)
participant observation teilnehmende Beobachtung
participate (v) teilnehmen
participating (päd) Beteiligung
participation Teilnahme
particulars Einzelheiten
part-time (adj) Teilzeit-, Halbtags-
part-time care Teilzeitbetreuung
part-time job Teilzeitarbeit
part-time vocational school Berufsschule
pass (Brit) Bestehen (*einer Prüfung, einer Aufgabe*); **to get a ~ in an exam** eine Prüfung bestehen
pass (v) bestehen einer Prüfung; **you can ~ or fail** man kann bestehen oder durchfallen
pass around (v) etwas herumreichen
pass mark (Brit) ein „Ausreichend" *(bei einer Prüfung)*; **to get a ~** eine Vier bekommen
pass rate Anzahl derer, die bei einer Prüfung etc. bestanden haben
passing Bestehen; **reasons**

for ~ the practical training Gründe für das Bestehen des Praktikums; **reasons for not ~ the practical training** Gründe für das Nichtbestehen des Praktikums

passing grade (US) ein „Ausreichend" *(bei einer Prüfung)*

passion Vorliebe, Leidenschaft

paste Kleister; **sticky ~** Klebstoff

paste (v) aufkleben

pastime Freizeitbeschäftigung, Freizeitbetätigung

pastoral care Seelsorge; Hilfe bei privaten Problemen

patch Revier, Bereich, Bezirk, Feld; **~ social work** feldorientierte Sozialarbeit

patch test Allergietest

patch together, patch up (v) etwas zusammenflicken

paternity Vaterschaft

paternity leave Vaterschaftsurlaub, Erziehungsurlaub für Väter

paternity suit Vaterschaftsprozess

paternity test Vaterschaftstest

pathetic (adj) Mitleid erregend, jämmerlich

patronise (v) bevormunden

pattern Struktur, Muster; **behavioural ~ , ~ of behaviour** Verhaltensmuster; **the ~ of family life** die Familienstruktur

pay Lohn, Gehalt

payee Zahlungsempfänger(in)

payment Zahlung, Lohn; **lump-sum ~** Pauschalzahlung

PE > physical education

peace education Friedenserziehung

pedagogic (adj) pädagogisch

pedagogically speaking pädagogisch gesehen

pedagogue Pädagoge(-in)

pedagogy Pädagogik

pediatric nurse (US) Kinderkrankenschwester

pediatrician (US) Kinderarzt/ärztin

pediatrics (US) Kinderheilkunde

pee (v) pinkeln; **to ~ (in) one's pants** in die Hose pinkeln; **to ~ oneself** sich bepinkeln; **to have a ~** pinkeln gehen

peek-a-boo "Wo-bin-ich"-Spiel

peer Ebenbürtiger, Gleichaltriger, Gleichrangiger

peer acceptance Anerkennung durch Gleichaltrige

peer group Peer Group,

informelle Gruppe von Gleichrangigen, Gleichaltrigen

peer interaction Kontakt mit Gleichaltrigen

peer support Unterstützung durch Gleiche

pen Stift, Schreibstift, Kuli

perambulator *(veraltet)* Kinderwagen

perception Wahrnehmung; **auditory** ~ akustische W.; **kinesthetic** ~ kinästhetische W.; **tactile** ~ taktile W.; **olfactory** ~ Geruchsw.; **gustatory** ~ Geschmacksw.; **depth** ~ Tiefenw.

perception of colour Farbensinn

perceptual development Entwicklung der Wahrnehmungsfähigkeit

perceptual disorders Wahrnehmungsverarbeitungsschwierigkeiten

performance Leistung

performance evaluation Leistungsmessung

perinatal (adj) während und unmittelbar nach dem Geburtsvorgang

period of quiet (after lunch) Mittagsruhe

peripatetic teacher Lehrer(in), der/die an mehreren Schulen unterrichtet, ambulanter Stützpädagoge

permanently disabled dauerhaft behindert

permissive society freizügige Gesellschaft

permissiveness Toleranz, Freizügigkeit

persistence Beharrlichkeit

person in need of help hilfsbedürftige Person

person under age Minderjährige(r)

pertussis Keuchhusten

petting zoo; ~ farm Streichelzoo

PGCE > Postgraduate Certificate in Education

PhD (Doctor of Philosophy) Doktor, Dr.

physical closeness körperliche Nähe

physical defect Körperbehinderung

physical development körperliche Entwicklung

physical education Sportunterricht; körperliches Training zur Entwicklung der Grobmotorik

physically challenged behindert

physically handicapped körperbehindert

physician Arzt, Ärztin

picture book Bilderbuch
pilot project Modellversuch
pilot study Pilotstudie, Vorstudie
pincer grasp Zangengriff
pincer prehension Daumen - Zeigefingergriff bei Säuglingen
pinkie, pinky (US) kleiner Finger
pinny Lätzchen
placement Vermittlung (einer Arbeit); Unterbringung (Heim, Anstalt); (Arbeits-)Stelle, **work** ~ Praktikum in einem Betrieb, einer Einrichtung
placement recordings Praxisberichte
placement service Ver-mittlungsdienst
placement supervisor Praxisanleiter(in)
placement test Einstufungstest
plan of practical training Arbeitsplan für das Praktikum
plastic cover for electrical outlets Kindersicherung an Steckdosen
Plasticine® (Brit) Knetmasse, -gummi
play age Spielalter
play area abgegrenztes Spielgebiet innerhalb eines Gruppenraums
play drive Spieltrieb
play leader Gruppenleiter(in); (Scot) päd. Mitarbeiter(in) im Elementarbereich, z.B. in *playgroups*
play tag (v) Fangen spielen
play therapy Spieltherapie
play truant (v) (die Schule) schwänzen
Play-Doh, play dough Knetmasse, auch: Salzteig
playground Spielplatz
playgroup (Brit) Spielgruppe, Krabbelgruppe (private Initiative, nur wenige Stunden/Woche)
playgroup leader (Brit) Spielgruppenleiter(in)
playing card Spielkarte
playing field Sportplatz
playmate Spielkamerad(in)
playpen Laufstall
plaything Spielzeug
pliable (adj) anpassungsfähig
plimsoll Turnschuh
PLOD > possible lines of direction
plywood Sperrholz
policy Programm, Grundsatz, Richtlinie
poliomyelitis Kinderlähmung
political asylum politisches

Asyl; **to seek / grant ~** politisches Asyl beantragen / gewähren

polling study *(soz)* statistische Erhebung; Umfrage

pollute (v) *(Umwelt)* verschmutzen, verunreinigen

polluter pays principle Verursacherprinzip *(im Umweltschutz)*

pollution *(Umwelt-)* Verschmutzung

polytechnic (Brit) Fachhochschule

poo, poop *(Kindersprache)* Kacke; **do a ~** kacken; **to ~ in the pants** in die Hose machen; **did you make a ~** hast du in die Hose gemacht?

poor *(päd)* schlecht, ungenügend; **~ behaviour** schlechtes Verhalten; **~ student** schlechter Schüler

poorly paid schlecht bezahlt

portfolio Mappe, Dokumentation

positive attribution positive Zuschreibung

positive discrimination Bevorzugung zum Ausgleich für soziale Benachteiligung

positive reinforcement positive Verstärkung

possible lines of direction (PLOD) mögliche Entwicklungslinien

postgraduate Student(in) nach Erreichen des ersten akad. Grades

postgraduate studies Aufbaustudium

postgraduate | course; ~ studies Graduiertenstudium; Studiengang, der einen akad. Abschluss voraussetzt

Postgraduate Certificate in Education (PGCE) (Brit) berufsqualifizierender Abschluss für Erzieher(innen) und Lehrer(innen), einjähriges Pädagogikstudium (mit Praktika) auf Hochschulniveau nach dem Fachstudium

postnatal (adj) nachgeburtlich

postnatal depression Wochenbettdepression

potty Töpfchen

potty-trained (adj) sauber sein; **is Mary ~ yet?** geht Mary schon aufs Töpfchen?

potty-training Sauberkeitserziehung

practical praktische Prüfung

practical attitude; to have a ~ praxisorientiert sein

practical experience praktische Erfahrung, Praxiserfahrung

practical placement Betriebspraktikum *(bezieht sich nicht nur auf Wirtschaftsbetriebe, sondern auch auf soz.-päd. Einrichtungen)*

practical studies Praktikum

practical term Praxissemester, Praktikum

practical training Praktikum

practical work experience Praktikum

practice teacher (US) Lehrer-Referendar

practice Übung; Handeln; Training; **in ~** in der Praxis; **private ~** Privatpraxis

practiced (adj) erfahren

practicum Praktikum; **~ abroad** Auslandspraktikum

practitioner Fachkraft, *i.w.S.* Erzieher/in

praise Lob

pram (Brit) Kinderwagen

precaution Vorsichtsmaßnahme

précis (schriftliche) Zusammenfassung

preconceived idea vorgefasste Meinung

predict (v) voraussagen, vorhersagen

prediction Vorhersage, Prognose

preference Vorliebe

pregnancy Schwangerschaft, **teenage ~** Schwangerschaft von Minderjährigen

pregnant (adj) schwanger; **she's seven months ~** sie ist im siebten Monat; **she is ~ with twins** sie erwartet Zwillinge

prehension Greifen (mit den Händen)

prehensory behaviour Verhalten (besonders Handmotorik) beim ersten Greifen des Säuglings

prejudice Vorurteil, Voreingenommenheit; **~ against...** Vorurteile gegen...

pre-kindergarten, pre-K (US) Kindergarten für 3 – 5-jährige Kinder, schließt nicht die Vorschule (> kindergarten) ein, Teil einer > pre-school

prelinguistic vorsprachliche Lautbildung

premature | baby zu früh geborenes Baby; **he was born six weeks ~** er wurde sechs Wochen zu früh geboren

premature birth Frühgeburt

premises Gebäude, Räumlichkeiten; **school ~** das Schulgelände

prenatal (adj) vorgeburtlich, pränatal; **~ care** vorgeburtliche Betreuung, Geburtsvorbereitung; ~ **development** vorgeburtliche Entwicklung

preparatory class Vorschulklasse

preparatory school, prep school (Brit) private Schule (8–13 Jahre) zur Vorbereitung auf eine > *public school*

prepare (v) vorbereiten

prepared environment vorbereitete Umgebung

preprimary class Schulkindergarten

preprimary schooling Vorschulerziehung, die vor der eigentlichen Vorschule *(preschool)* einsetzt

prerequisite Voraussetzung

Presbyterian Church, Church of Scotland schottische presbyterianische (protestantische) Kirche *(Trägerin von Schulen und Kindergärten in Schottland)*

preschool (adj) vorschulisch, Vorschul-; ~ **age** Vorschulalter; ~ **education** vorschulische Erziehung

pre-school (Brit) Elementarbereich ohne Vorschule, 3–5 Jahre, halbtags, nur während der Schulzeit (> *reception class*); (US) Kindergarten, Kindertagesstätte, die den Erziehungsbehörden untersteht, umfasst > *pre-kindergarten* oder > *nursery school*

preschool facilities vorschulische Einrichtungen

pre-school playgroup Eltern-Kind-Gruppe

presentation Präsentation, Ausstellung

pre-teen (adj) Kinder zwischen dem zehnten und zwölften Lebensjahr

pretend (adj) Spiel-; **this doll is Katie's pretend baby** mit dieser Puppe spielt Katie Baby

pretend play symbolisches Spiel

prevention Verhinderung, Vermeidung, Vorbeugung; *(med.)* Vorsorge

previous experience vorangegangene Erfahrungen

primary education Grundschulbildung

primary material Anfangsmaterial

primary school (Brit) Grundschule (5.–11. Lebensjahr)

primary stage of education Primarstufe, Primarbereich

primary teacher Grundschullehrer(in)

primary tooth Milchzahn

principal (of a nursery school) Leiter(in)
principal (of a school) Schulleiter(in)
private agencies freie Träger
private associations freie Verbände
private parts Geschlechtsteile
proactive (adj) initiativ; ~ **attitude** Eigeninitiative
proactivity (US) Initiative, Aktivität
probability Wahrscheinlichkeit
probation Probezeit; Bewährung; **to be on** ~ Probezeit haben, auf Bewährung sein
probation officer Bewährungshelfer(in)
probationary period Probezeit; *(für LehrerInnen)* Referendariat (D)
probationary year Berufspraktikum von einem Jahr, Jahrespraktikum
proficiency Leistung, Tüchtigkeit
profound (adj) *(im Zusammenhang mit Behinderungen)* sehr schwer
progressive educational approaches reformpädagogische Ansätze
promote (v) fördern

promote development Entwicklung fördern
promotion measures for highly gifted students Begabtenförderung
promotion prospects Aufstiegschancen
propensity Hang, Neigung **(to, for** zu)
proper care angemessene Sorge
proprioception Kinästhetik *(durch die Sinne wahrgenommene (Eigen-)Bewegung im Raum)*
props Requisiten, Verkleidungen
prosocial behaviour (positives) soziales Verhalten
protection of children Kinderschutz
protective legislation for working mothers Mutterschutzvorschriften
provide (v) anbieten, zur Verfügung stellen
provider Träger (einer Einrichtung)
provision Bereitstellung, Versorgung, Angebot; **educational** ~ schulische / Erziehungsmaßnahmen
provisions Einrichtungen, Summe aller Angebote
psychiatric [saiki'ætric]

(adj) psychiatrisch; ~ **child care worker** Psychagoge, Psychagogin

psychically ['saikik^eli] (adj) psychisch

psychological [,saike'lodjik^el] (adj) psychologisch

psychomotor learning objectives psychomotorische Lernziele

puberty Pubertät, Geschlechtsreife

pubescence der Pubertät vorausgehende Periode

public Öffentlichkeit, Allgemeinheit

public (adj) öffentlich

public agencies öffentliche Träger

public foundation Stiftung des öffentlichen Rechts

public funds öffentliche Gelder

public health service öffentliches Gesundheitssystem

public holiday gesetzlicher Feiertag

public law Öffentliches Recht

public ownership Staatsbesitz

public school (Brit) private Oberschule *(oft Internatsschule);* (Scot., US) staatliche Schule

public sector employees Angestellte im öffentlichen Dienst

public servant Angestellte(r) des öffentlichen Dienstes

public service öffentlicher Dienst

publicly funded öffentlich finanziert

publicly funded | provision; ~ **services** öffentlich finanzierte Einrichtungen; Angebote

Punch Kasper; ~ **and Judy (show)** Kasperletheater

punishment Bestrafung, Strafe

pupil Schüler(in) *(mst. im Grundschulalter) (teilw. veraltet)*

pupil-teacher ratio Lehrer-Schüler-Verhältnis, Gruppen-, Klassenstärke

puppet Marionette, Puppe; **finger** ~ Fingerpuppe; **glove** ~ Handpuppe

puppet show Marionetten-, Puppentheater

purchase-of-service system (US) kostenpflichtige Einrichtungen der Kinderbetreuung durch freie Träger oder Wirtschaftsbetriebe

purposeful play sinnvolles Spiel

pushbike Fahrrad, Drahtesel

pushchair (Kinder-) Sportwagen

push-up Liegestütze

puzzle Rätsel, Denksportaufgabe; **crossword** ~ Kreuzworträtsel; **jigsaw** ~ Puzzle; **solve a** ~ ein Rätsel lösen

pyjamas (Brit) Schlafanzug

Q

QTS > qualified teacher status

quadruplet Vierling

qualification Qualifikation; Schul-, Ausbildungsabschluss

qualification requirement Ausbildungsordnung

qualifications in education in the UK: GCSE / General Certificate of Secondary Education (Engl., Wales, N.I.) *entspricht dem Realschulabschluss in D.;* **SCE / Scottish Certificate of Education / ‚Standard Grade'** (Scot) *das schottische Äquivalent des* GCSE; **A Levels** (Engl., Wales, N.I.) *entspricht dem Abitur in D.,* **SCE ‚Highers'** (Scot) *das schottische Äquivalent der* A Levels; **GNVQ / General National Vocational Qualification** berufsqualifizierender Abschluss auf fünf verschiedenen Ebenen *(levels)*

qualified (adj) qualifiziert, geeignet, befähigt; **highly** ~ hoch qualifiziert; ~ **educator** staatlich anerkannte(r) Erzieher(in)

qualified teacher status (QTS) (Brit) Lehrer(in) mit akad. Grad (B.Ed., B.A., B.Sc., PGCE) (in jeder *nursery* muss ein(e) Mitarbeiter(in) QTS haben)

qualifying | examination, ~ test Eignungsprüfung, Aufnahmeprüfung *(Schule, Uni)*

quality Qualität, Wert, Güte; **high / low** ~ gute / mindere Qualität

quality development Qualitätsentwicklung

quality enhancement Qualitätsverbesserung

quantitative survey quantitative Befragung

quarrel Streit, Zank; **to have a ~** sich zanken, streiten
question (v) (be-)fragen, verhören, bezweifeln; **to ~ something** etwas bezweifeln
question Frage, Zweifel; Aufgabe *(Schule)*
questionnaire Fragebogen
quiet time Ruhezeit
quintuplet Fünfling

R

race relations Beziehungen zwischen verschiedenen ethnischen Gruppen
racial minority ethnische Minderheit
racial prejudice rassistische Vorurteile, Ausländerfeindlichkeit
racialism Rassismus
racialist Rassist(in); (adj) rassistisch
racism Ausländerfeindlichkeit; Rassismus; **overt ~** offener Rassismus
racist Rassist(in); (adj) rassistisch
racist attack rassistischer Angriff
racist remark rassistische Bemerkung
raffle ticket Los für eine Tombola
rag doll Stoffpuppe
random observation Zufallsbeobachtung
rape Vergewaltigung
rash (Haut)Ausschlag; **nettle ~** Nesselausschlag; **diaper ~** (US) Windelausschlag
rating Einstufung, Einschätzung
ratio *(zahlenmäßiges)* Verhältnis
RC *Abk. von* **Roman Catholic** römisch-katholisch *oder* **Red Cross** Rotes Kreuz
readiness for school Schulreife
reading age Lesealter; **to have a ~ of eight** wie ein/e Achtjährige/r lesen können
reading comprehension Leseverständnis
reading skill Lesefähigkeit
realize (v) sich klar werden, sich bewusst werden, zu der Erkenntnis gelangen
real-life situations Alltagssituationen

rear (v) aufziehen, großziehen
reason Vernunft
reasonable (adj) vernünftig, verstandesgemäß; angemessen
reasoning Logik, logisches Denken, Schlussfolgern
reassurance Bestärkung
reassure (v) jemanden (wieder) beruhigen
reassuring (adj) beruhigend
reception class (Brit) Vorschulklasse in einer Schule, erste Klasse
reception teacher Vorklassenleiter/in
receptive to teaching bildungsfähig
receptivity Aufnahmefähigkeit
reciprocal (adj) gegenseitig, beidseitig
reciprocal introduction gegenseitige Vorstellung *(im Sinne von „bekannt machen")*
reciprocity Wechselseitigkeit, Reziprozität
recognition Anerkennung
recognize (v) erkennen, anerkennen
recognized trainee occupation Ausbildungsberuf
reconcile (v) schlichten, versöhnen, vereinbaren
reconstituted family Patchwork-Familie, Stieffamilie
record Aufzeichnung, Unterlage, Akte, Protokoll, Bericht
record sheet Protokollbogen
recorder Blockflöte
records Unterlagen
recover (v) sich erholen
recreation Erholung
recreation ground Freizeitgelände
recreation room Aufenthaltsraum (für die Freizeit)
recreational facilities Einrichtung für Erholung und Spiel
recycling centre Wertstoffsammelstelle
red tape (Brit) Amtsschimmel; Bürokratie
redundancy Entlassung von Personal; ~ **payment** Abfindung bei Entlassung
re-educate (v) umerziehen
refectory Speiseraum in der Schule
reference Arbeitszeugnis, Referenz
reference group Bezugsgruppe
reflective parenting bewusste Elternschaft
refugee Flüchtling

register (v) (sich) anmelden, einschreiben, registrieren

registered association eingetragener Verein (e.V.)

registered charity eingetragene gemeinnützige Einrichtung, Hilfsorganisation

registered childminder professionelle, hauptberufliche Tagesmutter

registry office; **registry**; **register office** (Brit) Standesamt

regress (v) sich verschlechtern, Rückschritte machen

regression Regression, Verschlechterung, Rückentwicklung

regulation Verordnung, Vorschrift, Verfügung

rehabilitation centre Rehabilitationszentrum; **drug ~** Entziehungsanstalt

reinforce (v) bestätigen, verstärken

reinforcement Verstärkung, Bekräftigung, Belohnung; **negative ~** negative Verstärkung, Strafe

reintegration Wiedereingliederung, Resozialisierung

reject (v) zurückweisen

relate (v) in Beziehung treten; **she ~s well to young people** sie baut leicht Beziehungen zu jungen Leuten auf

relate to someone eine Beziehung zu jemandem herstellen

relation Beziehung, Verhältnis; Verwandte(r)

relationship Verhältnis, Verwandtschaftsverhältnis

relative Verwandte(r)

relaxation Entspannung

relevant work experience einschlägige Berufserfahrung

reliability Zuverlässigkeit, Genauigkeit

relief Unterstützung, Hilfeleistung

religious belief religiöser Glaube

religious instruction Religionsunterricht

remedial (adj) Förder-...; **~ education** Förderunterricht

remedial class Schulklasse mit Förderunterricht

remedial lessons Förderunterricht

remedial teaching Heilpädagogik

repeat a year, have to ~ sitzen bleiben, ein Schuljahr wiederholen

report Beurteilung, Bericht; **school ~** Zeugnis

represent (v) darstellen, symbolisieren

representation Stellvertretung, Darstellung

representative stage Periode, in der das Kind Objekte malt, wie es sie sieht

repression *(psych)* Unterdrückung, Verdrängung

research and development Forschung und Entwicklung

research department Forschungsabteilung

resentment Verbitterung, Groll

residence *(jur)* Aufenthaltsbestimmung

residence permit *(jur)* Aufenthaltserlaubnis

residency *(jur)* Aufenthaltsbestimmungsrecht; **grant a ~ order in one's favour** das Aufenthaltsbestimmungsrecht zugesprochen erhalten; **permanent ~** ständiger Wohnsitz

residential area Wohngebiet

residential care Heimerziehung

residential care worker Heimerzieher(in)

residential care officer Mitarbeiter(in) in einem Wohnheim

residential centre Wohnheim

residential childcare Fremdunterbringung

residential child care worker Heimerzieher(in)

residential district Wohngebiet

residential home Heim

residential provision Internatseinrichtung

residential school Internatsschule

residential unit Wohneinheit im Internat

resource person Bezugsperson

resource teacher (Irl) Sonderschullehrer(in)

resource room Medienraum

resources Hilfsquellen, Mittel

respond (v) reagieren, auf etwas antworten

responsibility Verantwortlichkeit, Verantwortung

responsiveness Empfindlichkeit, Empfänglichkeit

rest home Altersheim

rest time Ruhezeit

restrain (v) jmd. zurückhalten

restrained (adj) beherrscht

restraints Beschränkungen

restrict (v) beschränken, begrenzen

restrictive (adj) einschränkend, einengend

retardation Retardierung, Verzögerung

retarded (adj) entwicklungsgestört; zurückgeblieben; **mentally** ~ geistig zurückgeblieben

retire (v) in den Ruhestand gehen

retired (adj) im Ruhestand

retirement age Rentenalter; Altersgrenze

retraining Umschulung

reunion Treffen, Zusammenkunft; **family** ~ Familientreffen

revealing (adj) aufschlussreich

review Beurteilung

reward Belohnung

right of asylum Asylrecht

right of custody *(jur)* Sorgerecht

right to exist Recht auf Leben, Daseinsberechtigung

right-handedness Rechtshändigkeit

rightist Rechter, Rechtsradikaler

ring games Kreisspiele

risk factors Risikofaktoren

rite Ritus, Zeremoniell

road safety training Verkehrserziehung

rocking horse Schaukelpferd

role Rolle

role allocation Rollenzuweisung

role behaviour Rollenverhalten, Rollenhandeln

role conflict Rollenkonflikt

role model Rollenvorbild, Leitbild

role play, role playing Rollenspiel

role reversal Rollentausch

roller skate Rollschuh, Rollerskate

roller skating rink Rollschuhbahn

roller-coaster Achterbahn

roster (US) Dienstplan

rota Liste, Plan; **daily** ~ Tagesplan; **weekly** ~ Wochenplan; **duty** ~ Dienstplan

rota system Dienstplan

rotation schema das Verhaltensmuster der „Rotation"

rote learning; to learn by rote auswendig lernen, mechanisches Lernen, pauken

roundabout Karussell, Kreisverkehr

rubella Röteln

rude (adj) unhöflich

rule Regel, Vorschrift, Bestimmung

run (v) leiten, betreiben; **this institution is ~ by the state** diese Einrichtung wird vom Staat betrieben; **to ~ a**

nursery einen Kindergarten leiten
running translation Simultanübersetzung
runny nose „laufende Nase"
rural environment ländliche Umgebung

S

sabbatical, ~ leave, ~ year Sabbatjahr, einjährige Freistellung von der Arbeit
sack (v) jmd. kündigen, hinauswerfen
safeguard Vorsichtsmaßnahme
safety harness Sicherheitsgurt für Kinder
saliva Speichel
same-sex union gleichgeschlechtliche Ehe
sandman Sandmännchen
sandpail (US) Sandeimer
sandpit (Brit) Sandkasten
satchel (Schul)Ranzen
saying Sprichwort

schedule Fahrplan, Terminplan; **teaching ~** Lehrplan
schema [ski:ma] *(päd)* Schema, Verhaltensmuster, Handlungsmuster; > core and radial; > connection; > enveloping; > rotation; > transporting; > trajectory
schema cluster miteinander verbundene Verhaltensmuster
scheme [ski:m] Projekt, Plan, Programm
scholarship Stipendium
school Schule; **primary ~** (Brit), **elementary ~** (US) Grundschule; **secondary ~** (Brit) Oberschule, weiterführende Schule; **junior high ~** (US) 7. – 9. Klasse; **senior high ~** (US) 10. – 12. Klasse; **high ~** (US) Oberschule; > **infant ~**, **junior ~**
school attendance Schulbesuch
school country hostel Schullandheim
school drop-out Schulabbrecher(in)
school entrance age Schuleintrittsalter
school fees Schulgeld
school inspector (Brit) Schulrat

school leaver Schulabgänger
school magazine Schülerzeitung
school report (Schul)Zeugnis
school secretary's office Schulsekretariat
school trip Klassenfahrt
school-age (adj) schulpflichtig; ~ **children** schulpflichtige Kinder
school-age centre (Kinder-)Hort
school-age childcare worker Horterzieher(in) (D)
school-leaving | certificate Abschlusszeugnis; ~ **age** Abgangsalter von der Schule
scientific literacy naturwissenschaftliche Grundbildung
scooter Roller
Scottish Certificate of Education (SCE) schottisches Äquivalent des englischen > GCSE
Scottish Education Department schottisches Erziehungsministerium
Scottish Qualifications Authority (SQA) Schottisches Prüfungsamt
scrap book Sammelalbum
scribbling developmental stage Kritzelalter

second (v) *(meist passiv)* abgestellt, dienstlich befreit werden; **headteachers are ~ed from these duties** Leiter(innen) werden von dieser Pflicht befreit
second forename zweiter Vorname
second language erste Fremdsprache
second language learning Zweitspracherwerb
second name Nachname
secondary bonding Sekundärbeziehung
secondary education Erziehungsabschnitt für 12 – 17-Jährige
secondary school Oberschule, weiterführende Schule
secondment Abstellung, Versetzung *(für Arbeitnehmer(innen))*
secrecy Schweigepflicht
secure establishment geschlossene Einrichtung
see-saw Wippe; (v) wippen
segregate the sexes die Geschlechter trennen
segregated school Schule mit Rassentrennung
segregation Trennung, Segregation; **racial ~** Rassentrennung
select (v) auswählen

self-abasement Selbsterniedrigung
self-absorbed (adj) mit sich selbst beschäftigt
self-actualisation Selbstverwirklichung
self-assertion Selbstbewusstsein, Durchsetzungsvermögen, Geltendmachung seiner Rechte
self-assertive (adj) anmaßend, überheblich, sich behauptend
self-assessment Selbsteinschätzung
self-assurance Selbstsicherheit, Selbstbewusstsein, Selbstvertrauen
self-aware (adj) selbstkritisch
self-awareness Selbsterkenntnis
self-centred (adj) ichbezogen, egozentrisch
self-command Selbstbeherrschung
self-complacent (adj) selbstzufrieden
self-concept Selbstbild, Selbstverständnis
self-confidence Selbstbewusstsein, Selbstvertrauen
self-consciousness Befangenheit, Gehemmtheit
self-contained (adj) selbstständig, unabhängig

self-control Selbstbeherrschung
self-development Selbstentfaltung
self-directed activity Eigentätigkeit *(des Kindes)*, Selbsttätigkeit
self-efficacy Durchsetzungsfähigkeit, Selbstwirksamkeit
self-efficacy belief Glaube, dass man seine eigenen Lebensumstände kontrollieren kann
self-employed childminders selbstständige Tageseltern
self-esteem Selbstachtung
self-evaluation Selbstbewertung, Selbsteinschätzung
self-evident (adj) offensichtlich, selbstverständlich
self-expression Ausdruck der eigenen Persönlichkeit
self-fulfilling prophesy eine sich selbst erfüllende Voraussage; Verhaltenserwartung, die das erwartete Verhalten auslöst
self-governing selbstverwaltet
self-guided learning selbstgesteuertes Lernen
self-help-group Selbsthilfegruppe

self-indulgence Maßlosigkeit, Zügellosigkeit

self-inflicted selbstzugefügt; ~ **wounds** Selbstverstümmelung

selfish (adj) selbstsüchtig, eigennützig

self-mastery Selbstbeherrschung

self-possessed (adj) selbstbeherrscht

self-realization Selbstverwirklichung

self-respect Selbstachtung

self-restraint Selbstbeherrschung

self-worth Selbstwert; **feel ~** sich wertvoll fühlen

Sellotape ® (Brit) Tesafilm ®

semi-skilled (adj) angelernt

SEN-children > special educational needs

SENCO (Special Educational Needs Co-Ordinator) Koordinator für Integrationskinder an Schulen

senior citizens ältere Menschen

senior high school (US) Oberschule, 10. – 12. Schuljahr

sense Verstand, Bedeutung; Sinn; **hearing ~** Gehör; **~ of taste** Geschmackssinn, **tactile ~** Tastsinn

sense of achievement Erfolgserlebnis

sense of touch Tastsinn

sense organ Sinnesorgan

sensibility Verständnis, Einfühlungsvermögen

sensible (adj) vernünftig

sensitive (adj) verständnisvoll, sensibel

sensitive period sensible Phase

sensitivity Verständnis, Empfindsamkeit, Sensibilität

sensitize (v) jemanden für etwas sensibilisieren

sensorial, sensori-, sensory (adj) sinnes-, die Sinne betreffend

sensori motor *(adj)* sensomotorisch

sensorimotor development senso-motorische Entwicklung

sensorimotor period senso-motorische Phase

sensory development Entwicklung der Sinne

sensory exercise Sinnesübung

sensory materials Sinnesmaterialien

sensory organ Sinnesorgan

sensory perception Sinneswahrnehmung

sensory-motor sensomotorisch

sensual (adj) sinnlich; ~ **experience** sinnliche Erfahrung

separate (v) sich trennen

separate person eigenständige Person

separation Trennung *(auch ehelich)*

separation anxiety Trennungsangst

separation distress Trennungsschmerz

service Dienst, Dienstleistung; Angebot

session Sitzung, *(Unterrichts)* Stunde

set limits Grenzen setzen

setback Rückschlag

setting Umwelt, Umfeld; *(päd.)* Form der Leistungsdifferenzierung

settle in (v) sich eingewöhnen, einleben; **to ~ somebody** jemandem helfen, sich einzugewöhnen

settling-in Eingewöhnung

severe (adj) *(im Zusammenhang mit Behinderungen)* schwer

severely disabled schwerbehindert

sex *(biologisches)* Geschlecht

sex discrimination Diskriminierung aufgrund des Geschlechts

sex education Sexualerziehung

sex roles Geschlechtsrollen

sexual abuse sexueller Missbrauch

shadow (v) jemanden (bei der Arbeit) begleiten und beobachten

share (v) teilen, teilhaben, austauschen, weitergeben, gemeinsam...; ~ **a flat** in einer Gemeinschaftswohnung wohnen; ~ **in** teilnehmen an, ~ **information** mitteilen

sharing time Zeit, in der die Kinder über selbst gewählte Themen oder über mitgebrachte Dinge sprechen

sheltered accommodation betreutes Wohnen *(z.B. Behinderte)*

sheltered workshop Behindertenwerkstatt

shift Schicht, Dienstzeit; **early ~** Frühdienst; **late ~** Spätdienst

shift change-over Übergabe, Besprechung bei Schichtwechsel

shift hand-over Übergabe, Besprechung bei Schichtwechsel

short-term memory

Kurzzeitgedächtnis

Show and Tell Day Tag, an dem eigenes Spielzeug mit in den Kindergarten gebracht werden kann

show round einen Rundgang machen, eine Besichtigungstour durchführen

shuffle (v) schlurfen

sibling rivalry Geschwister-Rivalität

siblings *(meist pl) (Abk sib)* Geschwister

sick (adj) krank, **to be ~** sich übergeben müssen

sick certificate Krankenschein

sick leave krankheitsbedingte Abwesenheit von der Arbeit; **to be on ~** krank geschrieben sein

sick note Krankmeldung

sick pay Lohnfortzahlung (bei Krankheit)

sickness Krankheit, Übelkeit, Erbrechen

sickness benefit (Brit) Krankengeld

side effect Nebenwirkung

side trip Tagesausflug

SIDS > sudden infant death syndrome

sign language Gebärdensprache

significant (adj) beachtlich, bedeutsam, signifikant

significant difference deutlicher Unterschied

significant improvement beachtliche Verbesserung

single allein stehend, allein erziehend

single child family Familie mit einem Kind

single family Familie mit einem Elternteil; Ein-Eltern-Familie

single | mother; ~ father allein erziehende(r) Mutter / Vater

single parent allein erziehender Elternteil

sinusitis Nasennebenhöhlenentzündung

sit an exam eine Prüfung ablegen

sit in (on a class) (v) hospitieren

situation Situation

situation analysis Situationsanalyse

situational approach Situationsansatz

situation-oriented approach Situationsansatz

sixth form (Brit) letztes (12.) Schuljahr vor den > A Levels; **~er** Schüler(in) dieser Klasse

size constancy Größenkon-

skate (v) Schlittschuh laufen, Rollschuh fahren, Rollerskate fahren

skating rink Eisbahn; Rollschuhbahn

skill Geschick, Fähigkeit; **language ~s** Sprachkompetenz; **manual ~** Handgeschicklichkeit; **game of ~** Geschicklichkeitsspiel; **basic ~s** Grundfähigkeiten

skilled (adj) geschickt; gut ausgebildet

skilled worker Facharbeiter(in)

skin cancer Hautkrebs

skip (v) hüpfen, seilspringen

skipping Seilspringen

skipping rope Springseil

slap schlagen

sleeping in nächtlicher Bereitschaftsdienst von Mitarbeitern in Kinderheimen

sleepy (adj) schläfrig

slide (Kinder-) Rutsche

sliding scale progressive Skala

sling Tragetuch für Babys

slither (v) rutschen, schlittern

slow pupil Schüler, der in seinen Leistungen hinter der Klasse zurückbleibt

smack (v) prügeln; ~ somebody's bottom jemandem den Hintern versohlen

small-for-date baby zum korrekten Geburtszeitpunkt untergewichtiges Baby

small motor skills Feinmotorik

snakes and ladders Leiterspiel *(Brettspiel)*

Snoezelen Room Snoezelraum

snotty (adj) (F) rotzig, Rotz- *(in Zusammensetzungen)*

snotty-nosed (adj) (F) rotznasig

sociable (adj) gesellig

social (adj) Gesellschafts-, gesellschaftlich

social | office; ~ department Sozialamt

social adaptability soziales Anpassungsvermögen

social and economic issues soziale und wirtschaftliche Probleme

social aptitude soziale Anpassungsfähigkeit

social behaviour Sozialverhalten

social care Sozialpflege; ~ **orientation** sozialpflegerische Orientierung

social event gesellschaftliches Ereignis

social exclusion soziale Ausgrenzung
social insurance Sozialversicherung
social pedagogue Sozialpädagoge/-in
social pedagogy Sozialpädagogik
social problems soziale Probleme
social sciences Gesellschafts-, Sozialwissenschaften
social security (benefit) Sozialhilfe
social services staatliche Sozialleistungen
social skills soziale Fähigkeiten
social studies Sozialkunde, Gesellschafts-, Sozialwissenschaften
social work Sozialarbeit; **~er** Sozialarbeiter(in)
socialization Sozialisationsprozess
socially (adj) gesellschaftlich, das Sozialverhalten betreffend
society Gesellschaft; **multicultural ~** multikulturelle Gesellschaft
sociology of education Erziehungs-, Bildungssoziologie
sole parent allein erziehender Elternteil

solid food feste Nahrung
solvent Lösemittel; **to abuse ~s** Lösemittel missbrauchen, schnüffeln
somersault Purzelbaum; (v) einen Purzelbaum schlagen, sich überschlagen
soothe (v) beschwichtigen, lindern
sophomore Student im zweiten Studienjahr
sore throat Halsschmerzen
sorrow Kummer, Traurigkeit, Leid
sound | box; **~ cylinder** Rasselbüchse
sound basis solide Grundlage
source language Ausgangssprache
spank (v) verprügeln, jmd. einen Klaps geben
spatial (adj) räumlich
spatial awareness räumliches Bewusstsein
special (educational) needs Sondererziehungsanforderungen, sonderpädagogische Förderbedürfnisse; **SEN-children** Kinder mit besonderen pädagogischen Bedürfnissen z.B. wegen Behinderung
special education Sondererziehung; **~ teacher** Sonderschullehrer(in)

Special Educational Needs Co – Ordinator Koordinator für Integrationskinder an Regelschulen

special kindergarten Sonderkindergarten

special needs assistant (Brit) Assistenzkraft für Schüler/innen mit sonderpäda-gogischem Förderbedarf

special needs child Kind mit besonderen Bedürfnissen, z.B. wegen Behinderung

special needs education Sonderpädagogik

special needs kindergarten educator Erzieherin in einem Sonderkindergarten

special needs teaching Sonderschulwesen

special school Sonderschule

specific observation gezielte Beobachtung

speech defect Sprachfehler

speech disorder Sprachstörung

speech impediment Sprachfehler

speech therapist Logopäde/in, Sprachtherapeut(in)

speech therapy Logopädie, Sprachtherapie

spelling Rechtschreibung

spelling | error, ~ mistake Rechtschreibfehler

spending money Taschengeld

sphere Kugel

spinal column, spine Wirbelsäule

spinner Drehgrüst auf Spielplatz

split (v) (auf)teilen, sich trennen

split-up Trennung

spoilt (adj) verwöhnt, verzogen, verdorben

spontaneous unfolding selbsttätige Entfaltung

spoon-feed (v) jmd. mit dem Löffel füttern

spring rocker Spielgerät im Außenbereich: Sitz auf einer starken Feder zum Wippen

SQA > Scottish Qualifications Authority

stabilizers, stabilizing wheels Stützräder beim Fahrrad

staff (v) (*meist passiv*) beschäftigen; **nurseries are ~ed with qualified teachers** in den Kindergärten werden qualifizierte Lehrerinnen beschäftigt; **there are ~ed adventure playgrounds** es gibt Abenteuerspielplätze mit angestelltem Personal

staff Mitarbeiter, Kollegen, Kollegium; **teaching ~**

Lehrpersonal; **member of ~** Mitarbeiter(in)

staff meeting Mitarbeiterbesprechung, Dienstbesprechung

staff room Lehrerzimmer, Personalraum

staff training Ausbildung der Mitarbeiter(innen), des Personals

staff-child ratio zahlenmäßiges Verhältnis von Erziehern zu Kindern; Erzieher-, Personalschlüssel

staffing Personalausstattung; Stellenbesetzung

stakeholder Interessenvertreter

stand back (v) sich zurückhalten

Standard Grade / Scottish Certificate of Education / SCE mittlerer Schulabschluss in Schottland

standing conference ständige Arbeitsgemeinschaft, Ausschuss

state education staatliches Bildungswesen

state of marriage Ehestand

state school öffentliche Schule

state subsidized facility staatlich finanzierte Einrichtung

state subsidy staatliche Subvention

state support staatliche Unterstützung

state-funded staatlich finanziert

statement Darstellung, Behauptung, Feststellung

state-registered educator staatlich anerkannte(r) Erzieher(in) (D)

state-registered nursery worker staatlich anerkannte(r) Kinderpfleger(in) (D)

statute Satzung *(Verein, Organisation)*

statutory (adj) gesetzlich

statutory agency öffentlicher Träger

statutory body Körperschaft des öffentlichen Rechts

statutory school age gesetzliches Einschulungsalter

stay down a year sitzen bleiben

stepchild Stiefkind

stepmother Stiefmutter

stepping stones Teilziele, „Trittsteine" zur nächst höheren Stufe

stick figure Strichmännchen

stigma Stigma, Zeichen, Mal; **social ~** gesellschaftlicher Makel

stigmatize (v) jmd. abstempeln, brandmarken, stigmatisieren
stillbirth Totgeburt
stillborn (adj) tot geboren
stimulate (v) anregen
stimulating (adj) anregend, begeisternd, stimulierend; ~ **environment** anregende Umgebung
stimulation Anregung
stimulus *(psych)* Antrieb, Anreiz, Ansporn; **aversive** ~ unangenehmer Reiz
storybook Buch mit Kindergeschichten
storytime Vorlesezeit
strands of development Entwicklungsstränge
stranger anxiety Fremdeln, Angst vor Fremden
stream (Brit) *(päd)* Leistungsgruppe
streaming (Brit) *(päd)* Einteilung in Leistungsgruppen
street work Straßensozialarbeit
strive (v) streben, bemühen
stroke Strich; **brush** ~ Pinselstrich; Schlag, Hieb
stroller (US) (Kinder-) Sportwagen
stubborn (adj) dickköpfig, hartnäckig, störrisch
student Student(in), Studierende(r), Oberschüler(in); **university** ~ Student an einer Universität
student on placement Praktikant(in)
student teacher Praktikant(in) in der Lehrer(innen)- Ausbildung
study trip Exkursion
study visit Studienreise
stutter (v) stottern
subject lessons Fachunterricht
subject theory Fachtheorie
subsidies Subventionen, Zuschüsse
subsidize (v) mit öffentlichen Mitteln unterstützen
substandard (adj) unterhalb der Mindestanforderungen (z.B. Wohnen, Bildung)
substitution Ersatz, Austausch
subtenant Untermieter(in)
subtle intervention vorsichtiges, zurückhaltendes Eingreifen
sucking reflex Saugreflex
sudden infant death syndrome (SIDS) plötzlicher Kindstod
summative sheet Ergebnisbogen
summer school Ferienkurs

superego *(psych)* Über-Ich

supernormal entwicklungsmäßig über der Altersnorm liegend

supervise (v) beaufsichtigen, überwachen

supervised flats for young people betreutes Wohnen für junge Menschen

supervision Beaufsichtigung, Überwachung; **to be under** ~ unter Aufsicht stehen

supervisor Anleiter(in)

supervisory responsibility Aufsichtspflicht

supplementary benefit (Brit) Sozialhilfe für allein Stehende

supplementary service zusätzliches Angebot

supplementary training Zusatzausbildung

supply teacher Vertretungslehrer(in), Aushilfslehrer(in)

support (v) (unter-)stützen, fördern

support Unterstützung

supported | accommodation, ~ **living** betreutes Wohnen, betreute Wohngemeinschaft, betreutes Einzelwohnen

supportive environment anregende, unterstützende Umgebung

Sure Start (Brit) ein Programm der Regierung (seit 90er Jahre) zur Unterstützung junger Familien in den am stärksten sozial benachteiligten Gebieten in GB

surname Nachname, Familienname

surrogate mother Leihmutter

survey Übersicht, Kurzbeschreibung, (statistische) Untersuchung, Bericht

suspended sentence (Brit) *(jur)* Bewährungsstrafe

sustain interest Interesse aufrechterhalten

sustainable development nachhaltige, zukunftsverträgliche Entwicklung

sustained shared thinking anhaltendes gemeinsames Nachdenken

swaddle a baby ein Baby wickeln

swing Schaukel

swingset Schaukelgestell

syllabus Lehrplan

symbolic mode symbolische Methode

symbolic representation symbolische Darstellung

sympathetic (adj) verständnisvoll, teilnahmsvoll, sympathisch, wohlgesonnen

T

table Tabelle, Schaubild
tackle (v) *(ein Problem, eine Aufgabe)* angehen, in Angriff nehmen
tactile sense Tastsinn
take into account berücksichtigen, in Betracht ziehen
take into consideration berücksichtigen
take into effect in Kraft treten
take part (v) teilnehmen
take place (v) stattfinden
take turns (v) sich abwechseln
talk Vortrag, Bericht; **to give a ~** einen Vortrag halten
talk back (v) eine freche Antwort geben; **don't ~ to me!** sei ja nicht frech!
talk over (v) etwas besprechen
tantrum schlechte Laune, Wutanfall
target group Zielgruppe
task Aufgabe
ta-ta (F) tschüs, winke winke
tax benefits steuerliche Vergünstigungen
Tax Credits (Brit) Steuererleichterungen bzw. je nach Einkommenshöhe Beihilfen oder „negative Steuern" für z.B. Familien mit Kindern, Arbeitslose oder Personen mit niedrigem Einkommen
tax exemption Steuerbefreiung
tea (Brit) Zwischenmahlzeit am Nachmittag; **high ~** (warmes) Abendessen mit Brot und Tee
teacher Erzieher(in), Lehrer(in)
teacher talk Lehrervortrag
teacher training Lehrerausbildung
teacher training college pädagogische Hochschule
teacher's aide (pädagogische) Unterrichtshilfe
teacherese die Art, wie ein Lehrer mit seinen Schülern spricht
teacher-centred programme Lehrer (Erzieher-) zentriertes Programm
teaching certificate Lehrbefähigung
Teaching English as a Foreign Language (TEFL) Englischer Fremdsprachenunterricht; Englisch als Fremdsprache

Teaching English as a Second Language (TESL) das Unterrichten von Englisch als zweite Sprache

Teaching English to Speakers of Other Languages (TESOL) das Unterrichten von Englisch als Fremdsprache

teaching module Unterrichtseinheit

teaching practice (Brit) Schul-, Unterrichtspraktikum

teaching profession Lehramt

teaching staff Lehrerkollegium

teaching unit Unterrichtseinheit

team building Teamfortbildung

team effort Teamarbeit

technical college Fach(ober)schule

technical term Fachausdruck

teenage mother minderjährige Mutter

teenage pregnancy; teen pregnancy Teenager-Schwangerschaft

teethe (v) zahnen

teething stage Periode des Zahnens

TEFL > Teaching English as a Foreign Language

tell tales (v) petzen

tell off (v) jmd. tadeln

tell the facts of life to a child ein Kind aufklären

temp Zeitarbeitskraft

temper Naturell, Veranlagung

temper tantrum Wutanfall

template Schablone, Vorlage, Muster

temporary (adj) vorübergehend, zeitweise

temporary arrangement Übergangsregelung

temporary teacher Lehrer/in mit Zeitvertrag

tenant Mieter; **council** ~ Mieter einer Sozialwohnung

tendency Neigung, Hang, Anlage

tenement block Wohnblock

tension Spannung, Anspannung

tension reduction Spannungsreduktion

term Semester *bzw.* Trimester (das brit. Schuljahr ist in drei **terms** unterteilt: Autumn term, Spring term, Summer term); Amtszeit; **her ~ of office is 2 years** ihre Amtsperiode beträgt 2 Jahre

term time Schulzeit, Unterrichtszeit; **...they are open until 17:30 during**

~ ...während der Schulzeit sind sie bis 17.30 geöffnet
terminal illness unheilbare Krankheit
terminate (v) beenden; *(Vertrag)* aufheben
terminate a pregnancy eine Schwangerschaft abbrechen
terry nappy (Brit) Frotteewindel
tertiary | level Hochschulniveau; ~ **education** Hochschulbildung; ~ **sector** Dienstleistungsbereich
TESL > Teaching English as a Second Language
TESOL > Teaching English to Speakers of Other Languages
test Klassenarbeit, Test
thalidomide child Contergankind
theory days *etwa:* Seminartage (während eines Praktikums)
therapeutic (adj) therapeutisch, gesundheitsfördernd, heilend
therapeutic abortion Schwangerschaftsabbruch aus medizinischer Indikation
therapeutic community therapeutische Wohngemeinschaft
therapeutic education Heilerziehung
therapeutic support therapeutische Unterstützung
therapist Therapeut(in)
therapy Therapie, Behandlung; **behavioural** ~ Verhaltenstherapie; **occupational** ~ Beschäftigungstherapie
thick (adj) *(sl)* dumm; **to be** ~ begriffsstutzig sein
three Rs (reading, writing, arithmetic) Lesen, Schreiben, Rechnen als Basiswissen der Grundschule
through care Begleitung, Unterstützung während der Heimerziehung
throw up (v) sich erbrechen, kotzen
thumb sucker Daumenlutscher
tick-tac-toe (US) Zeichenspiel für zwei Personen
tiddlywink flacher Spielstein für Brettspiele; ~**s** Flohhüpfen
tidy up (v) aufräumen
tie-dye (v) mit Abschnürtechnik batiken
tie-dyeing Schnürbatik
time limit Frist
time off Dienstbefreiung, Freizeit
timetable Stundenplan;

Fahrplan
tissue Papiertaschentuch
toddle (v) wackeln, tapsen
toddler Kleinkind
toddler's pool Planschbecken
toilet training Reinlichkeitserziehung
toilet-trained (adj) sauber *(bezogen auf Kinder)*
tolerance Toleranz; ~ **of children** Nachsicht mit Kindern
tonus Muskelspannung
tooth fairy gute Zahnfee *(die den Kindern nachts kleine Geschenke im Tausch gegen ausgefallene Milchzähne bringt)*
tootsie (F) Füßchen
topic work Projektarbeit
topical aktuell
touch Berührung, Berührungssinn, Tasten, Tastsinn
touch, being in ~ with oneself Kontakt zu sich selbst haben, sich selbst spüren
toxic (adj) giftig
toxic waste Giftmüll
toy (v) (herum)spielen; ~ **with one's food** im Essen herumstochern; ~ **with something** mit etwas herumspielen
toy Spielzeug; **cuddly ~** Schmusetier; ~ **book** Kinderbuch; ~ **car,** ~ **animals etc.** Spielzeug-Auto, -Tiere usw.
toy bricks Bauklötze
toyshop Spielwarengeschäft
track Weg, Schiene, Gleis; **Germany has a three-track educational system** Deutschland hat ein dreigliedriges Schulsystem
tracking (US) *(päd)* Einteilung in Leistungsgruppen
tracksuit Trainingsanzug
trail observation Beobachtung der Bewegungsmuster in einem Raum
train (v) ausbilden, schulen
trainee Praktikant(in), Anlernling
trainee teacher Referendar(in)
traineeship Praktikum
trainer Turnschuh
training Ausbildung, Schulung; **on-the-job ~** Ausbildung am Arbeitsplatz
training allowance Ausbildungsvergütung
training college (Lehrer-) Ausbildungsstätte, Fachschule
training college for educators Fachschule / Fachakademie für Sozialpädagogik (D)

training regulations Ausbildungsordnung

training wheels (US) Stützräder

trajectory Flugbahn, gerade Linie; *i.w.S.* Bewegung in gerader Linie

trajectory schema das Verhaltensmuster „Bewegung in gerader Linie"

transformation Verwandlung, Umformung; **structural ~s in society** tiefgreifende gesellschaftliche Veränderungen

transient child Kind aus nicht sesshafter Familie

transition Übergang; **smooth ~** ein weicher, konfliktfreier Übergang

translate into practice in die Praxis umsetzen

translation Übersetzung; **simultaneous ~** Simultandolmetschen

transporting schema das Verhaltensmuster des „Transportierens"

treatment Behandlung

trial and error Versuch und Irrtum

tricycle Dreirad

triplet Drilling; **a set of ~s** Drillinge

trolley Servierwagen

troublemaker Störenfried

truancy unentschuldigtes Fehlen von der Schule

truant Schulschwänzer(in); **play ~** die Schule schwänzen

tuition Unterricht

tuition fee Schulgeld, Studiengebühr

tumbling Bodenturnen

tummy (F) Bauch

tummy ache Bauchweh

tummy button Bauchnabel

tutor Nachhilfelehrer(in); Privatlehrer(in); Tutor(in) an Universität

twin Zwilling; **identical ~s** eineiige Zwillinge, **fraternal ~s** zweieiige Zwillinge

U

ultrasound Ultraschall
umbilical chord Nabelschnur
umbrella organization Dachverband
unable (adj) unfähig
unaccompanied (adj) ohne Begleitung eines/einer Erwachsenen
unaccountable (adj) nicht verantwortlich, unerklärlich
unaccustomed (adj) selten, ungewohnt
unaltered (adj) unverändert
unambiguous (adj) eindeutig, unmissverständlich
unanimity Einstimmigkeit
unanimous (adj) einstimmig
unassuming (adj) bescheiden
unattached (adj) unabhängig, ledig, ungebunden
unattended (adj) unbeaufsichtigt, allein gelassen
unauthorized (adj) unerlaubt, nicht autorisiert
unavailable (adj) nicht erreichbar, nicht verfügbar
unbearable (adj) unerträglich, nicht auszuhalten
unbiased (adj) unvoreingenommen, unbeeinflusst
unbiased observations unvoreingenommene Beobachtungen
unborn (adj) ungeboren; **protection of the ~ child** Schutz des ungeborenen Lebens
uncared for (adj) vernachlässigt
uncaring (adj) gleichgültig; **an ~ mother** eine Rabenmutter
uncertainty Ungewissheit, Unsicherheit, Zweifel
uncharacteristic (adj) ungewöhnlich
uncompromising (adj) entschieden, kompromisslos
unconditional (adj) *(psych)* nichtkonditionell, unbedingt
unconscious (adj) unbewusst, bewusstlos; **the ~** das Unbewusste, das Unter-bewusste
uncountable (adj) unzählbar
under public law öffentlichrechtlich
underachiever leistungsschwache/r Schüler/in
underachieving child unterbegabtes Kind
underage (adj) minderjährig
underfed (adj) unterernährt
undergraduate Student(in) *(vor dem ersten akademischen Grad)*

underpaid (adj) unterbezahlt

underpin (v) zugrunde legen, eine Basis bilden, untermauern; **it is ~ned by...** umfasst, stellt eine Grundlegung dar

underprivileged child sozial benachteiligtes Kind

understanding Verständnis (von etwas haben), Übereinkunft

undivided attention ungeteilte Aufmerksamkeit

uneasy (adj) besorgt, unangenehm, unsicher

uneducated (adj) ungebildet

unemployed (adj) arbeitslos

unemployment benefit (Brit) Arbeitslosenunterstützung

unfamiliar (adj) unvertraut, fremd

unfold (v) sich entfalten

ungraded school nicht nach Jahrgängen oder Leistungen gegliederte Schule

unicycle Einrad

unimpaired (adj) unbeeinträchtigt; **~ hearing** ausgezeichnetes Gehör

unit Einheit, Abteilung, Wohneinheit

United Nations Educational, Scientific and Cultural Organization (UNESCO) UN-Organisation für Erziehung, Wissenschaft und Kultur

university student Student an einer Universität

unmanageable (adj) unkontrollierbar, außer Kontrolle

unobtrusively (adj) unaufdringlich, unauffällig

unpaid traineeship unbezahltes Volontariat

unprecedented (adj) beispiellos, noch nie dagewesen

unpredictable (adj) unvorhersehbar

unprepared (adj) unvorbereitet

upper secondary school-leaving examination Abitur, allg. Hochschulreife

unreliable (adj) unzuverlässig

unselfish (adj) selbstlos, uneigennützig

unskilled (adj) nicht ausgebildet, unqualifiziert

unstable behaviour labiles Verhalten

untapped educational potential Begabungsreserve

untrained (adj) ungeübt

unwanted (adj) unerwünscht, ungewollt

upbringing Erziehung (durch die Familie)

update (v) aktualisieren

upgrading Aufwertung; **~ of care professions** Aufwer-

tung pflegerischer Berufe
uproar Lärm, Tumult
upset (adj) aufgebracht, bestürzt
urban (adj) städtisch, urban; ~ **development** Stadtentwicklung, ~ **renewal** Stadtsanierung
urge starkes Verlangen, Trieb, Bedürfnis
urgent (adj) dringend, eilig
utterance Äußerung, Sprache; **a child's first ~s** die ersten Worte eines Kindes

V

vacancy Vakanz, freie Stelle *(Arbeitsplatz)*
vacation (US) (Schul-)Ferien, Urlaub
vaccinate (v) impfen; ~ **against** gegen etwas impfen
vaccination Schutzimpfung
vaccine Impfstoff
vacuum | bottle, ~ flask Thermosflasche
valentine card Valentinskarte
valid (adj) berechtigt, begründet, gültig
valuable (adj) wertvoll
valuation Bewerten, Wertung
value Wert, Bedeutung; ~**s** Werte; **basic ~s** Grundwerte
vandalism Zerstörungswut
variation Abweichung, Unterschied
variety Vielfalt, Verschiedenartigkeit
vast majority große Mehrheit, der überwiegende Teil
vegetarian Vegetarier; ~ **diet** vegetarische Kost
Venture Scout Pfadfinder über 16 Jahre
verbal expression mündlicher, verbaler Ausdruck
verbalize (v) etwas in Worten ausdrücken; **start to ~** *(bei Kindern)* anfangen zu sprechen
vicinity Nachbarschaft
vicious circle Teufelskreis
victim Opfer
victimize (v) jemanden schikanieren, ungerecht behandeln
view of | humanity; ~ **mankind** Menschenbild
vigorous (adj) energisch, kräftig
violence Gewalt, Heftigkeit; **domestic ~** Gewalt in der

Familie
violence against children Gewalt gegen Kinder
violence among children Gewalt unter Kindern
violent (adj) gewalttätig, gewaltsam, brutal; ~ **scene** Gewaltszene; ~ **crime** Gewaltverbrechen
virtue Tugend
vision Sehen, Sehvermögen
visit Besuch; **pay a** ~ jemandem einen Besuch machen
visit (v) besuchen, aufsuchen
visiting hours Besuchszeiten
visual disorder Sehstörung
visual impairment Sehschwäche
visual perception optische Wahrnehmung; visuelles Wahrnehmungsvermögen
visualize (v) sich etwas bildlich vorstellen, anschaulich machen
vital statistics Bevölkerungsstatistik
vitality Lebenskraft, Energie, Vitalität
vivid (adj) anschaulich, lebhaft, lebendig; ~ **imagination** lebhafte Fantasie
vocabulary, passive ~ passiver Wortschatz
vocal disorder Sprechstörung
vocational (adj) beruflich
vocational counselling Berufsberatung
vocational education Berufsausbildung
vocational further training berufliche Fortbildung
vocational grammar school Fachoberschule (D)
vocational practical studies Betriebspraktikum
vocational school Berufsschule
vocational training Berufsausbildung
vocational training college for social care Berufsfachschule für Sozialwesen (D)
vocational training institution Berufsfachschule *(in D. nicht berufsqualifizierend)*
voice, breaking of the ~ Stimmbruch
voluntary (adj) freiwillig; ~ **organization** Freiwilligenorganisation
voluntary | agency, ~ **organization** freier Träger
voluntary bodies for youth work freie Träger der Jugendhilfe
voluntary sector die freien Träger
voluntary welfare work freie Wohlfahrtspflege
voluntary youth leader Ju-

gendleiter
volunteer ehrenamtliche(r) Mitarbeiter(in), Freiwillige(r)
volunteer (v) sich als Freiwillige(r) melden, mitarbeiten, seine Mitarbeit anbieten
vomit (v) sich erbrechen, kotzen
voucher Gutschein
vulnerable families leicht verletzbare Familien, bedrohte Familien

W

wake up (v) jemanden aufwecken; aufwachen
wakened night staff, waking (night duty) nächtlicher Bereitschaftsdienst; Nachtwache
wall bars Sprossenwand
wall display Plakate, Bilder oder Collagen, die an der Wand aufgehängt werden
wallow (v) in etwas schwelgen, ganz absorbiert sein
wanted child Wunschkind
ward (Stadt-)Bezirk
warden Heimleiter, Aufseher
warm supportive environment anregende, unterstützende Umgebung
waste Verschwendung, Vergeudung
waste disposal Abfallbeseitigung
waste materials Abfallmaterial
water play area Fläche mit Wasserspielen
watering can Gießkanne
waterwings Schwimmflügel
wax crayon Wachsmalstift
wax paper Wachspapier
wean a baby ein Baby abstillen
weaning Entwöhnung
wedding Hochzeit; ~ **anniversary** Hochzeitstag
wee; wee-wee *(Kindersprache)* Pipi
weekly rota Wochenplan
welcome (v) jemanden begrüßen, herzlich willkommen heißen
welfare Sozialhilfe, Wohlfahrt, Fürsorge
welfare | benefits; ~ services Sozialleistungen
welfare | officer; ~ worker Sozialarbeiter(in)

welfare assistant (Brit) *(etwa:)* pädagogische Unterrichtshilfe (D)

welfare association Wohlfahrtsorganisation

welfare state Wohlfahrtsstaat

well behaved (adj) brav, gut erzogen

well done! gut gemacht!

well-being Wohlbefinden, Wohlergehen

Welsh Office walisisches Erziehungsministerium

wet (v) nass machen; ~ **the bed** ins Bett machen; ~ **one's pants** in die Hose machen

wheelbarrow Schubkarre

wheelchair Rollstuhl; ~ **user** Rollstuhlfahrer

whizzkid (F) Wunderkind, kleines Genie

wholefood Vollwertkost; ~ **shop** Bioladen

whooping cough Keuchhusten

wide age-range große Altersmischung

wishful thinking Wunschdenken

withdrawn (adj) in sich gekehrt, introvertiert, verschlossen, kontaktarm, zurückgezogen

women's refuge Frauenhaus

wooden block Holzblock, Holzbaustein; ~ **area** Spielecke für Holzbausteine

word game Buchstabenspiel

work contract Arbeitsvertrag

work creation | plan, ~ scheme Arbeitsbeschaffungsmaßnahme

work experience Betriebs-, Schulpraktikum; *auch:* Berufserfahrung; **to do** ~ ein Praktikum machen

work in shifts in Schichten *oder* zeitversetzt arbeiten

work permit Arbeitserlaubnis

work placement Arbeitspraktikum; **~s cover four weeks during the first year of study** im ersten Studienjahr sind vier Wochen Praktikum

work therapy Arbeitstherapie

workers (*pl*) Mitarbeiter(innen), Kollegen, Kolleginnen

workers' committee Betriebsrat

working conditions Arbeitsbedingungen

working day Arbeitstag

working with parents Arbeit mit Eltern

workload allocation Zuweisung von Arbeit

workplace Arbeitsplatz

workplace crèche Betriebskindergarten /-krippe
workplace setting Arbeitsfeld
workschool-philosophy Arbeitsschulgedanke
workshop Werkstatt; Seminar
wrap-around provision umfassende Angebote
written paper Klausur, schriftliche Prüfung
written plans and reports schriftliche Pläne und Berichte
written test schriftliche Arbeit, Klausur

X

xenophobia Fremdenfeindlichkeit
xerox ® (v) etwas kopieren
Xerox ® Fotokopie

Y

young adulthood frühes Erwachsenenalter
young child Kleinkind
young offender jugendlicher Straffälliger
young offenders' institution Jugendstrafanstalt
young person (Brit) *(jur)* junger Mensch zwischen 14 und 17 Jahren
youth | centre, ~ **club** Jugendzentrum
youth and child welfare Jugendwohlfahrt
youth and community worker Sozialpädagoge / Sozialpädagogin, Jugend- und Gemeinwesenarbeiter(in)
youth association Jugendorganisation, -verband
youth custody (Brit) *(jur)* Jugendstrafe
youth custody centre (Brit) *(jur)* Jugendstrafanstalt
Youth Training (YT) (Brit) Berufsfindungsprojekt für Jugendliche ohne Arbeit, Jugendausbildungsprogramm
youth unemployment Jugendarbeitslosigkeit

youth welfare Jugendhilfe
youth work Jugendarbeit;
 detached ~ mobile Jugendarbeit

Z

zap (v) *(im Fernsehen)* die Kanäle wechseln
zero tolerance null Toleranz
zone of actual development Zone der aktuellen Entwicklung
zone of proximal development Zone der nächsten Entwicklung

A

Abbild (n) image
Abendschule (f) evening school, evening classes, night school
Abenteuerpädagogik (f) adventure education
Abenteuerspielplatz (m) adventure playground
Abfall (m) waste
Abfallbeseitigung (f) waste disposal
Abfallmaterial (n) waste materials
Abgangsalter (n) *(von der Schule)* school-leaving age
Abgangszeugnis (n) (school-)leaving certificate (Brit); diploma (US)
abgelenkt (adj) distracted
abhängig (adj) dependent; **abhängiges Kind** dependent child
Abhängigkeit (f) dependency
abholen (v) *(jemanden)* to collect; *(mit dem Auto auch)* to pick up
Abitur (n) (D) (upper secondary) school-leaving examination / university entrance qualification; *(entspricht A level in Brit, Highers in Scot);* **das ~ machen** to take one's A levels (> fachgebundene Hochschulreife)
Abiturzeugnis (n) (D) school-leaving certificate, high-school diploma
ablenken (v) to distract
Ablösungsprozess (m) *(psych)* detachment process
Abneigung (f) aversion, dislike
abschaffen (v) to abolish, to get rid of
Abschlussklasse (f) final-year class
Abschlussprüfung (f) final examination
Abschlusszeugnis (n) school-leaving certificate (Brit); diploma (US)
Abstammungsfamilie (f) parental family
abstillen (v) *(Baby)* to wean a baby
abstrakte Operationen formal operations
Abtreibung (f) abortion; **eine ~ vornehmen** to carry out an abortion, to have an abortion; **legaler Schwangerschaftsabbruch** (m) legal abortion; **~ im fortgeschrittenen Stadium der**

Schwangerschaft partial-birth abortion
Abtreibungsversuch (m) attempt at an abortion
abwechseln, sich (v) to take turns
Abwehrmechanismus (m) defence mechanism
abweichend (adj) *(soz)* deviant
abweichendes Verhalten (n) aberrant behaviour, deviant behaviour
Abweichung (f) *(soz)* variation, deviation
abwesend (adj) absent
Abwesende(r) (m,f) absentee
Achterbahn (f) roller-coaster
Achtung (f) esteem
adaptierte Babynahrung (f) formula
Adoleszenz (f) adolescence
adoptieren (v) to adopt
Adoptionsberatung (f) adoption counselling
Adoptionsstelle (f) adoption agency
Adoptionsvermittlung (f) adoption procedures
Adoptiveltern (pl) adoptive parents
Adoptivkind (n) adopted child
Adressenliste (f) contact list, mailing list

ADS > Aufmerksamkeitsdefizitsyndrom
affektive Lernziele (n,pl) affective objectives
Aggression (f) aggression
Akademie (f) *(Fachschule)* college
Akademie für Sozialpädagogik (f) training college for educators
Akkulturation (f) acculturation
Akte (f) file; **zu den Akten nehmen** to file; **Aktenführung** file keeping
Aktivferien (pl) activity and adventure holiday
aktualisieren (v) to update
aktuell (adj) topical, up to date, current
Akzeleration (f) (päd) acceleration
Akzeptanz (f) acceptance
akzeptieren (v) to accept
Alimente (pl) > Unterhaltszahlung für Kinder
Alkoholmissbrauch (m) alcohol abuse
allein erziehende Eltern (pl) single parents
allein Erziehende(r) (f,m) single parent, lone parent
allein erziehende(r) Mutter (Vater) (f,m) single mother / father

allein erziehender Elternteil (m *oder* n) single parent

Allergietest (m) patch test, allergy test

Allgemeinbildung (f) general education, all-round education

allgemeine Schulpflicht (f) compulsory education

Allgemeinwissen (n) general knowledge

allseitig (adj) comprehensive

Alltag (m) daily routine, everyday life

Alltagssituation (f) real-life situation

Alltagswissen (n) common sense knowledge

Alphabetisierung (f) alphabetization, anti-illiteracy programme

Alphabetisierungskampagne (f) literacy campaign

Alptraum (m) nightmare

Altenheim (n) old people's home

Altenpflege (f) care for the elderly

Altenpflegeheim (n) home for the elderly, nursing home

Altenpfleger(in) (m,f) geriatric nurse

Altentagesstätte (f) day care centre for the elderly

Altenwohnheim (n) sheltered housing

Alter (f) age; **im ~ von 5 Jahren** at the age of 5; **Kinder im ~ von 2 – 5 Jahren** children aged 2 – 5 years

ältere Menschen (m,pl) senior citizens

altern (v) to get older

Alternativbewegung (f) alternative life style, alternative movement

altersgemäße Eingruppierung (f) grouped according to age, age-grade placement

altersgemische Angebote (n,pl) mixed-age provision

altersgemischt (adj) age-integrated

Altersgliederung (f) age distribution

Altersgrenze (f) age limit

Altersgruppe (f) age-group, age bracket; **die ~ der 0- bis 3-Jährigen** the 0- to 3 age bracket

Altersheim (n) rest home

altersheterogene Gruppierung (f) mixed age grouping

altershomogene Gruppe (f) age appropriate group, age homogeneous group

Altersmischung (f) mixed-age grouping, age-integrated groups for children 3 – 5 years (including schoolchildren up to 10 years)

Altersmischung, große (f) wide age-range

Alterssitz (m) retirement home

Altersspanne (f) age band

Altersspannweite (f) age-range

Altersteilzeit (f) (D) system of part-time working for people approaching retirement

altersübergreifend (adj) age-integrated

altersübergreifende Tageseinrichtung (f) extended-age centre

Altglascontainer (m) bottle bank

Altlasten (f,pl) burdens of the past

Ambiguitätstoleranz (f) ambiguity tolerance

Ambivalenz (f) ambivalence

ambulant (adj) non-residential

ambulante Erziehungshilfen (f,pl) non-residential provision for children with problems

Amme (f) wet nurse

Ammenmärchen (n) nursery tale

Amt (n) *(Behörde)* authority, department, office; *(Aufgabe)* duty, task; *(Stellung)* office, post

Amtspflegschaft (f) authority guardianship

Amtsvormund (m) local authority guardian, official guardian

Amtsvormundschaft (f) authority guardianship

anale Phase (n) anal stage

Analphabet(in) (m,f) illiterate

Analphabetentum (n) illiteracy

Anamnese (f) case history

Andragogik (f) adult education

aneignen, sich etwas ~ (v) to acquire; *(Lerninhalte)* to learn; *(Gewohnheiten)* to pick up

Aneignung (f) acquisition

anerkannt (adj) approved, established, accepted

anerkennen (v) *(akzeptieren)* to recognize; *(würdigen)* to appreciate

Anerkennung (f) appreciation, recognition; acceptance; respect; **~ durch Gleichaltrige** peer acceptance

Anerkennungsjahr (n) probationary year, full-time work placement

anerzogen (adj) acquired

Anfangsmaterial (n) primary material

Anfangsphase (f) initial stage, initial phase

angeboren (adj) inborn, innate, hereditary; **angeborenes Verhalten** innate behaviour

Angebote (n,pl) *(soz-päd)* activities, provision; ~ **der Kinderbetreuung** childcare provisions

angelernt (adj) *(Arbeiter)* semi-skilled

angelerntes Verhalten (n) *(päd)* learned behaviour

angemessen (adj) appropriate, adequate, fair

angemessene Sorge (f) proper care

angepasst (adj) conformist, adaptive

angepasstes Verhalten (n) adaptive behaviour, conformist behaviour

Angestellte(r) (f,m) employee; *(im öffentlichen Dienst)* public sector employee, civil service employee

Angestellte(r) (f,m) **auf Stundenlohnbasis** (f) hourly paid employee

angewöhnt (adj) acquired

angleichen (v) to grow closer together; *(soz) to* assimilate, to adjust

angriffslustig (adj) aggressive

Angst (f) anxiety, fear, worry; ~ **haben** to be afraid (of), scared

Anlage (f) (päd) genetic heredity

Anlage oder Umwelt nature or nurture

Anlaufstelle (f) first contact, drop-in centre

anleiten (v) to instruct, to teach

Anleiter(in) (m,f) supervisor, instructor; *(während der praktischen Ausbildung)* guidance instructor

Anleitergespräch (n) introduction talk, supervision talk

Anleitung (f) guidance, instruction

Anleitungsgespräch (n) introduction talk, supervision talk

anmaßend (adj) self-assertive, arrogant

Anmeldeformular (n) enrolment form, registration form, entry form, application form

Anmeldegebühr (f) enrolment fee, registration fee

anmelden (v) *(sich registrieren lassen)* to register; *(vormerken)* to enrol; **ein Kind bei einer Kita ~** to enrol a child at a nursery

Anmeldung (f) enrolment

annehmen (v) *(vermuten)* to assume; *(entgegennehmen)* to accept; *(sich aneignen)* to adopt, to pick up; *(zulassen)* to accept, to take on

anpassen, sich (v) to adapt to, to conform, to adjust

Anpassung (f) adaptation, accomodation; **soziale ~** social adaptation, adjustment, conformity

Anpassungsfähigkeit (f) adaptability

Anpassungsschwierigkeit (f) (psych) maladjustment, difficulty in adapting

anregen (v) to stimulate

anregend (adj) stimulating; **eine anregende Umgebung** stimulating environment

anregende, unterstützende Umgebung (f) warm supportive environment

Anregung (f) stimulation

Anreiz (m) *(psych)* stimulus; incentive

Ansatz (m) *(soz, psych)* approach

anschaulich (adj) vivid

anschaulich machen (v) to visualize

Anschlussstudie (f) follow-up study

Ansprechpartner(in) (m,f) contact person

Anspruchsberechtigte(r) (f,m) person entitled to receive benefits

Anstaltsfürsorge (f) institutional care

Anteil (m) share, interest, coverage rate; **wie hoch ist der ~ der Kinder in Krippen?** what is the coverage rate for children in day nurseries?

Anthroposophie (f) anthroposophy

antiautoritäre Erziehung (f) antiauthoritarian upbringing

Antrag (m) application (form), request; *(Konferenz)* motion, **einen ~ stellen** *(Konferenz)* propose a motion; *(Verein, Behörde etc.)* make an application

Anwendung (f) implementation

anwendungsorientierte Erziehungsforschung (f) application-oriented pedagogic research

anwesend (adj) present
Anwesenheit (f) attendance
Anwesenheitspflicht (f) compulsory attendance
Anzahl der aufgenommenen Kinder intake of children
April|scherz (m) April fool's trick; **jmd. in den ~ schicken** to make an April's Fool of somebody; **der erste ~** April Fool's Day; **April, April!** April fool!
Arbeit mit Eltern working with parents
Arbeitgeber (m) employer
Arbeitnehmer (m) employee
Arbeitsamt (n) employment service agency, job centre
Arbeitsbedingungen (f,pl) working conditions
Arbeitsberater(in) (m,f) job counsellor
Arbeitsbeschaffungsmaßnahme (f) (**ABM**) (D) job creation scheme
Arbeitserlaubnis (f) work permit
Arbeitsfeld (n) workplace setting
Arbeitskreis (m) working party
arbeitslos (adj) unemployed
arbeitslos sein to be on the dole, to go on the dole
Arbeitslosengeld (D) unemployment benefit
Arbeitslosenhilfe (f) (D) reduced unemployment benefit
Arbeitslosenunterstützung (f) job seekers allowance, unemployment benefit
Arbeitsplan (m) assignment plan
Arbeitsplan für das Praktikum plan of practical training
Arbeitsplatz (m) job, workplace; **Zufriedenheit mit dem ~** job satisfaction; > **Stelle**
Arbeitsplatzbeschreibung (f) job description, job specification
Arbeitsschulgedanke (m) workschool-philosophy
Arbeitstag (m) working day
Arbeitstherapie (f) work therapy
Arbeitsvertrag (m) contract of employment, work contract
Arbeitszeugnis (n) reference
Ärger (m) trouble, anger, irritation
ärgerlich (adj) annoyed, cross
Arzneimittelmissbrauch (m) drug abuse
Arzt, Ärztin (m,f) physician, doctor

ärztliches Attest (n) doctor's certificate, medical certificate

ASP > Abenteuerspielplatz

Assimilationsschemata (n) *(psych)* assimilatory schemata

Asyl (n) asylum; **~bewerber** asylum seeker; **~ beantragen** apply for asylum; **politisches ~** political asylum

Asylrecht (n) right of asylum

Attest (n) (doctor's) certificate

Aufbaugymnasium (n) (D) combined grammar school with sixth form college

Aufbaustudium (n) postgraduate studies

Aufbaustufe (f) (D) sixth form college

Aufenthaltsbestimmung (f) *(jur)* residence

Aufenthaltsbestimmungsrecht (n) *(jur)* residency; **das ~ zugesprochen bekommen** to grant a residency order in one's favour

Aufenthaltserlaubnis (f) residence permit

Aufenthaltsraum (m) recreation room, lounge

Aufgabe (f) *(Verpflichtung)* task, job; *(Übung)* exercise, homework

aufgebracht (adj) upset

aufklären (v) *(ein Kind)* to tell the facts of life to a child; *(Sexualkunde)* to give children sex education

Aufklärung (f), **sexuelle** sex instruction, sex education

aufkleben (v) to stick, to paste, to glue

Auflagen (f,pl) *(jur) (Bedingungen)* directions, conditions

aufmerksam (adj) attentive, observant

Aufmerksamkeit (f) attention, attentiveness

Aufmerksamkeitsdefizitsyndrom (n) (ADS) *(psych)* attention deficit hyperactivity disorder (ADHD), attention deficit disorder

Aufnahme (f) intake

Aufnahmefähigkeit (f) receptivity

Aufnahmeprüfung (f) entrance examination, qualifying examination

Aufnahmequote (f) intake, quota

aufpassen (v) *(pflegen)* to take care of somebody, *(beaufsichtigen)* to mind, to watch, to look after; *(Aufsicht führen)* to supervise;

(aufmerksam sein) to pay attention, *(vorsichtig sein)* to look out

aufräumen (v) to tidy up

aufschlussreich (adj) informative, revealing

Aufseher(in) (m,f) attendant, supervisor, warden

Aufsicht (f) supervision; **unter ~ stehen** to be under supervision

Aufsichtspflicht (f) *(der Eltern)* (parental) duty of supervision; parental responsibility; supervisory responsibilities, legal responsibility to keep children properly supervised

Aufstiegschancen (f,pl) promotion prospects

aufstoßen (v) *(rülpsen)* to burp

Aufwertung (f) upgrading; **~ pflegerischer Kräfte** upgrading of care professionals

Aufzeichnung (f) recording

aufziehen (v) *(erziehen)* to rear, to bring up, to raise

Aula (f) hall

ausbilden (v) to train

Ausbildung (f) training

Ausbildung am Arbeitsplatz on-the-job training

Ausbildungsbeihilfe (f) training grant, education grant

Ausbildungsberater(in) (m,f) educational counsellor

Ausbildungsberuf (m) recognized trainee occupation

Ausbildungsförderung (f) education grant

Ausbildungsordnung (f) qualification requirement, training regulations

Ausbildungsplan (m) plan of practical training, plan of training objectives

Ausbildungsvergütung (f) training allowance

Ausbruch (m) *(emotionaler)* outburst, explosion

Ausdauer (f) perseverance

auseinander leben (v) to grow apart

Auseinandersetzung (f) *(Streit)* argument; *(Diskussion)* discussion, debate

Ausflug (m) outing, (field) trip, walk; **einen ~ machen** to go on an outing / field trip / walk

Ausführungsvorschrift (f) code of practice

Ausgaben (f,pl) expenses; **~kürzungen** (f,pl) expenditure cuts

Ausgangssprache (f) source language

Ausgebranntsein (n) burn-out

Ausgestoßene(r) (f,m) outcast
ausgewogen (adj) balanced
ausgezeichnetes Gehör (n) unimpaired hearing
ausgleichen (v) *(Mangel)* to compensate for; *(Konflikt)* to mediate, to reconcile
ausgrenzen (v) to exclude
Ausgrenzung (f) *(soz)* marginalization, exclusion
Ausgrenzung, soziale (f) social exclusion
Aushilfskraft (f) temporary worker
Aushilfslehrer(in) (m,f) supply teacher
Aushilfspersonal (n) auxiliary staff
Ausländer(in) (m,f) foreigner; *(jur)* alien
Ausländerfeindlichkeit (f) xenophobia, hostility to foreigners
ausländische(r) Arbeitnehmer(in) (m,f) migrant worker, foreign worker
Auslandsaufenthalt (m) stay abroad
Auslandspraktikum (n) work experience abroad, practicum abroad
Ausreichend (n) *(in einer Prüfung)* a pass mark; a passing grade (US); **ein „ausreichend" bekommen** to get a pass mark
Ausschlag (m) *(Haut)* rash; **Nesselausschlag** nettle rash; **Windelausschlag** nappy rash; diaper rash (US)
ausschließen (v) to segregate
Ausschluss (m) exclusion
Ausschuss, ständiger (m) standing conference
Außen(spiel)bereich (m) *(im Kindergarten)* outdoor area, outside play area
Außenseiter(in) (m,f) misfit, outsider
außerfamiliäre Kinderbetreuung (f) non-parental child care, extrafamilial child care
außerfamiliäre Einflüsse (m,pl) extrafamilial influences
außerfamiliäre Kinderbetreuung (f) extrafamilial care
Äußerung (f) utterance
aussetzen (v) *(Kind)* to abandon; **ausgesetztes Kind** abandoned child
Aussetzung (f) *(eines Kindes)* abandonment, exposure
Aussiedlerkinder (n,pl) ethnic German children
aussondern (v) to separate

Aussteiger(in) (m,f) drop-out
ausstellen (v) to display, to exhibit
Ausstellung (f) display, exhibition
auswerten (v) to evaluate; *(Statistiken)* to analyse
Auswertung (f) evaluation; *(Statistiken)* analysis
Auswertungsgespräch (n) evaluation
Auszeichnung (f) award, distinction
ausziehen (v) *(aus dem Elternhaus)* to leave home
Auszubildende(r) (f,m) apprentice, trainee
Autismus (m) autism
autoritärer Führungsstil (m) directive style of leadership, authoritarian leadership

B

Babybrei (m) (F) pap, baby food
Babynahrung baby food; > adaptierte ~
babysitten (v) to babysit
Babysprache (f) baby talk
Bafög > Bundesausbildungsförderungsgesetz
barischer Sinn (m), **Beurteilung des Gewichts** *(Montessori)* baric sense (judging weights)
Barrieren-freie Umwelt (f) barrier-free environment
Basale Pädagogik (f) basal pedagogy
Basiswissen (n) basics, basic knowledge, fundamentals
Bastelkurs (m) handicraft class
Basteltisch (m) handicrafts table
Batik (f) batik; *(Schnürbatik)* tie-dyeing
batiken (v) to batik; *(mit Abschnürtechnik)* to tie-dye
Baubereich (m), **Bauecke** (f) block area
Bauch (m) stomach; tummy, belly (F)

Bauchlandung (f) pancake landing

Bauchnabel (m) navel; bellybutton, tummy button (F)

Bauchschmerzen (m,pl) stomach ache, tummy-ache (F)

Bauecke (f) building corner

Bäuerchen (n) (F) burp; ~ **machen** to burp

Bauklötze (m,pl) toy bricks

Beachtung (f) attention, consideration; ~ **schenken** to pay attention to; ~ **finden** to receive attention

Beamter (m), **Beamtin** (f) civil servant

beaufsichtigen (v) to supervise, to look after

Beaufsichtigung (f) supervision

Beaufsichtigung (f) **und Pflege** (f) custodial care

Beaufsichtigung durch die Eltern parental control

bedeutsam (adj) *(soz)* significant; important

bedingt (adj) *(psych)* conditioned

Bedingung (f) *(Voraussetzung)* condition; *(Erfordernis)* requirement

Bedürfnis (n) need, necessity; *(Verlangen)* desire; **ein ~ erfüllen** to satisfy a need

Beeinträchtigung (f) disability; ~ **des Gehörs** hearing disability; ~ **des Sehens** visual disability; ~ **des Sprechens** speech and language disability; language impairment

Befangenheit (f) self-consciousness, inhibition; *(Voreingenommenheit)* biased, prejudiced

befreien (v) *(von Gebühren, Pflichten)* to exempt sb. from s.th.; **jdn. von etwas ~** *(erlösen)* to free / release sb. from s.th.; *(freistellen, entschuldigen)* to excuse sb. from s.th; **sich ~** to free oneself

Befürchtung (f) fear, apprehension

Begabtenförderung (f) promotion measures for highly gifted students / children

begabtes Kind (n) gifted child

Begabung (f) talent, ability, aptitude

Begabungsreserve (f) untapped educational potential

begeistert (adj) enthusiastic; *(leidenschaftlich)* keen

begleiten (v) to accompany; to provide (individual) guidance and support

Begleiter(in) (m,f) compan-

begreifen (v) to understand, to grasp

Begriff (m) concept, idea

Begriffsbildung (m) concept formation

Begründung (f) reason

begrüßen (v) to welcome, to say hello to somebody

Begünstigung einer Person discrimination in favour of someone

Behandlung (f) treatment

Beharrlichkeit (f) persistence, perseverance

Behauptung (f) assertion

beherrscht (adj) restrained

behindert (adj) disabled, handicapped *(wird oft als abwertend empfunden)*, physically challenged; **behinderte Kinder** disabled children

Behinderte(r) (f,m) disabled person, physically *or* mentally challenged person, handicapped person *(s.o.)*; differently abled person (US) *(politisch korrekte Bezeichnung)*

behindertengerechte Wohnung (f) adapted housing, adapted accommodation

Behindertenwerkstatt (f) sheltered workshop

Behinderung (f) disablement, ion, attendant handicap *(s.o.)*, disability, impediment; **geistige ~** mental disability; **körperliche ~** physical disability; **Lernbehinderung** learning disability, learning difficulty

Behörde (f) authority, office

Behördenzentrum (n) civic centre

Beihilfe (m) allowance, subsidy, financial assistance

Beirat (m) advisory board, advisory committee

beispiellos (adj) unprecedented

Beitrag (m) contribution; *(Aufsatz)* article; **Mitgliedsbeitrag** fee

beitragsfrei (adj) free of charge

Beitragsfreiheit (f) non-contributory

beitreten (v) to join

bejahrt (adj) elderly

Bekannte(r) (f,m) friend, acquaintance

Bekenntnisschule (f) denominational school

Belohnung (f) reward; *(psych)* reinforcement

benachteiligen (v) to discriminate against

benachteiligt (adj) disadvantaged, underprivileged; *(soz)* deprived

benachteiligt, soziokulturell ~ culturally alienated

Benachteiligung einer Person discrimination against someone

benoten (v) *(Schule)* to grade s.o. (US), to mark s.o. (Brit)

beobachten (v) to observe

Beobachter(in) (m,f) observer; **teilnehmender** ~ participant observer; **nicht teilnehmende(r)** ~ external observer

Beobachtung (f) observation; > teilnehmende ~; > nichtteilnehmende ~; > gezielte ~; > Zufalls-~; > Verhaltensbeobachtung bei Kindern

Beobachtungsbogen (m) observation sheet

Beobachtungslernen (n) observational learning

beraten (v) to advise, to give advice, to discuss, to counsel

beratend (adj) advisory

Berater(in) (m,f) advisor, adviser, counsellor

Beratung (f) advice, discussion, consultation, counselling, guidance

Beratungsdienste (m,pl) counselling services

Beratungslehrer(in) (m,f) adviser, advisory teacher

Beratungsstelle (f) advice centre

Berechtigung (f) entitlement

Bereich (m) area, field, domain

bereitstellen (v) to provide

Bereitstellung (f) *(Angebot z.B. an Kita-Plätzen)* provision

Bericht (m) report, record

berücksichtigen (v) to take into account

Beruf (m) job, occupation; **akademischer / freier** ~ profession; **handwerklicher** ~ trade

beruflich (adj) vocational

berufliche Bildung (f) vocational education and training

berufliche Erwachsenenbildung (f) adult vocational education

berufliche Fortbildung (f) (vocational) further training

Berufsausbildung (f) training; *(Handwerk)* vocational training, *(akademisch)* (professional) training

Berufsaussichten (pl) job prospects

berufsbegleitende Fortbildung (f) in-service training

berufsbegleitende Weiterbil-

dung (f) in-service training

Berufsberater/in (m,f) careers guidance counsellor, careers officer, careers adviser

Berufsberatung (f) vocational counselling, careers guidance, vocational guidance

Berufsbild (n) job outline, requirements of a profession

Berufserfahrung (f) (professional) experience, work experience

Berufsfachschule (f) (D) vocational training college (attended full-time), full-time vocational school; ~ **für Sozialwesen** vocational training college for social care

Berufskolleg (n) (D) vocational college

Berufskrankheit (f) occupational disease

Berufspraktikum (n) (D) *(einjährig)* probationary year, full-time work placement, work experience

Berufsschule (f) (part-time) vocational school, technical college, further education college

Berufsschüler(in) (m,f) student at vocational school / technical college

Berufsschulpflicht (f) compulsory part-time vocational education

Berufstätigkeit von Müttern maternal employment

Berufsvorbereitungsjahr (n) pre-training course of one year

beruhigen (v) *(ruhig machen)* to pacify, to calm (down); *(beschwichtigen)* to reassure, to comfort; to chill out *(coll)*

beruhigend (adj) reassuring

Berührung (f) touch, contact

beschäftigt (adj) occupied, busy

Beschäftigung (f) activity, occupation; *(Arbeit)* job, employment

Beschäftigungs- und Ausbildungsprogramm (n) employment and training programme

Beschäftigungstherapeut(in) (m,f) occupational therapist

Beschäftigungstherapie (f) occupational therapy

bescheiden (adj) unassuming, modest

bescheinigen (v) to certify; to confirm; **hiermit wird bescheinigt, dass...** this is to certify that...

Bescheinigung (f) certificate,

written confirmation, receipt

Beschränkungen (f,pl) restraints, restrictions, limitations

Beschulung (f) educational placement

beschützende Werkstatt (f) sheltered workshop

beschwichtigen (v) to soothe

besorgt (adj) anxious, worried, apprehensive, concerned

besprechen (v) to talk something over

Beständigkeit (adj) consistency, constancy

Bestärkung (f) reassurance, support

bestätigen (v) *(psych)* to reinforce; to confirm, to support; > bescheinigen

Bestätigung (f) confirmation; *(psych)* affirmation, validation

Bestehen (n) *(einer Prüfung)* passing; **Gründe für das ~ des Praktikums** reasons for passing the practical training; **Gründe für das Nichtbestehen...** reasons for not passing...

bestehen (v) *(einer Prüfung, Aufgabe)* to pass; **man kann ~ oder durchfallen** you can pass or fail

Bestrafung (f) punishment

Besuch (m) visit; **jemandem einen Besuch machen** to pay a visit to somebody; **~ zum Kennenlernen** familiarization visit

besuchen (v) to visit, *(eine Schule etc)* to attend

Besuchszeiten (f,pl) visiting hours

betagt (adj) aged

Beteiligung (f) *(seelische)* involvement; *(päd)* participation

Betrachtungsweise (f) *(theor. Ansatz)* approach

betreffen (v) to affect; **das ~ mich nicht** that does not affect me

betreuen (v) to care for, to look after somebody, to take care of somebody

Betreuer(in) (m,f) care-giver, carer; *(jur)* custodian, *(soz)* case worker

betreutes Leben im Wohnumfeld community care

betreutes Wohnen (n) assisted living, supported accommodation; *(z.B. für Behinderte)* sheltered accommodation

betreutes Wohnen für junge Menschen supervised flats for young people

Betreuung (f) (child-)care; **gemeindenahe ~** community care; **frühkindliche ~** early childhood care

betriebliche Ausbildung (f) in-house training

Betriebskindergarten (m) crèche

Betriebspraktikum (n) work experience, work placement, practical placement; **ein ~ machen** to do work experience; *(in einem Wirtschaftsbetrieb)* vocational practical studies

Betriebsrat (m) workers' committee

betroffen (adj) *(etw. angehen)* concerned; *(bestürzt)* shocked

Bettnässen (n) bed-wetting; **ins Bett machen** to wet the bed

beurteilen (v) to assess

Beurteilung (f) appraisal, assessment, report, review

Bevölkerungsstatistik (f) vital statistics

bevormunden (v) to patronise, to domineer over

Bevorzugung zum Ausgleich für soziale Benachteiligung positive discrimination

Bewährungshelfer(in) (m,f) probation officer

Bewährungsstrafe (f) suspended sentence

Bewegungsspiele *(pl)* *(Fröbel)* Movements

Bewegungstherapie (f) therapeutic exercises, exercise therapy

Bewerbung (f) application

Bewerbungsformular (n) application form

Bewertung (f) appraisal, assessment

bewilligen (v) *(z.B. Finanzmittel)* to allocate, to grant

bewusst (adj) *(willentlich)* deliberate, intentional; *(psych)* conscious; **sich über etwas ~ werden** to become aware of, **sich etwas ~ machen** to realize; **~ leben** to live with great awareness

bewusstlos (adj) unconscious

Bewusstsein (n) awareness, consciousness

Beziehung (f) relationship, connection

Beziehungen zu jemandem herstellen to relate to someone; **sie baut leicht Beziehungen zu jungen Leuten auf** she relates well to young people

Bezirksamt (n) (D) local authority

Bezirksjugendamt (n) area youth office
Bezugserzieher(in) (m,f) key-worker, main carer
Bezugserzieher(in) für Kind und Eltern *(in einem Familienzentrum)* family worker
Bezugsgruppe (f) reference group
Bezugsperson (f) resource person, care-giver, attachment person; *(psych)* role model; **die wichtigste ~ des Kleinkindes** the person to whom the small child relates most closely
bezweifeln (v) to question, to doubt
Bikulturalität (f) belonging to two cultures
bikulturell (adj) bicultural
Bilderbuch (n) picture book
Bildung (f) education
Bildungsansprüche (m,pl) educational aspirations
bildungsfähig (adj) receptive to teaching
Bildungsgang (m) educational career
Bildungsministerium (n) Department of Education
Bildungsniveau (n) educational level, level of education
Bildungsnotstand (m) educational misery
Bildungsprogramm (n) educational programme
Bildungsurlaub (m) educational leave
Bildungswesen (n) educational cereer
bilingual (adj) bilingual
Bilingualität (f) bilingualism
Billigung (f) approval, acceptance
Bindung (f) *(Beziehung)* relationship, commitment, attachment; *(psych)* bonding
Bindungen herstellen *(psych)* to attach, to form an attachment, to bond
Bindungsbegriff (m) the concept of attachment
Biogemüse (n) organic vegetable
biographische Methode (f) biographical method
Bioladen (m) wholefood shop
biologisch abbaubar biodegradable
biologische Vaterschaft (f) biological paternity
biologischer Anbau (m) organic farming
Blockflöte (f) recorder
Bockspringen (n) leapfrog; *(Sport)* vaulting; *(Spiel)* to play a game of leapfrog
Bodenturnen (m) tumbling,

floor exercises

böse (adj) *(verägert)* angry, cross; **auf jmd. ~ sein** be angry with / at somebody

brandmarken (v) *(soz)* to stigmatize

Brauch (m) custom, tradition

Brauchtum (n) folkways

brav (adj) well behaved, good

Brennpunkt (m), **sozialer ~** socially deprived area

Brettspiel (n) board game

Brutkasten (m) *(für Babys)* incubator

Buchstabenspiel (n) word game

Bulimie (f) bulimia

Bundesangestelltentarif (m) (BAT) (D) Federal Employees Salary Scales Agreement

Bundesausbildungsförderungsgesetz (n) (Bafög) (D) Federal Educational Grants Act

Bundessozialhilfegesetz (n) (D) Federal Social Assistance Act

Buntstift (m) crayon, coloured pencil

Bürgerberatungsstelle (f) citizens advice bureau *(Brit)*

Bürgerinitiative (f) community action group, citizens' group

Bürgerliches Gesetzbuch (n) (BGB) (D) German Civil Code

Bürgerrechte (n,pl) civil rights

C

Cerebralparese cerebral palsy

Chancengleichheit (f) equal opportunities; **~ für Männer und Frauen fördern** gender mainstreaming

Computerfreak (m) computaholic

Computergeneration (f) e-generation

Computerkenntnisse (f,pl) computer literacy

Contergankind (n) thalidomide child

D

Dachverband (m) umbrella organization
darstellen (v) *(symbolisieren)* to represent
Daseinsberechtigung (f) right to exist
Datenschutz (m) data protection
Daumen (m) thumb; **jemandem die Daumen drücken** to keep one's fingers crossed for someone
Daumenlutscher (m) thumb sucker
Daumen-Zeigefinger Griff *(bei Säuglingen)* pincer prehension
Defizit (n) deficit
defizitärer Blick deficit oriented view
demokratischer Führungsstil (m) democratic style of leadership
Deutsch als Fremdsprache (DaF) teaching German as a foreign language
Deutschkenntnisse (f,pl) knowledge of German
Devianz (f) (psych) deviation
Dezentrierung (f) decentration
dickköpfig (adj) stubborn
Didaktik (f) principles of teaching
didaktisch (adj) didactic
Dienst (m) service
Dienstbefreiung (f) time off
Dienstbesprechung (f) staff meeting
Dienstleistung (f) service
Dienstleistungsbereich (m) tertiary sector
Dienstpflichten (f,pl) official duties
Dienstplan (m) duty rota; (work) schedule
Dienstvertrag (m) > Arbeitsvertrag
Diffamierung (f) defamation
Differenz (f) difference
differenzieren (v) to distinguish
Diplom-Pädagoge / Pädagogin (m,f) Graduate in Education
diskriminieren (v)) to discriminate against someone
Diskriminierung (f) discrimination
Diskriminierung aufgrund des Geschlechts sex discrimination
Dokumentation (f) *(als Mappe)* portfolio

Dokumentationsbogen (m) monitoring sheet

dokumentieren (v) to monitor, to demonstrate

dolmetschen (v) to interpret; **simultan ~** simultaneous interpreting

Dolmetscher(in) (m,f) interpreter

doppelte Staatsbürgerschaft (f) dual citizenship

Down-Syndrom (n) Down's Syndrome

Dozent(in) (m,f) instructor

dreigliedrig (adj) tripartite

Dreirad (n) tricycle

dreizügig (adj) three form entry

Drilling (m) triplet; **Drillinge** a set of triplets

dringend (adj) urgent

Droge (f) drug

Drogenabhängigkeit (f) drug dependency

Drogenberatung (f) drug counselling

Drogenentzug (m) withdrawal treatment

Drogenmissbrauch (m) drug abuse

Drogensüchtige(r) (f,m) drug addict

Dummerchen (n) (F) silly billy

durchfallen (v) *(in einer Prüfung)* fail; **er ist in Englisch durchgefallen** he failed in English

durchführen (v) to carry out, to implement

Durchlässigkeit (f) (fig) free interchange, mobility (between schools...)

Durchschnitt (m) average; **im ~** on average; **über / unter dem ~** above / below average

Durchschnittsfamilie (f) average family

Durchsetzungsfähigkeit (f) self-assertion

Durchsetzungsvermögen (n) self-assertion, assertiveness, ability to assert oneself

Dyade (f) dyad

E

e.V. > eingetragener Verein
Egoismus (m) egoism
egozentrisch (adj) self-centred, egocentric
Ehe (f) marriage; **arrangierte ~** arranged marriage; **gleichgeschlechtliche ~** same-sex marriage; **~ ohne Trauschein, eheähnliche Gemeinschaft** common law marriage; **Ehestand** state of marriage
Eheberater(in) (m,f) marriage guidance counsellor
ehelich geborenes Kind legitimate child
Ehemündigkeitsalter (n) age of consent
Ehename (m) married name
Ehescheidung (f) divorce
Ehestand (m) state of marriage, matrimony
ehrenamtliche Arbeit (f) voluntary work
ehrenamtliche(r) Helfer(in) (m,f) unpaid part-time worker
ehrenamtliche(r) Mitarbeiter(in) (m,f) volunteer
Eifersucht (f) jealousy
eifrig (adj) busy, enthusiastic, eager
Eigeninitiative (f) proactive attitude, initiative of one's own
eigenständige Person (f) separate person
Eigentätigkeit (f) *(des Kindes)* self-directed activity
Eignung (f) aptitude
Eignungsprüfung (f) aptitude test
Eignungstest (m) eligibility test, ability test
Einberufung (f) conscription, call-up papers *(Brit)*
Einbildungskraft (f) imagination, fantasy
einbürgern (v) *(jur)* to naturalize
Einbürgerung (f) *(jur)* naturalization
eindeutig (adj) unambiguous, clear
Ein-Eltern-Familie (f) one-parent-family, single parent family
Einfühlungsvermögen (n) empathy, sensitivity
Einführungsbericht (m) induction report
Einführungsgespräch (n) introductory dialogue
Einführungskurs (m) induc-

tion course

Einführungsphase (f) initial stage, initial phase, induction period

Einführungstreffen (n) introductory meeting, introductory dialogue

Einführungsveranstaltung (f) induction conference

Eingangsvoraussetzung (f) entrance qualification

eingetragener Verein (m) (e.V.) (D) registered association

eingewöhnen (v) to grow into something

eingewöhnen, sich ~ (v) to settle in; **jemandem helfen, sich einzugewöhnen** to settle somebody in

Eingewöhnung (f) settling-in, adaptation, adjustment

Eingewöhnungszeit (f) *(päd)* settling-in time / period

Eingliederung (f) integration

Eingreifen (n) intervention; **vorsichtiges, zurückhaltendes ~** subtle intervention; **zielgerichtetes ~** focused intervention

Eingrenzung (f) (schema) enclosure

Einhalten (n) **der Vorschriften** compliance with rules

Einheit (f) unit

Einhorn (n) unicorn

Einkommen (n) income

Einmaleins-Tafel (f) multiplication table

Einmalwindel (f) disposable nappy

Einmalzahlung (f) one-off payment

Einrad (n) unicycle

einrichten (v) *(gründen)* establish, to set up; (Zimmer ausstatten) to fit out, to furnish

Einrichtung (f) *(Institution)* establishment, organization, institution; **offene ~** establishment without fixed membership; *(Wohnung)* (fittings and) furnishings

Einsatzfigur (f) *(Montessori)* inset

Einsatzzylinder (m) *(Montessori)* cylinder inset

Einschätzung (f) *(einer Leistung)* assessment, evaluation

einschlägige Berufserfahrung (f) relevant work experience

einschränkend (adj) restrictive

Einschulung (f) enrolment at primary school, starting school; **eingeschult werden** to be sent to school; **Kin-**

der werden mit 6 Jahren eingeschult children start school at 6

einstellen (v) *(anstellen)* to employ, to take on; *(beenden)* to stop, to discontinue; *(sich richten nach)* to adapt oneself to somebody / something

Einstellung (f) *(Anstellung)* employment; *(Gesinnung)* attitude, **elterliche ~** parental attitude

Einstimmigkeit (f) unanimity

Einstufung (f) *(leistungsmäßige ~)* rating

Einstufungstest (m) placement test

Eintauchen (n) *(fig: Unterrichtsmethode, bei der nur in der Zielsprache gesprochen wird)* immersion

einverstanden sein to agree, to consent

Einwand (m) objection

Einwandererfamilie (f) immigrant family

Einwanderungsgesetze (n,pl) immigration laws

einwickeln (v) to envelop

Einzelarbeit (f) one-to-one work

Einzelberatung (f) individual counselling

Einzelbetreuung (f) one-to-one attention / care

Einzelfallanalyse (f) case study

Einzelfallhilfe (f) case work

Einzelgänger(in) (m,f) loner

Einzelgespräch (n) individual talk

Einzelkind (n) only child

Einzelleistung (f) individual performance

Einzelunterricht (m) one-to-one lessons

Ein-Zimmer-Wohnung (f) bedsitter

Einzugs|gebiet (n), **~bereich** (m) catchment area

Elementarbereich (m) foundation stage, pre-school level

Elfe (f) fairy

elterliche Aufsichtspflicht (f) (parental) duty of supervision, parental responsibility, supervisory responsibilities, legal responsibility to care

elterliche Einstellung (f) parental attitude

elterliche Pflege (f) parental care, family care

elterliche Rechte (n,pl) parental rights

elterliche Sorge (f) *(jur)* parental rights and duties, parentage

elterliche Zustimmung (f) parental consent

elterliches Verhalten (n) parenting

Eltern (pl) parents; **von den ~ betrieben** parent-run

Eltern..., elterlich (adj) parental

Elternabend (m) parents' meeting

Elternarbeit (f) working with parents

Elternbeirat (m) parents' council

Elternbeiträge (m,pl) *(finanziell)* parental contributions

Elternberatung (f) parent counseling

Elternbeteiligung (f) parent participation

Elternhaus (n) parental home

Elterninitiative (f) parents' action group

Eltern-Initiativ-Kindertagesstätte (f) (EIKita) (D) parent-managed children's centre

Eltern-Kind-Beziehung (f) parent-child-relation

elternlos (adj) parentless

Elternschaft (f) parenthood

Elternteil (m) parent

emotionale Bindung (f) emotional dependency

Empathie (f) empathy

Empfang (m) *(Sekretariat)* front office

Empfängnisverhütung (f) contraception

Empfindsamkeit (f) sensitivity

Empfindungsvermögen (n) sensory perception, faculty of sensation

empirisch (adj) empirical, experiential

energisch (adj) vigorous, energetic

Engagement (n) *(sich einsetzen)* commitment; **soziales ~** community involvement

engagiert sein to be involved in

Engagiertheit (f) *(päd)* involvement

Enkel(in) (m,f) grandchild; grandson, granddaughter

Entbehrung (f) deprivation

entbinden (v) to deliver, to give birth

Entbindungsklinik (f) maternity clinic, nursing home

entdeckendes Lernen active discovery learning

Entfaltung (f) self-realization, self-enrichment

entfremdet (adj) alienated; **sich der Gesellschaft ~ fühlen** to feel alienated from society

Entfremdung (f) alienation
Entlassung von Personal redundancy; **finanzielle Abfindung bei Entlassungen** redundancy payment
entlausen (v) to disinfest
Entlausung (f) delousing
Entschlossenheit (f) determination
Entschuldigungsschreiben (n) letter of excuse
entsetzlich (adj) appalling, dreadful
Entspannung (f) relaxation
Entwicklung (f) development, evolution, progress; **sich in der ~ befinden** to be in the development stage; **~ der kreativen Fähigkeiten** creative development; **geistige ~** mental development, **~ fördern** to promote development
Entwicklungsalter (n) developmental stage
Entwicklungsaufgaben (f,pl) developmental tasks
Entwicklungsfortschritt (m) developmental progress
Entwicklungsgespräch (n) development report
entwicklungsgestört (adj) retarded
Entwicklungslinie (f) developmental line, **mögliche Entwicklungslinien** possible lines of direction (PLOD)
entwicklungsmäßig angemessen developmentally appropriate
Entwicklungsordner (m) development file
Entwicklungspsychologie (f) developmental psychology
Entwicklungsstörung (f) developmental disorder
Entwicklungsstrang (m) strand of development
Entwicklungsstufe (f) developmental level, developmental stage, level of development
Entwicklungsverzögerung (f) developmental delay
Entwöhnung (f) *(Baby)* weaning
Entwurf (m) concept, draft
Entziehungsanstalt (f) drug rehabilitation centre
Entziehungskur (f) withdrawal therapy
Entzugserscheinungen (f,pl) withdrawal symptoms
Entzündung (f) inflammation
erblich (adj) hereditary
erbrechen (v) to throw up, to vomit
erfahren (adj) practiced, experienced
Erfahrung (f) experience,

~en machen to learn by experience; in ~ bringen to discover

Erfahrungsfeld (n) experiential arena

Erfahrungslernen (n) operational learning

erfahrungsorientierter Ansatz (m) experiential approach

Erfahrungstatsache (f) fact of experience

erfassen (v) *(begreifen)* to grasp

Erfolgserlebnis (n) sense of achievement

Erfolgskontrolle (f) follow-up control

ergänzend (adj) complementary; **familienergänzende Einrichtung** an establishment complementary to life at home

Ergebnisbogen (m) summative sheet

erholen (v) to recover

Erholung (f) recreation

Erholungsreisen für Kinder und Jugendliche holiday schemes for children and young people

Erkältung (f) cold; **eine ~ haben** to be ill with a cold

Erkenntnis (f) cognition, understanding

Erklärung (f) explanation

Erkundung (f) *(im Sinne e-r Exkursion)* exploratory trip

Erlass (n) circular

Erlebnisgesellschaft (f) adventure society

Erlebnispädagogik (f) adventure pursuits, outdoor pursuits

Ernährung (f) diet, nutrition; **vegetarische ~** vegetarian diet

Errungenschaft (f) achievement

Erstausbildung (f) initial training; **berufliche ~** initial vocational training

erste Fremdsprache (f) second language

erste Klasse in der Grundschule infant class, reception class

Erstleselehrgang (m) initial reading scheme

Erstspracherwerb (m) first language acquisition

Ersttäter(in) (m,f) *(Straftäter)* first offender

erwachsen (adj) adult, grown up, mature

erwachsen werden (v) to grow up, mature

Erwachsene(r) (f,m) adult, grown-up

Erwachsenenalter (n) adulthood
Erwachsenenalter, frühes (n) young adulthood
Erwachsenenbildung (f) adult education
Erwachsenenbildung (f), **berufliche** adult vocational education
erwerben (v) to acquire, *(Ansehen etc.)* to earn
erworben (adj) acquired
erworbene Rolle (f) achieved role
erziehen (v) to educate, to bring up
Erzieher(in) (m,f) (D) *(Ausbildung mit (Fach-) Hochschulreife)* early childhood educator, (nursery school-) teacher, kindergarten teacher, family worker, social pedagogue, educator (nursery worker); (eine englische Übersetzung des deutschen Begriffs ist schwierig, da das Berufsfeld der/des deutschen Erzieherin / Erziehers unterschiedliche Ausbildungsberufe in anderen Ländern umfasst); (Brit): teacher (nursery and primary education bzw. preschool and primary education bzw. primary and secondary education); meist 4 Jahre Ausbildung auf Hochschulniveau, Abschluss BEd. (Bachelor of Education) *oder* PGCE (Postgraduate Certificate in Education) *mit mittlerem Schulabschluss:* nursery nurse, nursery worker, nursery assistant; (Brit): 2-jährige Ausbildung für die Altersgruppe 0 – 5 Jahre, arbeitet als Hilfskraft (auxiliary worker) in der nursery school, nursery class, reception class, als Gruppenerzieherin im family centre oder local authority nursery, im Privathaushalt als nanny. Ausbildung: 2-jährig, National Nursery Examination Board (NNEB) *oder* Council for Awards in Children's Care and Education (CACHE) *oder* National Diploma in Caring Services (BTEC)
Erzieher(in) (m,f), **staatlich anerkannte(r)** ~ (D) qualified educator; social pedagogue, state-registered educator
Erzieher-Schlüssel (m) child-teacher-ratio
erzieherisch (adj) educational, educative

erzieherzentriertes Programm (n) teacher-centred programme

Erziehung (f) education, upbringing, teaching; **gute ~** manners

Erziehung (f), **gefühlsbetonte** affective education

Erziehungsberatung (f) child guidance, educational counselling

Erziehungsberatungsstelle (f) *(mit Therapie)* child guidance clinic / centre

erziehungsberechtigt (adj) acting as legal guardian

Erziehungsberechtigte(r) (f,m) legal guardian; **Unterschrift des / der Erziehungsberechtigten** signature of parent or legal guardian

Erziehungsgeld (n) (D) *(Geldleistung während der Elternzeit)* child benefit, child care allowance, child raising allowance

Erziehungsheim (n) community home

Erziehungshilfen (f,pl) socio-educational provision for children with problems

Erziehungsmaßnahmen (f,pl) educational measures

Erziehungsmaßregeln (jur) educational court orders

Erziehungsmittel (n,pl) educational methods, corrective measures

Erziehungssoziologie (f) sociology of education

Erziehungsstil (m) way of education

Erziehungsurlaub (m) child care leave, child raising leave, paid leave for new parent

Erziehungsurlaub für Väter paternity leave

Erziehungswissenschaft (f) educational studies

Erziehungswissenschaftler(in) (m,f) educationalist

Es (n) *(psych)* id

Essen auf Rädern meals on wheels

Essensvorschriften (f,pl) dietary requirements

Essstörung (f) eating disorder

ethnische Minderheit (f) ethnic minority, racial minority

Etikettierungsansatz (m) *(soz)* labelling approach

Europäische Union (EU) (f) European Union (EU)

Europäisches Abitur (m) European Baccalaureate

Examen (n) (final) exam(ination); **mündliches ~** oral examination; **schrift-**

liches ~ written examination; **das ~ bestehen** to pass one's finals; **durch das ~ fallen** to fail one's finals; **das ~ machen** to take one's finals

Examensangst (f) pre-exam anxiety; **unter ~ leiden** to suffer from pre-exam anxiety

exhibitionistische Handlungen (f,pl) indecent exposure

Exkursion (f) field trip, study trip

F

Fachabitur > fachgebundene Hochschulreife

Fachakademie für Sozialpädagogik (f) (D) training college for educators

Facharbeiter(in) (m,f) skilled worker

Fachausdruck (m) technical term, specialist term

Fachberater(in) (m,f) *(päd)* educational advisor

Fachbereichsleiter(in) (m,f) head of department

fachgebundene Hochschulreife (f) (D) subject-tied university entrance qualification (may be taken at a > Fachoberschule)

Fachhochschule (f) (D) technical college for higher education, polytechnic, advanced technical college; university for applied sciences, technical university

Fachhochschulreife (f) entrance qualification for > Fachhochschule

Fachleiter(in) (m,f) course supervisor

Fachoberschule (f) (D) vocational grammar school, technical college; **~ für Gesundheit und Soziales** advanced technical school for social care

Fachschule (f) training college; **~ für Sozialpädagogik** (D) training college for educators, college for social pedagogics, college for social education

Fachsprache (f) technical language

Fachtheorie (f) subject theory

fachübergreifendes Lernen (n) cross-disciplinary learning

Fachunterricht (m) subject lesson

Fähigkeit (f) ability, capability, aptitude, faculty

Fahrplan (m) timetable

Fahrrad (n) bicycle, bike, pushbike (F)

Fahrtkosten (pl) travel expenses

fakultativ (adj) optional

Fall (m) case

Fallbericht (m) case report

Fallbesprechung (f) discussion of the case (report)

Fallstudie (f) case study

Familie (f) family; **eine vierköpfige ~** a family of four; **eine ~ gründen** to start a family; **zur ~ gehören** to be family; **praktisch zur ~ gehören** to be like one of the family; **vaterlose ~** fatherless family

Familie mit einem Kind single child family

Familie mit geringem Einkommen low-income family

Familienausflug (m) family outing

familienbegleitende Erziehungshilfen (f,pl) socio-educational support provided to complement the family

Familienberatung (f) family counselling

Familienberatungsstelle (f) family advice centre

Familienbindung (f) family ties

familienergänzende Einrichtung (f) an establishment complementary to life at home

familienergänzende Erziehungshilfen (f,pl) socio-educational support provided to supplement the family

familienersetzende Erziehungshilfen (f,pl) socio-educational support provided to replace the family

Familienfürsorge (f) family welfare work

Familienhelfer(in) (m,f) family aide

Familienleben (n) domestic life, family life

Familienname (m) surname, last name, family name

familienorientierte Politik (f) family-oriented policy

Familienstand (m) marital status

Familienstruktur (f) the pattern of family life
Familientagespflege (f) family daycare
Familientreffen (n) family reunion
Familienunterbringung (f) family placement
familienunterstützende Maßnahmen (f,pl) family support measures
Familienzeit (f) (D) parental leave
Familienzentrum (n) family centre
Familienzusammenführung (f) family reunion
Fantasieren (n) imagining
Fangen spielen to play tag
Farbensinn (m) perception of colour
Farbtäfelchen (n) *(Montessori)* colour tablet
Fastnachtsdienstag (m) Pancake Day (Brit)
Fee (f) fairy
Fehlanpassung (f) maladaptation
Fehlen (n) *(unentschuldigt)* truancy
Fehlentwicklung (f) maldevelopment
Fehlgeburt (f) abortion, miscarriage
feiern (v) celebrate

Feiertage (m,pl) holidays
Feinmotorik (f) fine motor skills, small muscle skills
feinmotorische Entwicklung (f) fine motor development
Ferien (pl) holidays (Brit), vacation (US), **seine ~ in ... verbringen** to spend one's holidays in ...
Ferienkurs (m) summer school
Fernbleiben (n) absence; **unerlaubtes ~** absence without leave
Fernsinne (m, *meist* pl) far senses
Fernunterricht (m) distance learning
Fertigkeit (f) skill, competence, craft
feste Nahrung (f) solid food
festhalten (v) *(sich)* to hold on, *(etwas ergreifen)* to grab
Feststellung (f) statement
Feuerschutzübung (f) fire drill
Filzschreiber (m) felt-tip pen; *(dicker ~)* marker pen
Finanzierung (f) funding; **Finanzierungsprobleme** funding problems
Findelhaus (n) foundling hospital
Findelkind (n) foundling
Finger (m) finger; **Zeige-,**

Mittel-, Ring-, kleiner ~ first (*or* index-) finger, second, third, fourth (*or* little) finger; **kleiner ~** auch pinkie, pinky (US)

Fingerfarbe (f) fingerpaint; **mit ~ malen** to fingerpaint

Fingerpuppe (f) finger puppet

Fingerspitze (f) fingertip

Fläschchen (n) *(für Babys)* feeding bottle

Flaschenbürste (f) bottle brush

Flaschenkind (n) bottle-fed child; **mit der Flasche füttern** to bottle feed

Flaschenwärmer (m) bottle heater

Flüchtling (m) refugee

fordern (v) to challenge

Förder... remedial; **Förderunterricht** (m) remedial education, remedial lessons

Förderangebote (n,pl) *(für benachteiligte Kinder)* compensatory education

Förderdiagnostik (f) educational diagnostics

Förderlehrer(in) (m,f) learning support teacher

Fördermaßnahmen (f,pl) measures for support and advancement

fördern (v) *(unterstützen)* to support, *(voranbringen)* to advance, *(ermutigen)* to encourage, *(steigern)* to promote, to boost

fordern und fördern to challenge and support

Förderung (f) *(päd)* support, advancement, encouragement, promotion; *(finanziell)* grant-aid; **Förderungsantrag** application for grant-aid

Förderzentrum (n) support centre

formbare Materialien (n,pl) malleable materials

forschendes Handeln (n) exploratory experiences

Forschung (f) **und Entwicklung** (f) research and development

Forschungsabteilung (f) research department

fortbilden (v) to take further education courses, to go on further education courses

Fortbildung (f) further education, further training, advanced training, in-service training

Fortbildung für Mitarbeiter einer Einrichtung staff training

Fortbildungskonzept (n)

further education programme

Fortbildungskurs (m) (further) training course, evening classes

Fortbildungsveranstaltung (f) further training course

FOS > Fachoberschule

Fotokopie (f) photocopy, Xerox®

fotokopieren (v) to photocopy, to xerox

Fötus (m) fetus (US), foetus (Brit)

Fragebogen (m) *(soz)* inventory; questionnaire

Frauenbildung (f) female education

Frauenhaus (n) battered wives' shelter, house for battered women, women's refuge

frech (adj) cheeky

Freiarbeit (f) free work, self determined activities

freiberuflich (adj) freelance

freie Stelle (f) *(Arbeitsplatz)* vacancy

freie Träger (m,pl) private agencies, voluntary bodies

freie Träger der Jugendhilfe (pl) voluntary bodies fpr youth work

freie Verbände (m,pl) private associations

freie Wohlfahrtspflege (f) voluntary welfare work

freie(r) Mitarbeiter(in) freelancer

Freier Träger (m) voluntary agency, voluntary organization; **die Freien Träger** the voluntary sector

Freigelände (n) *(im Kindergarten)* outdoor area, outside play area

Freiheitsstrafe (f) *(für Jugendliche)* detention

Freispiel (n) free play

Freistellung (f) leave of absence

freiwillig (adj) voluntary

Freiwillige(r) (f,m) volunteer

Freiwilligendienste (m,pl) voluntary services, volunteering

Freiwilliges Soziales Jahr (n) (FSJ) (D) year of voluntary work and community service

Freizeit (f) leisure time

Freizeitangebot (n) leisure provision

Freizeitbeschäftigung (f) leisure activities, pastime,

Freizeiteinrichtungen (f,pl) recreational facilities

Freizeiterziehung (f) education of leisure

Freizeitgelände (n) recreation

ground
Freizeitgesellschaft (f) leisure society
Freizeitpädagogik (f) education of leisure
Freizeitzentrum (n) amenity centre, leisure centre, leisure complex
freizügige Gesellschaft (f) permissive society
Freizügigkeit (f) permissiveness
fremd (adj) alien, strange
Fremdeln (n) stranger anxiety, shyness with strangers
fremdeln (v), sie fremdelt: she's got stranger anxiety
Fremdenfeindlichkeit (f) xenophobia
Fremdsprachen lernen second language learning
Fremdsprachenerwerb (m) foreign language acquisition
Fremdunterbringung (f) *(von Kindern)* boarding out, residential child care
Freudsche Fehlleistung (f) Freudian slip
Friedenserziehung (f) peace education
Frist (f) time limit
Frontalunterricht (m) chalk and talk, direct teaching, whole-class teaching
Frotteewindel (f) terry nappy (Brit)
Fruchtbarkeit (f) fertility
Fruchtbarkeitsklinik (f) (in)fertility clinic
Frühdienst (f), **~schicht** (f) early shift
Frühförderung (f) early childhood special education
Frühgeburt (f) *(Vorgang)* premature birth; *(Kind)* premature baby; sie hatte eine ~ she gave birth prematurely
frühkindliche Entwicklung (f) early childhood development
Frühpädagogik (f) early years education
FSJ > Freiwilliges Soziales Jahr
Führungszeugnis (n) certificate of (good) conduct
Fülle (f) affluence
Fünfling (m) quintuplet
Fürsorge (f) *(Betreuung)* care, *(Amt)* welfare services
Fürsorgepflicht (f) duty to give assistance
Füßchen (n) tootsie
füttern (v) to feed

G

ganzheitlich (adj) holistic; **ganzheitlicher Ansatz** holistic approach; **ganzheitliche Pädagogik** holistic pedagogics

ganztags (adj) full-time; **sie arbeitet ~** she works full-time

Ganztagsbetreuung (f) full-time care

Ganztagseinrichtung (f) all-day institution

Ganztagsschule (f) all-day school

Ganztags-Schulwesen (n) full-day schooling

Ganztagsstellung (f) full-time job

Garderobenraum (m) cloakroom

Gastfamilie (f) host family

Gastfreundschaft (f) hospitality

Gastgeber(in) (m,f) host

Gebärdensprache (f) *(für Gehörlose)* finger spelling, sign language, manual alphabet

gebären (v) to give birth (to); **geboren werden** (v) to be born

gebildet (adj) educated

geborene(r)... née

Gebühr (f) fee

Geburt (f) birth, childbirth; **natürliche / sanfte ~** natural childbirth; **von ~ an** from *or* since birth

Geburten|regelung (f), **~ beschränkung** (f) birth control

Geburtenanstieg (m) rise in the birth rate

Geburtenrate (f) fertility rate

Geburtenrückgang (m) decline in the birth rate

Geburtenziffer (f) birth rate, natality

Geburts... *(in Zusammensetzungen)* natal

Geburtsfehler (m) congenital defect

Geburtshilfe (f) midwifery

Geburtsklinik (f) maternity hospital

Geburtsschaden (m) birth injury

Geburtstermin (m) due date

Geburtsurkunde (f) birth certificate

Geburtsvorbereitung (f) prenatal care, ante-natal preparation

Geburtsvorgang (m) natal period; **während des Geburtsvorganges** perinatal

Geburtswehen (f,pl) to be in labour, labour pains; > Wehen

Geburtszimmer (n) birthing room

Gedächtnisverlust (m) amnesia

gedemütigt (adj) humiliated

gefährdete Person (f) person at risk

gefühlsbetonte Erziehung (f) affective education

gegenseitige Anerkennung nationaler Berufsabschlüsse mutual recognition of national professional qualifications

Gegenstand (m) *(fig)* item

Gegenstände (m,pl) *(bearbeitete)* artifacts

gegenwärtig (adj) currently

gehemmt (adj) *(psych)* inhibited

Gehirnerschütterung (f) concussion (of the brain)

Gehör (n) hearing sense, hearing

gehorchen (v) to obey

gehörlos (adj) deaf

Gehörlose(r) (f,m) deaf person

gehorsam (adj) obedient

geistesabwesend (adj) absent-minded

Geisteskräfte (f,pl) mental faculties

geisteskrank (adj) insane

Geisteswissenschaften (f,pl) humanities

geisteswissenschaftliche Fächer (*in Oberschule und Hochschule*) arts and humanities

geistig behinderte Person (f) mentally handicapped person

geistige Arbeit (f) intellectual work

geistige Behinderung (f) mental retardation, mental handicap

geistige Entwicklung (f) mental development

Gelbsucht (f) jaundice

Geldleistung (f) cash benefit

Geldstrafe (f) fine

Gelegenheitsarbeit (f) casual labour, odd job

Gemeinderat (m) local council

Gemeindezentrum (n) community centre

gemeinnützig (adj) charitable; non-profit making

gemeinnützige Arbeit (f) community service

gemeinnützige Einrichtung (eingetragene) (f) (registered) charity

gemeinnützige Organisation (f) non-profit organization

Gemeinnützigkeit (f) non-profit status

gemeinsames Sorgerecht (n) joint custody

Gemeinschaftseinrichtung (f) community centre

Gemeinschaftskunde (f) social studies, civic education

Gemeinschaftswohnung (f), **in einer ~ wohnen** to share a flat

Gemeinwesen (n) community

Gemeinwesenarbeit (f) community work

Gemeinwesenarbeiter(in) (m,f) youth and community worker

Gemeinwesenorientierung (f) community orientation

Genehmigung (f) authorization, approval, licence

Generationsunterschied (m) generation gap

Generationszyklus (m) generational cycle

Genesungsurlaub sick leave

genitale Phase (f) genital stage

Genossenschaft (f) cooperative (society)

gerecht (adj) fair, just, even-handed; **sie behandelt alle Kinder ~** she is fair / even-handed with all the children

Gesamtelternvertretung (f) parents' council

Gesamthochschule (f) comprehensive university

Gesamtschule (f) comprehensive school

Gesamtschule mit Oberstufe (f) all-through comprehensive school

Gesamtzahl (f) overall number

Geschäftsfähigkeit (f) legal capacity

gescheit (adj) bright; **ein ~es Kind** a bright child

Geschicklichkeitsspiel (n) game of skill

Geschiedene(r) (f,m) divorcee

Geschlecht (n) *(biologisches)* sex; *(soziales und grammatisches)* gender

Geschlechtertrennung (f) *(Schule)* segregation of sexes

Geschlechtserziehung (f) sex education

Geschlechtsidentität (f) gender identity

Geschlechtsrollenklischee (n) gender stereotypes

geschlossene Abteilung (f) secure unit

geschlossene Einrichtung (f)

secure establishment
Geschmackssinn (m) sense of taste, taste
Geschwister (pl) siblings, brothers and sisters
Geschwister-Rivalität (f) sibling rivalry
gesellig (adj) sociable
Gesellschaft (f) society; **multikulturelle ~** multicultural society
gesellschaftlich (adj) socially
gesellschaftliches Ereignis (n) social event
Gesellschafts-, gesellschaftlich social
Gesellschaftswissenschaften (f,pl) social sciences, social studies
gesetzlich (adj) statutory
gesetzliche Verpflichtung (f) legal obligation
gesetzlicher Feiertag (m) public holiday
gesetzliches Einschulungsalter (n) compulsory school age, statutory school age
Gesichtsausdruck (m) facial expression
Gesprächsführung (f) client-centred counselling; discussion leading
Gesprächstechnik (f) communication techniques
Gesten (f,pl) gestures

Gesundheitsamt (n) health authority
Gesundheitsamt-Mitarbeiter(in) (m,f) health visitor
Gesundheitsberatung (f) health guidance
Gesundheitserziehung (f) health education
Gesundheitsfürsorge (f) health care
Gesundheitslehre (f) health education
Gesundheitszeugnis (n) health certificate
Gewalt (f) *(Gewalttätigkeit)* violence; *(gewaltsames Vorgehen)* force; *(Macht)* power; **~ in der Familie** domestic violence
Gewalt gegen Kinder violence against children
Gewalt unter Kindern violence among children
Gewaltanwendung (f) use of violence
gewaltsam (adj) violent
Gewaltszene (f) violent scene
gewalttätig (adj) violent
Gewaltverbrechen (n) violent crime
geweckt werden von to be awakened by
Gewichtsbrettchen (n) *(Montessori)* baric sense tablet

Gewissen (n) conscience
gewöhnen (v), **sich an etwas ~** to adapt, to become used to something
gezielte Beobachtung (f) specific observation
giftig (adj) poisonous, toxic
Giftmüll (m) toxic waste
Gitterbett (n) crib
Gleichaltrige(r) (f,m) peer; **Anerkennung durch Gleichaltrige** peer acceptance; **Kontakt mit Gleichaltrigen** peer interaction
Gleichaltrigengruppe, informelle (f) peer group
Gleichbehandlung (f) equal treatment, non-discrimi-nation
gleichberechtigt (adj) equal, to have equal rights
Gleichberechtigung (f) equality (of rights), equal rights
Gleichberechtigung der Frau equal rights for women
Gleiche (pl) *(soz)* peers
gleichgeschlechtliche Ehe (f) same-sex union
Gleichheitsgrundsatz (m) equal protection clause
Graduiertenstudium (n) postgraduate studies
Greifalter (n) *(in der Säuglingsentwicklung)* manipulative stage
greifen (v) to grasp
Greifreflex (m) *(Babys)* grasp(ing) reflex
Grenzen (f,pl) boundaries
Grenzen setzen to set limits
Grenzfall (m) *(psych)* borderline case
grobe Fahrlässigkeit (f) gross negligence
Grobmotorik motor skills; large muscle skills; **Training zur Entwicklung der Grobmotorik** physical education
grobmotorische Entwicklung (f) gross motor development
Großfamilie (f) extended family
Grund- und Leistungskurse (pl) basic and extension courses
Grundannahmen (f,pl) basic assumptions
Grundausbildung (f) basic training
Grundbedürfnisse (n,pl) bare necessities, basic needs
gründen (v) to found *(past tense: founded, p.p.: founded)*
Grundfähigkeiten, Grundfertigkeiten (f,pl) basic

skills, fundamental skills
Grundgedanke (m) key note
Grundidee (f) basic belief
Grundlagenwissen (n) grounding
grundlegend (adj) basic, fundamental
Grundmisstrauen (n) basic mistrust
Grundprinzipen (n,pl) basic principles
Grundschulbildung (f), **Grundschulerziehung** (f) elementary education, primary education
Grundschule (f) primary school *(5. – 11. Lebensjahr)* (Brit); elementary school, grade school (US)
Grundschullehrer(in) (m,f) primary teacher, infant teacher (*eigentlicher Titel in Brit:* teacher (nursery and primary education *bzw.* preschool and primary education *bzw.* primary and secondary education); meist 4 Jahre Ausbildung auf Hochschulniveau, Abschluss BEd. (Bachelor of Education) *oder* PGCE (Postgraduate Certificate in Education))
Grundüberzeugung (f) basic belief
Grundvoraussetzung (f) basic requirement
Grundwerte (m,pl) basic values
Grundwissen (n) core knowledge, basic knowledge
Gruppenstärke (f) child-teacher ratio
Gruppe von Gleichaltrigen (pl) peer group
Gruppenberatung (f) group counselling
Gruppenbetreuer(in) (m,f) group escort
Gruppendynamik (f) group dynamics
Gruppenerzieher(in) (m,f) group leader, main carer
Gruppengespräch (n) group discussion
Gruppengröße (f) group size
Gruppenkreis (m) group circle time
Gruppenleiter(in) (m,f) play leader
Gruppenpädagogik (f) group pedagogics
gruppenübergreifende Arbeit (f) open plan work
Gruppenzeit (f) sharing time
gültig (adj) valid
gut erzogen (adj) well behaved
gut gemacht! well done! good job!

Gutachter (m) consultant
Gutachterkommission (f) advisory board, advisory committee
Gutenachtgeschichte (f) bedtime story
Gutmensch (m) do-gooder
Gutschein (m) voucher
Gymnasium (n) (D) grammar school (Brit); high school (US)

H

Halbschwester (f) half sister
Halbtags... part-time
Hallenschwimmbad (n) indoor pool
Hallensport (m) indoor sport
Halsschmerzen (m,pl) sore throat
Halt (m) **geben** holding; **der Begriff des Halt-Gebens** the concept of holding
Hampelmann (m) jumping jack
Handarbeit (f) handicraft, needle work
Händeklatschen (n) clapping hands; **Spiel mit ~** clapping game
Handeln (f) (päd) being active
Handgeschicklichkeit (f) manual skills
Handlungsforschung (f) action research
Handlungskompetenz (f) performance skills
Handlungsmuster (n) action pattern, schema
Handlungsorientierung (f) hands-on approach, task-based approach
Handmotorik beim ersten

Greifen des Säuglings prehensory behaviour
Handpuppe (f) glove puppet
Handzettel (m) leaflet
Hansdampf (m) jack-of-all-trades
Häufigkeit (f) frequency
hauptamtliche(r) Mitarbeiter(in) (m,f) full-time worker, full-timer
hauptberuflich (adj) full-time
Hauptschulabschluss (m) (D) *etwa* > GCSE (Brit)
Hauptschule (f) (D) *etwa* secondary modern school (Brit); junior high school (US)
Hausarbeit (f) housework
Hausarzt (m), **Hausärztin** (f) family doctor, general practitioner (GP)
Hausaufgaben (f,pl) homework
Hausfrau (f) housewife; *(Hausmütterchen)* homemaker
Hausgeburt (f) home birth
Haushalt (m) **führen** keep house
häuslich (adj) domestic
häusliche Angelegenheiten domestic affairs
häuslicher Kinderbetreuungsdienst (m) in-home childcare service

Hausmann (m) house husband
Hauspflegedienst für Behinderte home help service
Hauspfleger(in) (m,f) home help
Hausstand (m) **gründen** to set up house
Hauswirtschaftslehre (f) domestic science, domestic economy, home economics
Hautfarbe (f) skin colour
Hautkrebs (m) skin cancer
Hebamme (f) midwife
Heftpflaster (n) sticking plaster, Band-Aid ® (US)
Heilerziehung (f) remedial education, therapeutic education
Heiligabend (m) Christmas Eve
Heilpädagogik (f) remedial education
heilpädagogische Betreuung (f) child guidance
Heim (n) residential home; **in ein ~ einweisen** to institutionalize; **durch Heimaufenthalt unselbstständig sein** to be institutionalized
Heimeinweisung (f) care-order
Heimerzieher(in) (m,f) residential child care worker
Heimerziehung (f) residenti-

al care, upbringing in foster care; **Begleitung, Unterstützung während der ~** through care

Heimkind (n) boarding child, child in residential care

Heimleiter(in) (m,f) warden

Heimunterbringung (f) residential care

Helfersyndrom (n) helper syndrome

Hemmung (f) *(psych)* inhibition

Heranwachsende(r) (f,m) adolescent; *(pl)* rising generation

Herkunftsfamilie (f) parental family

Herkunftsland (n) home country, country of origin

Herkunftssprache (f) language of origin

herumspielen (v) to toy with something

Heterogenität (f) heterogeneity, diversity

Hilfe zur Erziehung nach § 27 Sozialgesetzbuch VIII (D) socio-educational provision under a care order

Hilfebedürftige(r) (m,f) person in need of help

Hilfekonferenz (f) (päd) panel

Hilfeleistung (f) relief, assistance

Hilfestellung, praktische (f) (practical) guidance

Hilfspersonal (n) auxiliary staff, temporary staff, ancillary worker, ancillary staff

Hilfsquellen (f,pl) resources

Hirnschädigung (f) brain injury

hitzefrei *(gibt es nur in D.!)* school closure due to very high temperatures

hochbegabt (adj) highly gifted

hochbegabtes Kind (highly) gifted child

Hochdeutsch (n) standard German

Hochschulabsolvent(in) (m,f) graduate

Hochschulausbildung (f) higher education

Hochschulbildung (f) tertiary education

Hochschule (f) institution of higher education

Hochschulniveau (n) tertiary level

Hochschulreife (f) > Abitur

Hochstühlchen (n) **für Kinder** highchair

Hochzeit (f) wedding; **Hochzeitstag** wedding anniversary

Holzbaustein (m) wooden

block
hörbar (adj) audible
Hörbehinderung (f) hearing defect, impaired hearing
Hörgerät (n) hearing aid
hörgeschädigt (adj) hearing impaired
Hörhilfe (f), **Hörgerät** (n) hearing aid
Hörschädigung (f) hearing impairment
Hort (m) (D) centre for school-age children, after-school provision, after-school care, after-school facilities, out-of-school educational daycare facility
Horterzieher(in) (m,f) (D) school-age childcare worker
Hörverlust (m) hearing loss
Hörvermögen (n) faculty of hearing
Hospitalismus (m) hospitalism, institutionalization
Hospitation (f) observation visit, sitting in on a class
Hospiz (n) hospice
hospitieren (v) to observe in action, to sit in
hüpfen (v) to skip
hyperaktiv (adj) hyperactive

I

Ich (n) *(psych)* ego
ichbezogen (adj) self-centred
Identität (f) identity
Imitationslernen (n) imitative learning
immanent (adj) intrinsic
impfen (v) to vaccinate, to inoculate; **gegen etwas ~** to vaccinate against
Impfstoff (m) vaccine
Informationsfluss (m) flow of information
Inhaltsanalyse (f) content analysis
Inklusion (f) inclusion, mainstreaming
inklusive Kultur (f) inclusive culture
inklusive Leitlinien (f,pl) inclusive policies
inkonsequent (adj) inconsistent
Innen... indoor, *z.B.* **Innenaktivitäten durchführen** to do indoor activities
innere Hemmung (f) internal inhibition
innere Ruhe (f) inner peace
innerlich (adj) *(psych)* intrinsic

innewohnend (adj) intrinsic
Inobhutnahme (f) provision of shelter and protection
Insidergruppe (f) in-group
institutionelle Diskriminierung (f) institutional discrimination
Integration (f) *(von behinderten und nichtbehinderten Kindern)* mainstreaming, integration, inclusion
Integrationsgruppe (f) *(für behinderte und nicht behinderte Kinder)* integrative group, inclusive group
Integrationskindergarten (m) inclusive nursery
Integrationspädagogik (f) inclusive pedagogy / education
integrative Erziehung (f) *(behinderter und nicht-behinderter Kinder)* joint education, inclusive education
integrieren (v) to mainstream, to integrate
Interaktion (f) interaction
Interdependenz (f) interdependence
interdisziplinäres Lernen (n) cross-disciplinary learning
Interesse aufrechterhalten to sustain interest
Interessengebiet (n) field of interest

Interessengleichheit (f) identity of interest
Interessenvertretung (f) advocacy
interkonfessionell (adj) inter-denominational
interkulturell (adj) cross-cultural, intercultural
interkultureller Ansatz (m) intercultural approach
Internalisierung (f) internalization
Internat (n) boarding school
Internatseinrichtung (f) residential provision
Internatsschule (f) residential school
interventionistischer Ansatz (m) *(päd)* hands on approach
Intoleranz gegen Mehrdeutigkeit od. Unterschiedlichkeit intolerance of ambiguity
intrinsische Motivation (f) intrinsic motivation
introvertiert (adj) withdrawn, introverted

J

Jahrespraktikum (n) probationary year
Jahresurlaub annual leave
Jugend (f) adolescence
Jugend... *(in Zusammensetzungen)* juvenile
Jugendamt (n) (D) youth welfare (and youth service) office, youth office
Jugendamt (n) child welfare department
Jugendarbeit (f) youth work, youth and community work; **mobile Jugendarbeit** detached youth work
Jugendarbeitslosigkeit (f) youth unemployment, entry unemployment
Jugendarbeitsschutzgesetz (n) (D) Protection of Young Persons at Work Act
Jugendcafé (n) drop-in centre
Jugendfreizeitstätte (f,pl) leisure centre for young people
Jugendfürsorge (f) child / youth welfare
Jugendfürsorger(in) (m,f), child / youth worker
Jugendgericht (n) juvenile court
Jugendgruppenleiter(in) (m,f) youth leader
Jugendhilfe (f) child and youth welfare (services)
Jugendkriminalität (f) juvenile delinquency
Jugendleiter(in) (m,f) voluntary youth leader
Jugendliche(r) (f,m) adolescent, young person, youth
jugendlicher Straftäter (m) juvenile delinquent, young offender
Jugendorganisation (f) youth association
Jugendpfleger(in) (m,f) youth worker
Jugendpsychiatrie (f) child guidance clinic
Jugendrecht (n) youth legislation
Jugendrichter(in) (m,f) juvenile court magistrate
Jugendstrafanstalt (f) young offender's institution, youth custody centre (Brit)
Jugendstrafe (f) youth custody (Brit)
Jugendwohlfahrt (f) youth and child welfare
Jugendzentrum (n) youth centre, youth club

junge Menschen (m,pl) young persons (14–17 years); young adults (17–25 years) (Brit)

K

Kacke (f) poo, poop *(Kindersprache)*
kacken (v) to poo. to poop *(Kindersprache)*; **in die Hose machen** to poop in the pants
Kaiserschnitt (m) caesarean (section); **Kaiserschnittgeburt** caesarean delivery
Kartenspiel (n) cardgame
Karussell (n) roundabout (Brit), merry-go-round, carousel
Kasper (m) Punch
Kasperletheater (n) Punch and Judy show
Kern (m) *(auch fig)* core
Kernfamilie (f) nuclear family, basic family, elementary family
Keuchhusten (m) whooping cough, pertussis

Kieferorthopäde (m), **Kieferorthopädin** (f) orthodontist
Kinästhetik (f) kinesthesia, proprioception
Kind (n) child, (pl) children, infant; **uneheliches ~** illegitimate child; **vom ~ ausgehend** child initiated; **Schutz des Kindes** child protection
Kindchenschema (n) baby schema
Kinder- und Jugendfürsorge (f) child care
Kinder- und Jugendhilfe (f) (D) child and youth services
Kinder- und Jugendhilfegesetz (n) (KJHG) (D) Child and Youth Services Act
Kinder- und Jugendpsychotherapie (f) child and adolescent psychotherapy
Kinderarbeit (f) child labour
Kinderarzt / Kinderärztin (m,f) paediatrician (Brit), pediatrician (US)
Kinderbetreuung (f) child minding
Kinderbett (n) cot
Kinderfreibetrag (m) child allowance
kinderfreundlich (adj) child-orientated
Kindergarten (m) nursery school, nursery class, nurs-

Kindergeld (n) child benefit, children's allowance, family allowance, family benefit

Kinderheilkunde (f) paediatrics (Brit), pediatrics (US)

Kinderheim (n) children's home

Kinderhort (m) (D) after-school provision, after-school care, after-school facilities, centre for school-age children

Kinderklinik (f) children's clinic

Kinderkonferenz (f) children's planning meeting

Kinderkram (m) kid('s) stuff

Kinderkrankenhaus (n) children's hospital

Kinderkrankenschwester (f) childrens's nurse; paediatric nurse (Brit); pediatric nurse (US)

Kinderkrankheit (f) childhood disease; *(fig)* teething troubles

Kinderkrippe (f) day nursery; > Krippe

Kinderladen (m) (D) parent-managed children's centre, antiauthoritarian playgroup

ery, preschool (US); kindergarten *(Brit: meist private Einrichtung; US: meist Vorschule)*

Kinderlähmung (f) poliomyelitis, polio, infantile paralysis

Kinderlied (n), Kinderreim (m) nursery rhyme

Kindermädchen (n) nurse; *(im Privathaushalt)* nanny

Kindernotdienst (m) emergency services for (mistreated or neglected) children

Kinderpflege (f) child care

Kinderpfleger(in) (m,f) (D) childcare worker, nursery nurse, nursery worker, nursery assistant, childcare assistant; *(med)* children's nurse; > Erzieher(in)

Kinderrechte (n,pl) children's rights; **Bewegung zur Wahrung der Rechte der Kinder** children's rights movement

Kinderreim (m) nursery rhyme

Kinderschänder (m) child molester, child abuser

Kinderschutz (m) protection of children

kindersicher (adj) childproof

Kindersitz (m) *(Auto)* child safety seat, *(Fahrrad)* child-carrier seat

Kinderspiel (n) *(fig)* child's play

Kinderspielplatz (m) playground

Kindersterblichkeit (f) infant mortality

Kinder-Tageseinrichtung in Trägerschaft der Gemeinde local authority nursery

Kindertagesbetreuung (f) day care (establishment) for children

Kindertagesstätte (f) day care centre (for children and young people); child care centre

Kinderwagen (m) pram, buggy; pushchair (Brit); baby carriage, baby stroller (US)

Kinderzimmer (n) *(für Kleinkinder)* nursery; children's room

Kinderzulage (f) child benefit

Kindesaussetzung (f) exposure, child abandonment

Kindesmisshandlung (f) child abuse

Kindesvernachlässigung (f) child neglect

Kindeswohl (n) the child's well-being

kindgemäß (adj) suitable for children

Kindheit (f) childhood; **zweite ~** *(Senilität)* second childhood

kindisch (adj) babyish, childish

kindlich (adj) childlike

Kind-orientierter pädagogischer Ansatz (m) child-oriented educational approach

Kindschaftsverhältnis (n) filiation

kindzentriert (adj) child-centred

kirchlich geführt church-run

Kita-Berater(in) (m,f) educational advisor (for nursery school teachers)

KJHG > Kinder- und Jugendhilfegesetz

Klasse (f) *(Schule)* class, form (Brit); grade (US); **Klasse(n) überspringen** skipping classes

Klassenarbeit (f) test, written paper

Klassenausflug (m) class outing

Klassenfahrt (f) school trip

Klassengröße (f) class size

Klassenlehrer(in) (m,f) form teacher

Klausur (f) written paper, written test

Klebstoff (m) sticky paste

kleiner Finger (m) pinky, pinkie (US)

Kleinfamilie (f) nuclear family

Kleingruppenunterricht (m) small-group teaching

Kleinkind (n) infant, toddler, young child

Kleinkindalter (n) infancy, early childhood

Kleinkindpädagogik (f) early childhood education / pedagogics

Kleinstkindpädagogik (f) infant pedagogics / education

Kleister (m) paste

Klettergerüst (n), **Klettergestell** climbing frame, climbing equipment; jungle gym (US)

Klient(in) (m,f) client

Knete, Knetmasse (f) dough, play-dough, Play Doh ®, Plasticine ® (Brit)

kneten (v) to mould

Koedukation (f) coeducation

kognitive Entwicklung (f) cognitive development; **kognitive Lernziele** (n,pl) cognitive objectives

Kollegin (f), **Kollege** (m) colleague

Kolloquium (n) colloquium; *(mündliche Abschlussprüfung)* oral examination (as part of the finals)

kommunal (adj) local, municipal, community...

kompensatorische Erziehung (f) compensatory education

Kompetenzen erweitern upgrade competencies

Kompetenzmodell (n) competence model

Kompetenztransfer (m) shared learning

kompromisslos (adj) uncompromising

konditioniert (adj) *(psych)* conditioned

konfessionell (adj) denominational; **nicht-konfessionsgebunden** non-denominational

Konfliktvermeidung (f) conflict avoidance

konkrete Operationen concrete operations

Konrektor(in) (m,f) deputy headmaster

kontaktarm (adj) withdrawn

Konvention über die Rechte des Kindes (f) Convention on the Rights of the Child

Konzentrationsvermögen (n) attention span

Konzept (n) *(Entwurf)* draft

Konzeption (f) concept

kooperativ (adj) cooperative

Kopfläuse (f,pl) head lice

Kopfrechnen (n) mental arithmetic
Kopftuch (n) headscarf, veil
kopieren (v) to photocopy, to xerox
Korbkinderwagen (mit Verdeck) (m) bassinet
Korbwiege (mit Verdeck) (f) bassinet
Kordel (f) *(an Kleidungsstücken)* drawstring
körperbehindert (adj) invalid, physically disabled, physically handicapped
Körperbehinderung (f) disability, physical defect
Körperbewusstsein (n) body awareness
Körperhaltung (f) composure
körperliche Behinderung (f) physical handicap
körperliche Bestrafung (f) corporal punishment
körperliche Entwicklung (f) physical development
körperliche Nähe (f) physical closeness
Körperschaft (f) *(jur)* body
Körperschaft des öffentlichen Rechts (f) *(jur)* statutory body, body corporate under public law
Körpersprache (f) non-verbal communication and posture

Krabbelkind (n) crawler
krabbeln (v) to crawl
Kraftausdrücke (m,pl) **benutzen** use bad language
krank (adj) ill, sick
krank geschrieben sein to be on sick leave
krank werden (v) to fall ill
Krankengeld (n) sick pay, sickness benefit
Krankengeschichte (f) case history
Krankenhaus (n) hospital, clinic
Krankenhauseinweisung (f) hospitalization
Krankenkasse (f) health company
Krankenpfleger (m) **in einer Sozialstation** (f) health visitor
Krankenpfleger (m) male nurse
Krankenschein (m) health insurance voucher, sick certificate
Krankenschwester (f) nurse
Krankenschwester (f) **in einer Sozialstation** (f) health visitor
Krankenstation (f) infirmary
Krankenversicherung (f) health insurance
Krankheit (f) illness, sickness, disease; *(ansteckende)*

contagious disease
krankmelden (v) to report sick, to call in sick
Krankmeldung (f) sick note
krankschreiben (v) to give someone a sick note
Kreativität (f) creativity
Kreisgespräch (n) (group) circle time
Kreisspiel (n) ring game
Kreißsaal (m) delivery room, labour ward
Kreuzworträtsel (n) crossword-puzzle
Kriminalität (f) delinquency
Krippe (f) day nursery *(als Tageseinrichtung)*; crèche *(für nicht ständige Einrichtungen benutzt, z.B. für Kinderbetreuung bei Veranstaltungen, sowie für betriebliche Einrichtungen);* baby nest
Krippenspiel (n) nativity play
Kritzelalter (n) scribbling developmental stage
Kugelbahn (f) bowling alley, ball alley
kulturelle Anpassung (f) acculturation
kulturelle Vielfalt (f) cultural diversity
kündigen (v) *(Arbeitsverhältnis)* to sack someone

Kunsterzieher(in) (m,f) arts teacher
Kunsterziehung (f) art education
Kuratorium (n) board of trustees
Kurzbeschreibung (f) brief presentation
Kürzung (f) *(von finanziellen Mitteln und Leistungen)* cutback, cuts (pl)
Kurzzeitgedächtnis (n) short-term memory
Kuscheltier (n) cuddly toy

L

labiles Verhalten (n) unstable behaviour
Laienspiel (n) pantomime
Laientheater (n) amateur theatre
laissez-faire Führungsstil (m) non-directive / liberal style of leadership
ländliche Umgebung (f) rural environment
Langzeitgedächtnis (n) long-term memory

Latenzperiode (f) latency period
Lätzchen (n) bib, pinny
Laubsäge (f) jigsaw
Laufbahn (f) career
laufende Nase (f) running nose
Laufstall (m) playpen
Laufstuhl (m) baby walker
Lebensbedingungen (f,pl) living conditions
Lebensgefährte (m), **Lebensgefährtin** (f) partner
Lebensgrundlagen (f,pl) basic necessities
Lebenskraft (f) vitality
lebenslang (adj) life-long
Lebenslauf (m) curriculum vitae (C.V.)
Lebenspraxis (f) experience of life
Lebenszyklus (m) life cycle
lebhaft (adj) lively, *(Unterhaltung, Gebärden)* animated
lebhafte Phantasie (f) vivid imagination
Legasthenie (f) dyslexia
Lehramt (n) teaching profession
Lehramtsanwärter(in) (m,f) trainee teacher
Lehrbefähigung (f) teaching certificate
Lehrer(in) (m,f) teacher; *(der/die an mehreren Schulen unterrichtet)* peripatetic teacher
Lehrerausbildung (f) teacher training
Lehrerkollegium (n) teaching staff
Lehrervortrag (m) teacher talk
lehrerzentriertes Programm (n) teacher-centred programme
Lehrerzimmer (n) staff room
Lehrgang (m) course of study
Lehrplan (m) curriculum, syllabus, teaching schedule; **~gestaltung** curriculum design; **heimlicher ~** hidden curriculum
Lehrprobe (f) assessed teaching practice, demonstration lesson
lehrreiches Spielzeug (n) didactic toys
Lehrstelle (f) traineeship
leibliche Schwester (f) full sister
Leidensdruck (m) desire to change
Leihmutter (f) surrogate mother
leisten (v) *(vollbringen)* achieve, *(sich etwas ~)* be able to afford

Leistung (f) achievement, performance, result

Leistungsbeurteilung (f) assessment, achievement report

Leistungsdifferenzierung (f) ability grouping; streaming *(Niveaudifferenzierung)*; setting *(Fachleistungsdifferenzierung)*

Leistungsfähigkeit, unterschiedliche mixed ability; **Schulklasse mit unterschiedlicher Leistungsfähigkeit, ohne > Leistungsdifferenzierung** mixed ability class

Leistungsgruppe (f) *(päd)* stream; **in Leistungsgruppen einteilen** to stream

Leistungsmessung (f) performance evaluation

leistungsorientiert (adj) achievement oriented

leistungsschwache(r) Schüler(in) (f,m) underachiever

Leistungstest (m) achievement test

Leistungswille (m) motivation

Leitbegriff (m) key concept

Leitbild (n) image, role model

Leitbildfunktion (f) role model function

leiten (v) *(betreiben)* to run; **diese Einrichtung wird vom Staat betrieben** this institution is run by the state; **einen Kindergarten leiten** to run a nursery

Leiter(in) (m,f) *(einer Kindertagesstätte)* principal (of a nursery school); headteacher, head

Leitfaden (m) guidelines, s.a. > pädagogischer Leitfaden

Leitgedanke (m) central idea, central theme

lernbehindert (adj) with special needs, ineducable, with learning difficulties

lernbehindertes Kind (n) special needs child, educationally subnormal child, child with learning difficulties

Lernbehinderung (f) learning disability, learning handicap, learning difficulty

lernen (v) to learn, to study, to train; *(päd)* **aneignen** to acquire; **beiläufiges, unbeabsichtigtes Lernen** incidental learning; **auswendig ~** to learn by heart; **auf die harte Tour ~** to learn the hard way; **aus Erfahrung ~** to learn by experience; **aus seinen Fehlern ~** to learn by one's mistakes; **auswendig ~** to learn by heart; *(im Sinne von pauken)* to learn by rote

Lernmittel (n,pl) schoolbooks and equipment

Lernmittelfreiheit (f) free provision of schoolboks and equipment

Lernen (n), **aktives, selbstbestimmtes** active independent learning

Lernen am Modell modelling

Lernen durch Beobachtung observational learning

Lernen durch systematische Beobachtung und praktische Erfahrung experiential learning

Lernen durch Versuch und Irrtum learning by trial and error

Lernfähigkeit (f) learning aptitude

Lernfeld (n) area of learning

Lernmittelfreiheit (f) free provision of teaching materials

Lernprozess (m) learning process

Lernschwierigkeiten (f,pl) learning difficulties; **moderate ~** moderate learning difficulties; **schwere ~** severe learning difficulties; **schwerste ~** profound and multiple learning difficulties; **spezifische ~** specific learning difficulties

Lernspiele (n,pl) learning games, educational games

Lernstörung (f) learning disability

Lernziel (n) learning objective, learning goal

Lese- und Schreibfähigkeit (f) literacy

Lesealter (n) reading age; **wie ein Achtjähriger lesen können** to have a reading age of eight

Lesefähigkeit (f) reading skill

Lesekompetenz (f) reading ability

lesen und schreiben können to be literate

Leseverständnis (n) reading comprehension

Liebesentzug (m) deprivation, loss of love

liebevoll (adj) affectionate, loving

Lieblingsbeschäftigung (f) favourite occupation

Liegestütze (f) push-up

Linkshänder(in) (m,f) left-handed person

Linkshändigkeit (f) left-handedness

Literalität (f) literacy
Literaturhinweise (m,pl) further reading
Lob (n) praise
loben (v) to praise
Logopäde, Logopädin (m,f) speech therapist
Lohn (m) *(Gehalt)* pay, salary
Lohnfortzahlung bei Krankheit sick pay
Lohnfortzahlung für Mütter maternity pay
Lösemittel (n) solvent; ~ **missbrauchen** to abuse solvents
Lösemittelmissbrauch (m) abuse of solvents
loslassen (v) to let go
Lückentest (m) cloze test

M

Mädchenarbeit (f) work with girls
Mädchenname (m) maiden name
Makel (m) stigma; **gesellschaftlicher** ~ social stigma
Malkasten (m) paint box
Mangel (m) defect, deficit, deficiency, weakness
manische Depression (f) maniac depression
männlich (adj) male
Märchen (n) fairy tale
Märchenland (n) fairyland
Marionettentheater (n) puppet show
Masern (pl) measles, rubella
Mäßigung (f) moderation
Maßlosigkeit (f) self-indulgence, boundlessness
Mathematik (f) mathematics, maths; > Rechnen
mathematische Kompetenz (f) mathematical literacy
Matriarchat (n) matriarchy
maulen (v) to whine
Medienerziehung (f) media education
Medikament (n) medicine, medication; drug (US)
Mediothek (f) audiovisual library
Mehrdeutigkeit (f) ambiguity
Mehrfachbeeinträchti-gun-gen (f,pl) complex and severe learning difficulties
Mehrfachbehinderung (f) multihandicap, multiple handicap
mehrfache Benachteiligung (f) multiple deprivation

Mehrgenerationenfamilie (f) extended family
Mehrheit, große (f) vast majority
Mehrlingsgeburt (f) multiple birth
mehrsprachig (adj) multilingual
Mehrsprachigkeit (f) multilingualism
Meinung (f) opinion
Meinungsumfrage (f) opinion poll, opinion survey
Menschenbild (n) view of humanity, view of mankind
Menschenwürde (f) human dignity
Merkmal (n) feature, characteristic
Mietbeihilfe (f) housing allowance
Mieter(in) (m,f) tenant; ~ **einer Sozialwohnung** council tenant
Milchpulver (n) **für Babys** formula
Milchzahn (m) milk tooth, primary tooth, baby tooth
Mimik (f) gestures and facial expressions
Minderheit (f) minority
Minderheitsgruppe (f) minority group
minderjährig (adj) underage; ~ **sein** to be underage
Minderjährige(r) (f,m) minor, person under age, underage person
Minderjährigkeit (f) minority
Minderwertigkeitsgefühl (n) feeling of inferiority
Minderwertigkeitskomplex (m) inferiority complex
Mindestalter (n) minimum age
Miniclub (m) (D) parent-organized toddlers' group, play group
Missbrauch (m) abuse; **Alkohol~** (m) alcohol abuse; **sexueller ~** sexual assault
missbrauchen (v) to abuse; **sexuell ~** to abuse sexually
misshandeln (v) to batter, to maltreat; **misshandeltes Kind** abused *or* battered child *or* baby; **misshandelte Frau** battered wife
Misshandlung (f) maltreatment, ill-treatment, mistreatment, **körperliche ~** bashing
Missverhältnis (n) mismatch, imbalance
Mitarbeit (f) cooperation
Mitarbeiter (pl) *(Kollegium)* staff
Mitarbeiter(in) (m,f)

colleague, member of staff, worker
Mitarbeiterbesprechung staff meeting
Mitarbeiter-Fortbildung staff training
Mitbestimmung (f) participation, joint management
mitfühlend (adj) compassionate
Mitglied (n) member
Mitgliedsbeitrag (m) membership fee
mitmachen (v) to join in; **sich am Spiel beteiligen** to join in the game
Mittagessen (n) lunch
Mittagspause (f) lunch break
Mittagsruhe (f) period of quiet (after lunch), quiet hour
Mittagsschlaf (m) nap
Mittagszeit (f) lunchtime
mitteilen (v) to share information, to inform
Mittlere Reife (f) (D) *(veraltet, aber noch gebräuchlich,* > Realschulabschluss) *etwa*: General Certificate of Education (GCE), *früher* O-level (Ordinary level)
Mitverantwortung (f) joint responsibility
Mitwirkung (f) contribution
mobben (v) to bully

mobile Jugendarbeit (f) detached youth work
Modelliermasse (f) modelling compound
Modelllernen (n) learning from model, modelling
Modellprojekt (n), **Modellversuch** (m) pilot project, pilot scheme
Moderator(in) (m,f) facilitator
Monokultur (f) monoculture
monolingual (adj) monolingual
Moralerziehung (f) moral education
Morgenkreis (m) circle time
Motivationserschöpfung (f) burn-out
Motorik (f) motor behaviour, **Feinmotorik** fine motor skills, **Grobmotorik** motor skills
motorische Fähigkeit (f) motor ability
multikulturell (adj) multicultural
Mumps (m *oder* f) mumps
mündig (adj) of age, responsible
Mündigkeit (f) majority
mündliche Ausdrucksfähigkeit (f) oracy
mündliche Befragung (f) oral questioning

mündliche Prüfung (f) oral examination, oral test
mündlicher Ausdruck (m) verbal expression
musikalischer Sinn (m) musical sense
Muße (f) leisure
Mutter- und Koselieder *(pl) (Fröbel)* Mother-Songs
Mutter, minderjährige (f) teenage mother
Mütterberatung (f) counselling in child care
Mutter-Kind-Bindung (f) *(psych)* mother-child attachment, bonding
Mutter-Kind-Gruppe (f) pre-school playgroup, mother-toddler group
Mutter-Kind-Heim (n) home for single mothers and their children
mütterlich (adj) maternal; **mein Großvater mütterlicherseits** my maternal grandfather
Muttermal (n) birth mark
Muttermilch (f) mother's milk
Mutterschaft (f) maternity, motherhood
Mutterschaftsgeld (n) maternity allowance, maternity benefit
Mutterschaftsurlaub (m) maternity leave
Mutterschutz (m), **betrieblicher** maternity protection
Mutterschutzvorschriften, betriebliche protective legislation for working mothers
Muttersprache (f) first language, mother tongue, native language
Muttersprachler(in) (m,f) native speaker
Muttertag (m) Mother's Day

N

Nabelschnur (f) umbilical chord
Nachbarschaft (f) neighbourhood, vicinity
Nachbarschaftsheim (n) neighbourhood centre, community centre
Nachbarschaftshilfe (f) community care
Nachbarschaftsverein (m) community association
Nachbetreuung (f) after-care
Nachfrage (f) demand

nachgeburtlich (adj) postnatal

nachhaltig zukunftsverträgliche Entwicklung (f) sustainable development

Nachhaltigkeit (f) sustainability

Nachhilfe (f) coaching

Nachhilfelehrer(in) (m,f) tutor

nachlässig (adj) neglectful

Nachmittagsbetreuung (f) afternoon session

Nachname (m) last name, second name, surname, family name

Nachsitzen (n) *(in der Schule)* detention

nachsitzen lassen (v) to keep somebody in, to give somebody detention

Nachsorge (f) *(z.B. bei Heimerziehung)* after care

nachspielen (v) to act out (something); **eine Geschichte ~** to act out a story

nächste Angehörige (pl) next of kin

Nachteil (m) disadvantage

nächtlicher Bereitschaftsdienst (m) wakened night staff

Nachtwache (f) wakened night staff

Nahrungsaufnahme (f) intake of food

Nahsinne (m, *meist* pl) near senses

Namensband (n) *(bei Babys)* ID bracelet (for newborn babies)

Naturheilverfahren (n) nature cure

naturwissenschaftliche Grundbildung (f) scientific literacy

Naturschutz (m) (nature) conservation

Naturschützer (m) conservationist

Nebenräume (m,pl) ancillary rooms

Nebenwirkung (f) side effect

negative Verstärkung (f) *(psych)* escape conditioning, negative reinforcement

Neigung (f) tendency; *(Zuneigung)* affection, fondness

Nervenklinik (f) mental hospital

Nesselausschlag (m), **Nesselfieber** (n) nettle rash

Neugeborene(s) (n) newborn, newborn infant

Neugeborenen... *(in Zusammensetzungen)* neonatal; **~station** neonatal unit

neugeborenes Kind (n) *(bis zu einem Monat)* neonate;

newborn baby, newborn infant
Neugier (f) curiosity, (F) nosiness; **aus** ~ out of curiosity; **unstillbare** ~ insatiable curiosity
neugierig (adj) curious, (F) nosy
Nicht-Ausgrenzung (f) non-segregation
nicht ehelich geborenes Kind illegitimate child
Nicht-Behinderte (pl) able-bodied people, non-disabled person
nichtkonditionell (adj) *(psych)* unconditional
nicht-teilnehmende Beobachtung (f) non-participant observation
Nickerchen (n) nap; **ein ~ machen** to take a nap
non-verbale Interaktion (f) non-verbal interaction
Notdienst (m) emergency service, > Notruf
Note (f) *(Schule)* mark (Brit), grafe (US); **gute / schlechte Noten erhalten** to get good / bad marks
Notensystem (n) *(Schule)* marking / grading system
Notruf (m) helpline
null bis drei Jahre nought to three years
null Toleranz (f) zero tolerance

O

obdachlos (adj) homeless
Obdachlose(r) (f,m) homeless person
Obdachlosigkeit (f) homelessness
Oberschule (f) secondary school; high school (US)
Oberschüler(in) (m,f) student, high-school student
Oberstufenzentrum (n) (D) vocational secondary college
Objektpermanenz (f) object permanence
offene Angebote (n,pl) drop-in facilities
offene Arbeit (f) *(in der Kita)* open-plan work
offene Einrichtung (f) establishment without fixed membership
offene Jugendarbeit (f) open activities for young people

offenes Verhalten (n) overt behaviour
Offenheit (f) openness
offensichtlich (adj) self-evident
öffentlich (adj) public
öffentlich finanzierte Bildungseinrichtunge maintained educational provision
öffentlich finanzierte Einrichtungen publicly funded provisions / services
öffentlich finanzierte Schule maintained school
öffentliche Erziehungshilfen (f,pl) statutory socio-educational provision for children with problems
öffentliche Gelder (n,pl) public funds
öffentliche Schule (f) state school
öffentliche Träger (m,pl) public agencies, statutory agencies / bodies
öffentlicher Dienst (m) civil service, public service
öffentliches Gesundheitssystem (n) public health service; National Health Service (NHS) (Brit)
Öffentliches Recht (n) public law
Öffentlichkeit (f) public

öffentlich-rechtlich (adj) under public law
Öffnungszeiten (f,pl) opening hours, opening times
Ökologie (f) ecology
ökologisch (adj) ecological, environmental
Ökosystem (n) ecosystem
Opfer (n) victim
optische Wahrnehmung (f) visual perception
orale Phase (f) oral stage
oral-sensorische Phase (f) oral-sensory stage
örtliche Verwaltung (f) local administration

P

Paarverhältnis (n) dyad
Pädagoge / Pädagogin (m,f) pedagogue
Pädagogik (f) (theory of) education, pedagogy, pedagogics
pädagogisch (adj) educational, pedagogical
pädagogisch gesehen pedagogically speaking

Pädagogische Hochschule (f) college of education, teacher training college

pädagogische Unterrichtshilfe (f) teacher's aide, welfare assistant (Brit)

pädagogischer Leitfaden (m) educational guide

Papiertaschentuch (n) (paper) tissue, kleenex ®

Papierwindel (f) disposable nappy; > Windel

Pappe (f) cardboard

Pappkarton (m) cardboard box

Pappmaschee (n) papier-mâché

Partnerarbeit (f) peer work

Patchwork-Familie (f) (D) reconstituted family, blended family

Patient in ambulanter Behandlung out-patient

Patient in stationärer Behandlung in-patient

pauken (v) rote learning, to learn by rote

Pauschale (f), **Pauschbetrag** (m) flat rate

Pauschalzahlung (f) lump-sum payment

permanente Gegenstände (m,pl) object permanence

Personalausstattung (f) staffing

Personalraum (m) staff room

Personalschlüssel (m) *(Zahlenverhältnis Erzieher / Kinder)* staff-child ratio

Personensorge (f) *(jur)* care and control; care and custody of a person

Personensorgeberechtigte(r) (f,m) person who exercises the right of care and custody

persönlich (adj) one-to-one, individual(ly)

petzen (v) to tell tales

Pfadfinder(in) (m,f) (boy) scout, (girl) guide; ~ **über 16 Jahre** venture scout

Pfarrgemeinde (f) parish

Pflege (f) care

pflegebedürftig (adj) in need of care

Pflege|eltern, ~vater, ~mutter foster parents, foster father, foster mother

Pflegefall (m) nursing case

Pflegefamilie (f) foster family

Pflegeheim (n) nursing home

Pflegekind (n) foster child (in a family / in a home)

Pflegekosten (pl) nursing fees

Pflegekraft (f) carer, nurse, care-giver

pflegen (v) to nurse, to care for, to look after

Pfleger(in) (m,f) carer, enabler, assistant

pflegerische Orientierung (f) *(beruflich, Ausbildung)* paramedical orientation

Pflegesatz (m) daily allowance, daily rate

Pflegetochter (f) foster daughter

Pflegesohn (m) foster son

Pflegeversicherung (f) nursing insurance

Pflegschaft (f) (D) *(jur)* curatorship, guardianship

Pflicht- und Wahlfächer common curriculum

Pflichtfach (n) foundation subject, compulsory subject, *(im Pl.:)* core curriculum

Phantasie (f) imagination

Physiotherapeut(in) (m,f) physiotherapist

pinkeln (v) to pee; **in die Hose** ~ to pee (in) one's pants; ~ **gehen** to have a pee; **sich bepinkeln** to pee oneself

Pipi (n) *(Kindersprache)* wee, wee-wee; ~ **machen** to pee

Plan (m) *(Übersicht)* rota (Brit), roster (US); **Tagesplan** daily rota; **Wochenplan** weekly rota; **Dienstplan** duty rota

Planschbecken (n) toddler's pool

plötzlicher Kindstod (m) sudden infant death syndrome (SIDS)

Po (m) (F) butt

politisches Asyl (n) political asylum; ~ ~ **beantragen / gewähren** to seek / to grant political asylum

postnatale Depression (f) baby blues, post-natal depression

prägend (adj) formative; **die prägenden Jahre** the formative years

Prägung (f) *(psych)* imprinting, fixation

Praktikant(in) (m,f) student on placement, (student) trainee, student on work experience; *(Lehrer/innen-Ausbildung)* student teacher; intern (US)

Praktikantenberatung (f) counselling students in training

Praktikum (n) (practical) work experience, practical studies, practicum, period of practical training; *(in Betrieb oder päd. Einrichtung)* work placement, internship

Auslandspraktikum practicum abroad; **im ersten Studienjahr sind vier Wochen** ~ work placements cover four weeks during the first year of study

praktisch arbeiten (v) to do practical work

praktische Erfahrung (f) practical experience, work experience, hands-on experience

praktische Prüfung (f) practical

praktisches Beispiel (n) concrete example

Praxis (f) *(Erfahrung)* practical experience, work experience; *(Anwendung)* practice; **in der ~** in practice; **etwas in die ~ umsetzen** to put s.th. into practice, translate into practice; *(Arztpraxis)* surgery

Praxisanleiter(in) (m,f) placement supervisor

Praxisberichte (m,pl) placement recordings

Praxiserfahrung (f) practical experience

praxisnah (adj) closely concerned with practice

praxisorientiert sein to have a practical attitude

Praxissemester (n) practical term / semester

Primärbeziehung (f) early bonding

Primarstufe (f) primary school level, primary stage of education

Prinzipienstreit (m) fight over fundamental issues

Privatschule (f) private school; independent school (Brit), public school *(meist mit Internat)* (Brit)

Probezeit (f) probation, probationary period; **~ haben, auf Bewährung sein** to be on probation

professioneller Praktiker(in) (m,f) practitioner

Programm (n) scheme [ski:m]

progressive Skala (f) sliding scale

Projektarbeit (f) topic work

Protokoll (n) record; **Protokollbogen** (m) record sheet

prüfen (v) to examine, to test, to study, to check

Prüfung (f) examination

Prüfungs|arbeit (f), **~aufgabe** examination paper

Prügel bekommen to get a beating

Prügelstrafe (f) corporal punishment, flogging

Psychagoge (m), **Psychagogin** (f) psychiatric child care worker

psychiatrisch (adj) psychiatric
psychisch (adj) psychological
Psychologe (m), **Psychologin** (f) *(zur Beratung Jugendlicher)* guidance counselor; psychologist
Psychologie (f) psychology
psychologisch (adj) psychological
psychomotorische Lernziele (n,pl) psychomotor learning objectives
Pubertät (f) puberty
Puppe (f) *(Spielpuppe)* doll; *(Theater-, Handpuppe)* puppet
Puppenecke doll's corner
Puppenküche (f) kiddie kitchen
Puppenspiel (n) puppet theatre, puppet play
Puppenstube, **Puppenhaus** doll's house
Puppentheater (n) puppet show
Puppenwagen doll's pram
Purzelbaum (m) somersault; **einen ~ schlagen** to somersault
Putzplan (m) cleaning rota
Puzzle (n) jigsaw puzzle

Q

qualifiziert (adj) qualified; **hoch ~** highly qualified
Qualitätsentwicklung (f) quality development
Qualitätskontrolle (f) quality control
Qualitätsverbesserung (f) quality enhancement
quantitative Befragung (f) *(soz)* quantitative survey
quengelig (adj) whining, fretful; **sei nicht so ~** stop your whining
quengeln (v) to whine, to become fretful
Querschnitt (m) cross-section
querschnittsgelähmt (adj) paraplegic
Quote (f) proportion, quota
Quotenregelung (f) quota regulation, quota system

R

Rabenmutter (f) an uncaring mother, a cruel mother
Radweg (m) cycle way, cycle path
Rand (m) fringe; **am ~ der Gesellschaft** on the fringes of society
Randgruppe (f) *(soz)* fringe group, marginal group, minority group
Ranzen (m) satchel
Rasselbüchse (f) sound box, sound cylinder
Rassismus (m) racism, racialism; **offener ~** overt racism
Rassist(in) (m,f) racialist, racist
rassistisch (adj) racist, racialist; **rassistische Vorurteile** racial prejudice; **rassistischer Angriff** racist attac; **rassistische Bemerkung** racist remark
Rat (m) *(Ratsversammlung)* council
Rat(schlag) (m) advice
Rätsel (n) puzzle; **ein ~ lösen** to solve a puzzle
räumliches Bewusstsein (n) spatial awareness
Realschulabschluss (m) (D) intermediate school-leaving certificate; *entspricht etwa:* General Certificate of Education (GCE), *früher* O-level (Ordinary level) *in Engl, Wales, N.I.; in Schottland:* Standard Grade (Scottish Certificate of Education, SCE)
Realschule (f) (D) *etwa:* secondary modern school (Brit); junior high school (US)
Rechenkompetenz (f) numeracy skills
Rechenrahmen (m) counting frame
Rechnen (n) arithmetic, number work
rechnerische Fähigkeiten (f,pl) numeracy
rechtliche Verantwortung (f) legal responsibility
Rechtsanspruch (m) legal entitlement
Rechtsberatungsstelle (f) legal advice centre
Rechtsfähigkeit (f) legal responsibility
Rechtschreibfehler (m) spelling error, spelling mistake
Rechtschreibung (f) spelling
Rechtshändigkeit (f) right-handedness

Rechtsradikale(r) (f,m) rightist, right-wing extremist

Referat (n) *(univ)* seminar paper; *(school)* project; ~ **halten** read / present a paper

Referendar(in) (m,f) *(Schule)* trainee teacher; practice teacher (US)

Referendariat (n) *(für Lehrer/innen)* probationary period

Reformpädagogik (f) progressive education

reformpädagogische Bewegung (f) educational reform movement

Regelkita (f) mainstream childcare centre / daycare centre

Regelschule (f) mainstream school

reguläre Schule (f) regular school

Rehabilitationszentrum (n) rehabilitation centre

rehabilitierend (adj) rehabilitative

Reha-Klinik (f), **Reha-Zentrum** (n) rehab (clinic / centre)

Reifung (f) maturation

Reinlichkeitserziehung (f) toilet training

Reiz (m), stimulus; **unangenehmer** ~ aversive stimulus

Reizüberflutung (f) overstimulation, flooding

Religionsunterricht (m) religious instruction

religiöser Glaube (m) religious belief

Rentenalter (n) retirement age

Rentner(in) (m,f) old age pensioner (OAP)

Resozialisierung (f) reintegration, rehabilitation

Retardierung (f) retardation

Revier (n) *(Bezirk, Feld)* patch

Richtlinien (f,pl) guidelines

Risikofaktor (m) risk factor

Risikogruppe (f) high-risk group

Risikokind (n) delicate child

Risikoschwangerschaft (f) high-risk pregnancy

Rodelbahn (f) toboggan run

rodeln (v) to sledge

Rohrstock (m) cane

Rolle (f) *(psych)* role; **eine** ~ **übernehmen** to assume a role

Rollenkonflikt (m) role conflict

Rollenspiel (n) role play, role playing

Rollentausch (m) role reversal

Rollenverhalten (n) role behaviour
Rollenvorbild (n) role model
Rollenzuweisung (f) role allocation
Roller (Tret~) (m) scooter
Rollschuh (m) roller skate
Rollschuh fahren to rollerskate
Rollschuhbahn (f) roller skating rink
Rollstuhl (m) invalid chair, wheelchair
Rollstuhlfahrer(in) (m,f) wheelchair user
Röteln (pl) German measles, rubella
rotznasig (adj) snotty-nosed
Rückentwicklung (f) regression
Rückschlag (m) setback
Rückschritte machen to regress
Ruhestand (m) retirement; **in den ~ gehen** to retire; **im ~** retired; **vorzeitiger ~** *(aus arbeitsmarktpolitischen Gründen)* job release
Ruhezeit (f) quiet time, rest time
Rundschreiben (n) circular
Rutsche (f) *(Kinder-)* slide; *(Rummel)* helter skelter

S

Sabbatjahr (n) sabbatical, sabbatical leave, sabbatical year
Sachbearbeiter(in) (m,f) desk officer, *(Sozialamt)* case worker
Sachbuch (n) non-fiction book, factual book
Sachwalterschaft (f) advocacy
Sammelalbum (n) scrap book
Sandkasten (m) sandpit (Brit); sandbox (US)
Sandmännchen (n) sandman
Satzung (f) *(Verein etc.)* statute
sauber (adj) *(bezogen auf Kinder)* toilet-trained
sauber sein *(Kleinkinder)* potty trained; **ist Mary schon „sauber"?** is Mary potty-trained yet?
Sauberkeitserziehung (f) potty-training
Säugling (m) infant
Säuglingsalter (n) babyhood, infanthood, early infancy
Säuglingspflege (f) infant care, baby care

Säuglingspflegekurse (m,pl) classes on infant care

Säuglingsschwester (f) nursery nurse, baby nurse, infant nurse

Säuglingssterblichkeit (f) infant mortality

Saugreflex (m) suckling reflex

Säulendiagramm (n) bar graph, bar chart

Schablone (f) template

Schachtelmännchen (n) jack-in-the-box

Schädigung (f) impairment

Schaubild (n) chart

Schaukel (f) swing

Schaukelgestell (n) swingset

Schaukelpferd (n) rocking horse

scheiden (v) *(Ehe)* to divorce, **geschieden werden** obtain a divorce

Schema (n) *(päd)* schema [ski:ma]

Schicht (f) *(Arbeit)* shift; **in Schichten arbeiten** to work in shifts; to do shift work

Schicht (f) *(soz)* class, stratum, level

schikanieren (v) to bully, to harass

Schimpfwörter (n,pl) bad language, swear words

Schlafanzug (m) pyjamas, pajamas (US)

Schlafenszeit (f) *(am Mittag)* nap time

Schlafsaal (m) dormitory

schlechte(r) Schüler(in) poor student

schlechtes Verhalten poor behaviour

Schleife (f) *(auch päd)* loop

schlichten (v) to mediate, to settle, to arbitrate

schließen (v) *(auf Dauer)* to close down

Schließfach (n) locker; **abschließbares ~** lockable locker

Schließzeiten (f,pl) closing times

Schlitten (m) sledge; *(Pferde-)* sleigh

Schlittschuh (m) ice skate

Schlüssel > Erzieher-Schlüssel

Schlüsselbegriff (m) key concept, key word

Schlüsselfähigkeiten (f,pl) key competences

Schlüsselfrage (f) key question

Schlüsselqualifikation (f) core skill

Schlüsselkind (n) latch-key child

Schmerz (m) pain, ache; *(Kummer)* grief

schmerzen (v) to hurt, to ache
schmerzstillendes Mittel (n) pain-killer
schmollen (v) to pout
schmusen (v) to cuddle
Schmusetier (n) cuddly toy
Schmutz erzeugende Aktivitäten (manschen, planschen, kleistern) messy activities
Schnitzeljagd (f) paper-chase
Schnüffeln (n) *(bei Drogen)* abuse of solvents
schnüffeln (v) *(Lösemittelmissbrauch)* to abuse solvents, sniffing
Schnuller (m) pacifier, baby's dummy
Schnupperkurs (m) (one-off) bite size course, taster course
Schnürsenkel (m) shoe-lace; **die ~ zubinden** to lace up one's shoes
Schranke (f) barrier
Schreibkompetenz (f) literacy skills
schriftliche Prüfung (f) written paper
Schriftsprachenkompetenz (f) literacy
Schulabbrecher(in) (m,f) school dropout
Schulabgänger(in) (m,f) school leaver

Schulabschlusszeugnis (n) school-leaving ceritificate
Schulamt (n) (local) education authority
Schulanfang (m) beginning of term
Schulangst (f) school phobia
Schulbesuch (m) school attendance; **regelmäßiger ~** regular attendance at school
Schuldfähigkeit (f) legal responsibility
Schule (f) school; **Grundschule** primary school (Brit); elementary school (US); **Oberschule** secondary school (Brit); high school (US), **7.–9. Klasse** junior high school (US); **10.–12. Klasse** (senior) high school (US)
Schule in freier Trägerschaft private school; independent school (Brit)
Schuleintrittsalter (n) school entrance age
Schüler(in) (m,f) student; *(im Grundschulalter)* pupil *(veraltet)*
Schülerausweis (m) school identity card
Schülerladen (m) parent-run / private after-school provision
Schülerlotse (m), **Schüler-**

lotsin (f) lollipop man / lady / woman (Brit); crossing guard (US)

Schülervertretung (f) (SV) (D) pupils' council, students' council

Schülerzeitung (f) school magazine

Schulfach (n) (school) subject

Schulferien (pl) school holidays (Brit); summer vacation (US)

Schulgebühren (f,pl), **Schulgeld** (n) school fee

Schulgelände (n) premises

Schulgeld (n) school fee

Schulgesetz (n) education act

Schulheft (n) exercise book

schulische Integration (f) inclusion at school

Schulkindergarten (m) pre-primary class

Schulklasse (f) form, (school) class

Schulklasse mit Förderunterricht remedial class

Schulleiter(in) (m,f) head of school, principal, headmaster, headmistress

Schulpflicht (f) compulsory school attendance

schulpflichtig (adj) of school-age; **schulpflichtige Kinder** school-age children

Schulpraktikum (n) teaching practice, work experience; **ein ~ machen** to do work experience

Schulpsychologe (m), **Schulpsychologin** (f) educational psychologist

Schulpsychologie (f) educational psychology

Schulrat (m), **Schulrätin** (f) inspector of schools, school inspector

Schulreife (f) readiness for school

Schulschwänzer(in) (m,f) truant

Schulsekretariat (n) school secretary's office

Schulstunde (f) lesson, period

Schultafel (f) blackboard

Schulträger (m) body responsible for schools

Schulverweigerung (f) school refusal

Schulzeugnis (n) school report

schummeln (v) to cheat

Schutz des ungeborenen Lebens protection of the unborn child

Schutzimpfung (f) inoculation, vaccination

schwanger (adj) pregnant; **sie ist im siebenten Mo-**

nat ~ she's seven months pregnant; **sie ist mit Zwillingen** ~ she's pregnant with twins

Schwangerschaft (f) pregnancy; ~ **von Minderjährigen** teenage pregnancy

Schwangerschaft abbrechen to terminate a pregnancy

Schwangerschaftsabbruch (m) legal abortion, termination of a pregnancy

Schwangerschaftsabbruch aus med. Indikation therapeutic abortion

schwänzen (v) *(unentschuldigtes Fehlen)* to play truant

schwatzen (v) to chatter

Schweigepflicht (f) duty to maintain confidentiality, professional confidentiality, secrecy

schwer erziehbares Kind (n) disruptive child

schwerbehindert (adj) severely disabled, severely handicapped *(wird häufig als abwertend empfunden)*

Schwerbehinderte(r) (f,m) severely disabled person

Schwererziehbarkeit (f) disruptive behaviour

schwerhörig sein (adj) to be hard of hearing

Schwerpunkt (m) centre of gravity

Schwiegerkinder, ~ eltern, Schwager *etc.* in-laws

Schwimmflügel (m,pl) water-wings

seelische Grausamkeit (f) mental cruelty

Seelsorge (f) pastoral care

Segregation (f) segregation

Sehbehinderung (f) impaired vision

Sehschwäche (f) visual impairment

Sehstörung (f) visual disorder

Sehvermögen (n) vision

Seilspringen (n) skipping

seilspringen (v) to skip (rope)

Sekundärbeziehung (f) secondary bonding

Sekundärliteratur (f) secondary literature

Sekundarstufe (f) secondary school level

Sekundarstufe I (f) (D) junior high school *(7. – 9. Schuljahr)* (US); classes with students aged 10 to 15

Sekundarstufe II (f) (D) senior high school (US); fifth and sixth form classes

Sekundärtugend (f) secondary virtue

Selbstachtung (f) self-esteem, self-respect
selbstbeherrscht (adj) self-possessed
Selbstbeherrschung (f) self-command, self-control, self-mastery
Selbstbeobachtung (f) introspection
Selbstbestimmung (f) self-determination
Selbstbewertung (f) self-evaluation, self-assessment
Selbstbewusstsein (n) self-assurance, self-confidence, self-assertion, ego
Selbstbild (n) self-concept
Selbsteinschätzung (f) self-assessment
Selbstentfaltung (f) self-development
Selbsterkenntnis (f) self-awareness, self-knowledge
Selbsterniedrigung (f) self-abasement
selbstgesteuertes Lernen self-guided / self-directed learning
Selbsthilfegruppe (f) non-professional helping group
Selbsthilfegruppe (f) self-help-group
selbstkritisch (adj) self-aware
selbstlos (adj) unselfish
Selbstsicherheit (f) self-assurance
selbstständig (adj) self-contained, independent
Selbstständigkeit (f) autonomy, independence
selbstsüchtig (adj) selfish
selbsttätige Entfaltung (f) spontaneous unfolding
Selbsttätigkeit (f) *(des Kindes)* self-directed activity
Selbstverstümmelung (f) self-inflicted wounds
Selbstvertrauen (n) self-confidence
selbstverwaltet (adj) self-governing
Selbstverwirklichung (f) self-actualization
Selbstwahrnehmung (f) self-perception
Selbstwert (m) self-worth
Selbstwertgefühl (n) (sense of) self-esteem, feeling of self-worth
Selbstwirksamkeit (f) self-efficacy
selbstzufrieden (adj) self-complacent
selbstzugefügt (adj) self-indulged
Semester (n) term, semester
Seminar (n) workshop
Seminararbeit (f) seminar paper

Seminartage (m,pl) *(Schultage während eines Praktikums)* theory days
Senioren (pl) elderly people, senior citizens
sensibel (adj) sensitive
sensibilisieren (v), **jemanden für etwas ~** to sensitize
Sensibilität (f) sensitivity
sensible Phase (f) sensitive period / phase
sensomotorisch (adj) sensory-motor
Servierwagen (m) trolley
Sexualerziehung (f) sex education
sexuell missbrauchen (v) to abuse sexually
sexueller Missbrauch (m) sexual abuse
sexueller Übergriff (m) indecent assault
Sich-Ausdrücken (n) (päd) expressing
Sich-Entwickeln (n) (päd) becoming
Sicherheitsgurt (m) *(für Kinder)* safety harness
Simultanübersetzung (f) running translation, simultaneous interpretation
Sinn (m) sense; **Geschmackssinn** sense of taste; **Tastsinn** tactile sense, sense of touch
sinnes-, die Sinne betreffend sensorial, sensory
Sinnesentwicklung (f) sensory development
Sinnesmaterialien (n,pl) sensory materials
Sinnesorgan (n) sense organ, sensory organ
Sinnesübung (f) sensory exercise
Sinneswahrnehmung (f) sensory perception
sinnlich (adj) sensual; **sinnliche Erfahrung** sensual experience
Situationsanalyse (f) situation analysis
Situationsansatz (m) contextual (child development) approach, situational approach, situation-oriented approach
sitzen bleiben (v) *(Schule)* to repeat a year, to stay down a year
Sitzung (f) session
Sondererziehung (f) special education
Sondererziehungsanforderungen (f,pl) special (educational) needs (SEN)
Sonderkindergarten (m) special kindergarten; **Erzieher(in) in einem ~** special needs kindergarten

educator; **Kind mit besonderen Bedürfnissen in einem** ~ special needs child

Sonderpädagoge (m), **Sonderpädagogin** (f) special educational needs (SEN) teacher

Sonderpädagogik (f) special needs education (SEN), remedial education

Sonderschule (f) special (needs) school

Sonderschullehrer(in) (m,f) special education teacher, special school teacher

Sonderschulwesen (n) special needs teaching

Sorge (f) worry, trouble, anxiety

Sorgeberechtigter (m) person having custodial rights

sorgeberechtigter Elternteil (m) custodial parent

Sorgerecht (n) (legal) custody, custodial rights, right of custody; **die Mutter erhielt das** ~ the mother was given (the) custody of the children; **gemeinsames** ~ joint custody

Sorgerechtsanordnung (f) care-order

Sorgerechtsentzug (m) withdrawal of (the right of) custody

Sorgfalt (f) care

So-Sein (n) (päd) being

Sozialabbau (m) cutback in the social welfare system

Sozialamt (n) social office, social department, local welfare authority (Brit)

Sozialarbeit (f) social work

Sozialarbeit, feldbezogene patch social work

Sozialarbeiter für Einzelfälle (m) case worker

Sozialarbeiter(in) (m,f) social worker, welfare officer, welfare worker

soziale Anpassungsfähigkeit (f) social adaptability

soziale Benachteiligung (f) social discrimination

soziale Einrichtung (f) social institution

soziale Fähigkeiten (f,pl) social skills

soziale Integration (f) social inclusion

soziales Verhalten (n) social behaviour

sozialer Wohnungsbau (m) council housing

Sozialhilfe (f) social security (benefit), welfare, *(Hilfe zum Lebensunterhalt)* income support; **von** ~ **leben** to be on social security

Sozialisation(sprozess) (m) socialization

Sozialisierung (f) socialisation

Sozialkunde (f) social studies

Sozialleistungen (f,pl) welfare benefits, welfare services

Sozialpädagoge, Sozialpädagogin (m,f) social pedagogue, youth and community worker, social education worker

Sozialpädagogik (f) social pedagogy, ~ pedagogics, social education

Sozialpflege (f) social care

sozialpflegerische Orientierung (f) social care orientation

Sozialraum (m) community, neighbourhood; ~**orientierung** community orientation

Sozialstation (f) community care centre

Sozialversicherung (f) social insurance

Sozialwissenschaften (f,pl) social sciences

Sozialwohnung (f) council flat

soziokulturell (adj) socio-cultural

soziokulturell|benachteiligt, ~ **randständig** culturally alienated

Spannung (f) tension; **Spannungsreduktion** tension reduction

Spätdienst (m) **Spätschicht** (f) late shift, back shift

Speiseraum (m) *(Schule)* refectory, canteen

Spende (f) donation

Spenden sammeln fund-raising

Sperrholz (n) plywood

Spiel (n) game; *(Sport)* match

Spiel mit Matsch und Pampe messy play

Spiel- und Beschäftigungsgaben *(pl) (Fröbel)* Gifts and Occupations

Spielalter (n) play age

Spielecke (f) *(für künstlerische Aktivitäten)* creative corner

Spielecke (f) *(im Gruppenraum)* play area, interest area

spielen (v) to play

spielerisch (adj) playful

Spielfeld (n) playing field

Spielgebiet für Rollenspiele innerhalb eines Gruppenraums imaginative play area

Spielgelände (n) play space; **eingezäuntes ~** enclosed

play space
Spielgruppe (f) playgroup
Spielkamerad(in) (m,f) playmate
Spielkarte (f) playing card
Spielplatz (m) playground
Spieltherapie (f) play therapy
Spieltrieb (m) play drive
Spielwarengeschäft (n) toy shop
Spielzeug (n) toy, plaything, play materials; ~ **Auto**, ~ **Tiere** *usw.* toy car, -animals *etc.*
Spielzeugtag (m) show and tell day
Sport (m) *(Schulsport)* games; P.E. (physical education)
Sportplatz (m) playing field
Sportunterricht (m) physical education (PE)
Sportwagen (m) *(für Kinder)* pushchair, baby buggy *(Brit)*
Sprachbegabung (f) linguistic aptitude
Sprachenmischung (f) mixture of languages
Spracherwerb (m) language development, acquisition of language; language acquisition
Sprachfehler (m) speech defect, speech impediment
Sprachfertigkeit (f) language proficiency
Sprachgebrauch (m) use of language
Sprachkompetenz (f) language skills
sprachliche Entwicklung (f) linguistic development
Sprachschädigung (f) speech defect
Sprachstörung (f) speech disorder
Sprachtherapie (f) speech therapy
Sprachverlust (m) aphasia, loss of speech
Sprachvermögen (n) faculty of speech, speech faculty
sprechen (v) to speak, to talk; **kann das Kind schon ~?** can the baby talk yet?
Sprechstörung (f) vocal disorder
Springseil (n) skipping rope
Sprossenwand (f) wall bars
staatlich anerkannte(r) Erzieher(in) (m,f) (D) state-registered educator
staatlich anerkannte(r) Kinderpfleger(in) (m,f) (D) state-registered nursery worker
staatlich finanziert state-funded

staatlich finanzierte Einrichtung (f) state subsidized facility

staatliche Subvention (f) state subsidy

staatliche Unterstützung (f) state support

staatlicher Träger (m) statutory agency / body

staatliches Bildungswesen (n) state education

Staatsbesitz (m) public ownership

städtisch (adj) urban

Stadtrat (m) *(Behörde)* city / town council; *(Person)* city / town councillor

Stadtsanierung (f) urban renewal

Stadtverwaltung (f) municipal authority

Standesamt (n) registry office, registry

stationäre Erziehungshilfen (f,pl) residential provision for children with problems

statistische Erhebung (f) polling study

stattfinden (v) to take place

Steißgeburt (f) breech birth, breech delivery

Steißlage (f) breech presentation

Stelle (f) *(Arbeits-)* job; **volle / halbe ~** full-time / part-time job; **sich um eine ~ bewerben** to apply for a job; **eine ~ bekommen** to get a job; **eine ~ kündigen** to give up a job

Stellenbeschreibung (f) job description

Stellenbesetzung (f) staffing

Stellenvermittlung (f) employment agency, employment bureau

Steuerbefreiung (f) tax exemption

Steuerfreibetrag für Kinder children exemption (US)

Steuervergünstigung (f) tax benefit

Stieffamilie (f) blended family

Stiefkind (n) stepchild; **Stiefmutter** stepmother

Stift (m) pencil, pen

Stiftung (f) foundation; **gemeinnützige ~** charitable foundation, charity; **~ des öffentlichen Rechts** public foundation, foundation under public law

stillen (v) *(ein Baby)* to breast-feed, to nurse

stillende Mutter (f) nursing mother

Stillkind (n) breast-fed child

Stimmbruch (m) breaking of the voice

Stipendium (n) grant, fellowship, scholarship
Stoff (m) *(Textilien)* cloth, material; *(allgemein)* material; *(Chemie)* substance
Stoffpuppe (f) rag doll
Stoffwechselerkrankung (f) metabolic disease, ~ disorder
Störenfried (m) troublemaker
Störung (f) disturbance, *(psych)* disorder, *(techn)* fault, interruption
stottern (v) to stutter
Strafarbeit (f) written punishment, extra work
Strafe (f) punishment
Straffälligkeit (f) delinquency
Straftäter(in) (m,f) delinquent, criminal, offender; **jugendliche(r)** ~ young offender, juvenile delinquent
Strampler (m) Babygro ®
Straßensozialarbeit (f) street work
Streichelzoo (m) petting zoo, petting farm
Streit (m) quarrel
streiten (v) to argue, to quarrel, to fight
Strichmännchen (n) stick figure
Struktur (f) pattern
Stubenarrest haben be confined to one's room, to be grounded
Student(in) (m,f) *(Universität)* undergraduate, university student
Studentenheim (n) hall of residence
Studien zur Gleichstellung von Frauen und Männern gender studies
Studiengebühr (f) tuition fee
Studienreise (f) study visit
Studierende(r) (f,m) student
Stuhlkreis (m) circle time
stumm (adj) mute
Stunde (f) *(Unterrichts-)* session
Stundenplan (m) timetable, schedule
Stützräder (n,pl) *(Fahrrad)* stabilizers, stabilizing wheels; training wheels (US)
Subventionen (f,pl) subsidies
suchen (v) to look for somebody / something, to search
Sucht (f) addiction, *(fig)* obsession
süchtig sein (adj) be addicted
Süchtige(r) (f,m) addict
Supervision (f) **tutorial supervision**
süß (adj) *(fig)* cute
symbolische Darstellung (f) symbolic representation

T

Tabelle (f) table, chart
Tadel (m) reprimand
tadeln (v) to rebuke, to criticize, to disapprove
Tagebuch (n) diary
Tagegeld (m) daily allowance
Tagesablauf (m) daily routine, daily schedule
Tagesausflug (m) day trip, excursion
Tageseinrichtung (f) day unit
Tageseinrichtung für Kinder day care centre; day care establishment for children; day care institution
Tageseltern, selbstständige (pl) self-employed childminders
Tagesmutter (f) childminder, day care mother, family daycarer, babyminder
Tagesmutter, hauptberufliche, eingetragene (f) registered childminder
Tagesordnung (f) agenda
Tagesordnungspunkt (m) item
Tagespflege (f) child minding, day care
Tagespflegestelle (f) family daycare
Tagesplan (m) daily rota (Brit); daily roster (US)
Taschengeld (n) pocket money, allowance, spending money
Taschenlampe (f) penlight, torch
Taschenmesser (n) jackknife, penknife
Tastmaterialien (n,pl) heuristic play materials, tactile play materials
Tastsinn (m) sense of touch, tactile sense
taub (adj) deaf
tauber Mensch (m) person with a hearing impairment
taubstumm (adj) deaf-mute
Taufe (f) baptism, christening
taufen (v) to baptize, to christen
Taufname (m) Christian name
Teamarbeit (f) team effort
Teamfortbildung (f) team building
Teenager-Schwangerschaft (f) teenager pregnancy, teen pregnancy
teilen, sich etwas ~ (v) to share
Teilnahme (f) participation, *(Anteilnahme)* sympathy

Teilnahmebescheinigung (f) certificate of attendance

teilnahmslos (adj) listless, apathetic, uninterested

teilnehmen (v) to attend, to take part, to participate

teilnehmende Beobachtung (f) participant observation

Teilnehmer(in) (m,f) participant

teilstationäre Erziehungshilfen (f,pl) partly residential provision for children with problems

teilweise behindert partially disabled

teilzeit (adj) part-time

Teilzeitarbeit (f) part-time work, part-time job

Teilziele (n,pl) stepping stones

Teilzeitbetreuung (f) part-time care

Tempo-Taschentuch ® (n) paper tissue, kleenex®

Terminkalender (m) diary

tertiäres Bildungssystem (n) further education

Tesafilm ® (m) Sellotape ® (Brit); Scotch tape ® (US)

Teufelskreis (m) vicious circle

Theater|spiel (n) drama; **~gruppe** drama group

Themenfeld *(päd)* subject area

Therapeut(in) (m,f) therapist

therapeutisch (adj) therapeutic

therapeutische Unterstützung (f) therapeutic support

therapeutische Wohngemeinschaft (f) therapeutic community

Therapie (f) therapy

Toleranz (f) tolerance

Töpfchen (n) potty

tot geboren (adj) still born

Totgeburt (f) stillbirth

Träger (m) *(einer Einrichtung)* provider, agency, agency responsible for a sector of work; > freier ~; > öffentlicher ~; > staatlicher ~

Träger der öffentlichen Jugendhilfe bodies responsible for the statutory youth services

Tragetuch (n) *(für Babys)* sling

Trainingsanzug (m) track suit

Trauschein (m) marriage certificate

Trauung (f), **standesamtliche** civil marriage

Trennung (f) *(auch ehelich)* separation, splitting-up; *(soz)* segregation; **Rassen-**

trennung racial segregation; **Schule mit Rassentrennung** segregated school

Trennungsangst (f) separation anxiety

Trieb (m) *(psych)* drive, impulse

Trinkflasche (f) baby bottle

trösten (v) to comfort

Trotz (m) defiance

Trotzalter (n) difficult age

Trotzreaktion (f) act of defiance

Tugend (f) virtue

Tumult (m) uproar

Turnanzug (m) leotard

Turnhalle (f) gym, gymnasium

Turnschuh (m) trainer, plimsoll, gym-shoe

U

überängstlich (adj) overanxious

überbehütend (adj) overprotective

überbehütet (adj) overwatched

überbetriebliche Ausbildung (f) joint vocational training

Übereinkommen über die Rechte des Kindes Convention on the Rights of the Child (United Nations, 1989)

Übereinkunft (f) agreement, arrangement, understanding; ~ **erzielen** to reach an agreement

überempfindlich (adj) hypersensitive

Überempfindlichkeit (f) *(gegenüber Kritik)* defensiveness

Überfluss (m) abundance, affluence

überfordern (v) to expect too much of sb.

überfordert sein it's expecting too much of sb., it's too much for sb.

Übergabe (f) *(Schichtwechsel)* shift handover

Übergang (m) transition; **weicher, konfliktfreier ~** smooth transition

Übergangsregelung (f) temporary arrangement

übergewichtig (adj) obese, overweight

Überlegenheitsgefühl (n) feeling of superiority

Übersetzer(in) (m,f) translator > Dolmetscher(in)

Übersetzung (f) translation

Übersicht (f) survey

Überstunden (f,pl) overtime; **~ machen** to work overtime

Übung (f) *(Praxis)* practice, *(Aufgabe)* exercise

umarmen (v) to hug somebody, to embrace

umerziehen (v) re-educate

umfassend (adj) comprehensive

umfassende Angebote (n,pl) wrap-around provision

Umfeld (n) setting, environment

Umformung (f) transformation

Umgebung (f) environment; **anregende, unterstützende ~** warm, supportive environment

Umhüllung (f) *(päd)* envelopment

Umschulung (f) retraining

Umstandskleid (n) maternity clothes, maternity dress

Umwelt (f) *(natürliche)* environment; *(Umfeld)* setting

umweltbewusst (adj) ecology-minded

Umweltbewusstsein (n) environmental awareness

Umwelteinflüsse (m,pl) environmental influences

Umwelterziehung (f) environmental education

umweltfeindlich (adj) ecologically harmful

umweltfreundlich (adj) ecologically beneficial, beneficial to the environment

Umweltlabor (n) environment laboratory

Umweltschutz (m) environmental protection

Umweltschützer(in) (m,f) environmentalist

Umweltverschmutzung (f) environmental pollution

umziehen (v) *(Wohnungswechsel)* to move house, to move home

unabsichtlich (adj) involuntary; **unabsichtliche Bewegung** involuntary movement

unangenehmer Reiz (m) aversive stimulus

unangepasst (adj) non-conformist; *(gesellschaftlich)* alienated

unangepasstes Verhalten (n) maladjusted behaviour

unaufdringlich (adj) unobtrusively

unbeaufsichtigt (adj) unattended

unbeeinträchtigt (adj) unimpaired

unbeholfen (adj) awkward, clumsy

unbewusst (adj) unconscious

Unbewusste(s) (n) the unconscious

unbezahltes Volontariat (n) unpaid traineeship

unerlaubt (adj) unauthorized

unerreichbar (adj) unavailable

unerträglich (adj) unbearable

unerwünscht (adj) unwanted

unfähig (adj) unable, incompetent

Unfähigkeit (f) inability

unfreiwillig (adj) involuntary

Unfruchtbarkeit (f) infertility

Unfug (m) mischief; ~ **anstellen** to horseplay, to fool around

ungebildet (adj) uneducated

ungeboren (adj) unborn

ungebunden (adj) unattached

ungeschickt (adj) awkward, clumsy, careless

ungeteilte Aufmerksamkeit (f) undivided attention

ungeübt (adj) untrained, inexperienced

Ungewissheit (f) uncertainty

ungewöhnlich (adj) unusual, uncharacteristic

ungewohnt (adj) unaccustomed

ungezogen (adj) misbehaved, naughty, ill-mannered

Ungleichheit (f) inequality; **soziale** ~ social inequality

Ungültigkeit (f) *(soz)* invalidity

unheilbar (adj) incurable

unheilbare, tödlich verlaufende Krankheit terminal disease

unhöflich (adj) rude, impolite

Unklarheit (f) ambiguity, uncertainty

unkontrollierbar (adj) unmanageable

UN-Organisation für Erziehung, Wissenschaft und Kultur United Nations Educational, Scientific and Cultural Organization (UNESCO)

unqualifiziert (adj) unskilled, unqualified
unreif (adj) immature
Unstimmigkeit (f) inconsistency
unter vier Augen on a one-to-one basis
unterbezahlt (adj) underpaid
unterdrücken (v) to keep down, to suppress, to oppress
Unterdrückung (f) repression
unterernährt (adj) malnourished, underfed
Unterernährung (f) malnutrition
unterfordern (v) make too few demands on sb.; to not challenge somebody enough
Unterhalt (m) maintenance (payment)
Unterhalt leisten to maintain, to pay maintenance
Unterhaltshilfe (f) maintenance assistance
Unterhaltspflicht (f) maintenance responsibility
Unterhaltszahlung (f) alimony
Unterhaltszahlung für Kinder child maintenance, child support
Unterlagen (f,pl) records

untermauern (v) *(fig)* to underpin
Untermieter(in) (m,f) subtenant
unterprivilegiert (adj) deprived
Unterricht (m) lesson; **theoretischer ~** theoretical classes, **praktischer ~** practical classes; **~ nehmen** to take lessons
unterrichten (v) to instruct, to teach
Unterrichtseinheit (f) teaching module, teaching unit
Unterrichtserfahrung (f) teaching experience, teaching practice
Unterrichtsfach (n) subject
Unterrichtshilfe (pädagogische ~) teacher's aide
Unterrichtsstoff (m) subject matter
Unterrichtsstunde (f) lesson, period, session
unterscheiden (v) to discriminate, to distinguish, to tell the difference between things
Unterschicht (f) lower class
unterschiedlich behandeln to discriminate between
unterstellen (v) *(annehmen)* to assume
unterstützen (v) to encour-

age, to support, to back something

Unterstützung (f) *(Hilfe, auch finanziell)* support; *(Entlastung)* relief

untersuchen (v) to investigate

unverändert (adj) unaltered, unchanged

unveräußerliche Rechte inalienable rights

unvereinbar (adj) incompatible

unverheiratet zusammenlebendes Paar (n) cohabiting couple

unvertraut (adj) unfamiliar

unvollständige Familie (f) incomplete family

unvorbereitet (adj) unprepared

unvoreingenommen (adj) unbiased

unvorhersehbar (adj) unpredictable

unzählbar (adj) uncountable

unzuverlässig (adj) unreliable

Urenkel(in) (m,f) great-grandchild

Urgroßvater (m) great-grandfather

Urlaub (m) leave, holiday, vacation; **Jahresurlaub** annual leave; **Genesungsurlaub** sick leave; **Mutterschaftsurlaub** maternity leave; **auf ~ sein** to be on leave

Ururgroßvater (m) great-great-grandfather

Urvertrauen (n) basic trust

V

Vaterschaft (f) fatherhood, paternity

Vaterschaftsprozess (m) paternity suit

Vaterschaftstest (m) paternity test

Vaterschaftsurlaub (m) paternity leave

Vegetarier(in) (m,f) vegetarian

vegetarische Kost (f) vegetarian diet

verantwortlich (adj) responsible; **wer ist hier ~ ?** who's in charge here?

verantwortlich machen (v) blame somebody, hold somebody responsible

Verantwortliche(r) (f,m) person responsible; person in charge
Verantwortlichkeit (f) responsibility
Verantwortung (f) responsibility
Verarmung (f) impoverishment
verbaler Ausdruck (m) verbal expression
verbessern (v) to improve
verbieten (v) to ban, to forbid
Verbitterung (f) bitterness; *(Groll)* resentment
verbundene Augen blindfolded
verbundenes Verhalten (n) *(psych)* linked behaviour
Verbundenheit (f) (päd) connection
Verdrängung (f)(psych) repression
Vereinzelung (f) individuation
Verfügungszeit (f) non-contact time
Vergewaltigung (f) rape
vergleichend (adj) comparative
Verhalten (n) behaviour; **abweichendes** ~ deviant behaviour; **angeborenes** ~ innate behaviour; **unangepasstes** ~ maladjusted behaviour; **provozierendes / herausforderndes** ~ challenging behaviour
Verhaltensänderung aufgrund von Erfahrung operational learning
verhaltensauffällig (adj) maladjusted, disturbed, displaying behavioural problems
Verhaltensauffälligkeit (f) deviant behaviour, behavioural disorder, behavioural problems
Verhaltensbeobachtung (f) behaviour observation
Verhaltensbeobachtung bei Kindern child study
Verhaltenserwartung, die das erwartete Verhalten auslöst self-fulfilling prophecy
Verhaltensmuster (n) behavioural pattern, pattern of behaviour, schema [ski:ma]
Verhaltensschema (m) schema [ski:ma]
Verhaltensstörung (f) behavioural disorder, behavioural disturbance
Verhaltenstherapie (f) *(psych)* conditioning therapy, behavioural therapy
Verhältnis (n) relationship

Verinselung (f) *(soz)* islandization

Verkehrserziehung (f) road safety training

Verkleidungen (f,pl) *(Kleidung)* disguise, *(weitere Requisiten)* props, fancy dress

Verkleidungsecke (f) *(im Gruppenraum)* fancy dress corner

Verlangen (n) urge, desire, craving

verlassen (v) to leave, to desert, to abandon

Vermeidung (f) *(psych)* aversion; avoidance

Vermeidungsverhalten (n) *(psych)* avoidance behaviour

vermitteln (v) *(im Konflikt)* to mediate, to negotiate, to abitrate

Vermittler(in) (m,f) *(Konflikte)* moderator, mediator, facilitator

Vermittlung (f) *(Konflikte)* mediation

Vermittlungsausschuss (m) mediation committee

vernachlässigen (v) to neglect; **vernachlässigtes Kind** neglected child

vernachlässigt (adj) uncared for, neglected

Vernachlässigung (f) negligence

Vernachlässigung durch die Eltern parental neglect

Vernunft (f) reason, common sense

Vernunftehe (f) marriage of convenience

vernünftig (adj) reasonable, sensible

Verpflichtung (f) committment

verpfuschen (v) to mess up

Verrückte(r) (f,m) maniac, lunatic, madman (madwoman)

Versammlung (f) assembly, meeting

Verschiedenheit (f) diversity

verschlechtern (v) to make something worse, to get worse, to worsen, to aggravate

Verschlechterung (f) *(psych)* regression; deterioration

verschleiert (adj) *(Frau)* veiled

Verschluss (m) *(bei Kleidungsstücken)* fastening

verschmutzen (v) *(Umwelt)* to pollute

Verschwendung (f) waste
Versetzung (f) (päd) moving up
versöhnen (v) to reconcile
Verstand (m) (common) sense
Verständnis (n) *(Einfühlungsvermögen)* understanding, appreciation
verständnisvoll (adj) understanding, sympathetic
verstärken (v) *(psych)* to reinforce
Verstärkung (f) reinforcement; **negative ~** negative reinforcement
Versteck (n) hideaway, hiding place
Verstecken spielen to play hide-and-seek
Versuch und Irrtum trial and error
Vertrag (m) agreement, contract
Vertrauen (n) confidence, trust
vertraulich (adj) confidential
vertraut (adj) familiar; **~ sein mit** to be familiar with; **sich vertraut machen mit** to familiarize oneself with
Vertretung (f) *(päd) (fig)* advocacy
Vertretungslehrer(in) (m,f) supply teacher, substitute teacher
Verursacherprinzip (n) *(Umweltschutz)* polluter pays principle
verwahrlost (adj) destitute, neglected
Verwahrlosung (f) destitution, neglect
verwalten (v) to administer, to manage
Verwaltung (f) administration; **örtliche ~** local administration, **Gemeindeverwaltung** local authority
Verwaltungsrat (m) board of managers
Verwandte(r) (m,f) relation, relative
Verwandtschaftsverhältnis (n) relationship
verwöhnen (v) to pamper, to spoil
verwöhnt (adj) pampered, spoilt
Verzögerung (f) *(psych)* retardation
Vesper (f) *(Zwischenmahlzeit am Nachmittag)* (D) tea (Brit)
Vielfalt (f) diversity, variety
Vielvölkergesellschaft (f) multi-ethnic society
Vierfüßer-Gang (m) creeping on hands and feet
Vierling (m) quadruplet

visuelles Wahrnehmungsvermögen (n) visual perception

Volkshochschule (f) adult education centre

Volkskindergarten (m) people's day nursery

Volksmärchen (n) folktale

vollbringen (v) to achieve, to accomplish, to perform

volljährig (adj) of age; ~ **sein / werden** to be / to come of age; **volljährig werden** (v) to reach one's majority

Volljährigkeit (f) majority; **Volljährigkeitsalter** (n) age of majority

Vollwertkost (f) wholefood

Vor- und Nachbereitungszeit für Erzieher(innen) non-contact time

vorangegangene Erfahrungen (f,pl) previous experience

vorbereiten (v) to prepare

vorbereitete Umgebung (f) prepared environment

Vorbeugung (f) prevention

Vorbild (n) model

voreingenommen (adj) biased, prejudiced

Voreingenommenheit (f) bias, prejudice

vorgeburtlich (adj) antenatal, prenatal; **vorgeburtliche Betreuung** prenatal care

vorgefasste Meinung (f) preconceived idea

Vorkenntnisse (f,pl) previous experience

Vorklasse (f) reception class

Vorklassenleiter(in) (m,f) reception teacher

Vormittagsbetreuung (f) morning session (in childcare)

Vormund (m) guardian

Vormundschaft (f) guardianship

Vormundschaftsgericht (n) guardianship court

Vorname (m) first name, Christian name

Vorschrift (f) regulation

Vorschul-, vorschulisch (adj) preschool

Vorschulalter (n) preschool age

Vorschulerziehung (f) preschool education

vorschulische Einrichtungen (f,pl) pre-school facilities

vorschulische Erziehung (f) preschool education

Vorschulklasse (f) reception class, preparatory class, pre-school class

Vorsichtsmaßnahme (f) safeguard, precaution

vorstellen (v) **sich ~** to introduce oneself; *(sich etwas einbilden)* to think of, to imagine

Vorstellung (f) *(geistige)* idea, concept

Vorstellung, gegenseitige *(sich bekannt machen)* (reciprocal) introduction

Vorstellungskraft (f) powers of imagination

Vorstudie (f) pilot study

Vortrag (m) talk; **einen ~ halten** to give a talk

vorübergehend (adj) temporary

Vorurteil (n) prejudice, bias; **Erziehung gegen ~e und Rassismus** anti-bias education

vorurteilsbewusste Erziehung (f) bias awareness education

vorurteilsfrei (adj) unbiased, unprejudiced

W

wachsen (v) to grow; **bist du aber gewachsen!** haven't you grown!

Wachsmalstift (m) wax crayon

Wachspapier (n) wax paper

Wachstum (n) *(Zunahme)* growth, increase; *(Geschäft)* expansion

Wachstumsschmerzen (m,pl) growing pains

Wachstumsschub (m) growth spurt

Wachstumsstörung (f) disturbance of growth

Waghalsigkeit (f) audacity

Wahlfach (n) facultative subject

wahlfrei (adj) optional

Wahrnehmung (f) *(psych)* cognition; *(Sinneswahrnehmung)* perception; **Entwicklung der ~** development of perception

Wahrnehmungsfähigkeit (f) perceptual ability, perceptive faculty

Waise (m,f) orphan, parentless child

Waisenhaus (n) orphanage

Wasserspielfläche (f) water play area
Wechselseitigkeit (f) reciprocity
Wechselspiel (n) interplay
Wechselwirkung (f) interaction, interdependence
Wehen (f,pl) labour, contractions, pains (US); ~ **einleiten** induce labour; **in den ~ liegen** to be in labour
Wehrdienst (m) (national) military service
Wehrdienstverweigerer (m) *(aus Gewissensgründen)* (D) conscientious objector
weiblich (adj) female
Weihnachten (n) Christmas, Xmas; **erster Weihnachtstag** Christmas Day; **zweiter Weihnachtstag** Boxing Day
Weiterbildung (f) further education, further training, in-service further training
werdende Mutter (f) mother-to-be
Werkraum (m) craft shop
Werkstatt (f) *(Raum, Veranstaltung)* workshop
Werkunterricht (m) craft classes
Werte (m,pl) *(soz)* values; **Grundwerte** basic values
Wertschätzung (f) esteem
Wertorientierung (f) orientation in values
Wertung (f) valuation
wertvoll (adj) valuable
wesentlich (adj) essential, substantial
wesentlicher Bestandteil (m) intrinsic part
wickeln (v) *(ein Baby)* to swaddle a baby, to change a baby, to put on a baby's nappy (Brit) / diaper (US); > Windel
Wickelraum (m) baby's changing room, nursing room
Wickeltisch (m) baby's changing table
widersprechen (v) to answer back; **widersprich mir nicht!** don't answer back!
widersprüchlich (adj) inconsistent, contradictory
Widersprüchlichkeit (f) inconsistency
Wiedereingliederung (f) re-integration
wiederholen (v) *(ein Schuljahr)* repeat a year
Wiege (f) cradle
Windel (f) *(aus Stoff)* nappy (Brit); diaper (US); > wickeln, > Papierwindel
Windelausschlag (m) nappy rash; diaper rash (US)

Windeldermatitis (f) nappy rash

Windeleinlage (f) nappy liner

Windpocken (pl) chicken pox

Wippe (f) see-saw; *(für Babys)* baby rocker; cozy (US)

wippen (v) to see-saw

Wirbelsäule (f) spinal column, spine

wissenschaftliche Arbeit (f) academic work

Wochenbett (n) child-bed

Wohlbefinden (n) well-being

Wohlfahrt (f) welfare; **von der ~ leben** to live on welfare

Wohlfahrtsorganisation (f) welfare organization

Wohlfahrtsstaat (m) welfare state

Wohlfahrtsverband (m) charity, charitable institution

wohlhabend (adj) to be better off, affluent, well-to-do, prosperous

Wohlstandsgesellschaft (f) affluent society

Wohlstandsverwahrlosung (f) demoralization by affluence

wohltätig (adj) charitable

wohltätige Organisation (f) charity, charitable society

Wohnbereich (m) > Wohnecke

Wohnblock (m) block of flats, tenement block

Wohnecke (f) *(im Gruppenraum)* home play area, domestic play area

Wohngebiet (n) residential area, residential district

Wohngeld (n) housing benefit

Wohngemeinschaft (f) communal living, flat-sharing; **betreute ~** communal living with social worker support; assisted-living community

Wohnheim (n) residential centre

Wohnheim in einem Internat residential unit

Wohnheim-Mitarbeiter(in) (m,f) residential care officer

Wohnsiedlung (f) housing estate

Wohnsitz (m) *(ständiger)* residence, place of residence

Wohnung (f) flat, apartment; **sich eine ~ einrichten** to set up home

Wolfskind (n) *(in einer Tiergesellschaft aufgewachsenes Kind; wildes Kind)* feral child

wörtlich (adj) literal; **wörtliche Übersetzung** literal translation

Wortschatz (m) vocabulary; **passiver / aktiver** ~ passive / active vocabulary

Wunderkind (n) child prodigy, infant prodigy

Wundsein (n) *(beim Säugling)* diaper rash (US); nappy rash (Brit)

Wunsch (m) desire, wish, request

Wunschdenken (n) wishful thinking

Wunschkind (n) wanted child

Würde (f) dignity; **menschliche Würde** human dignity

würdigen (v) to appreciate, to *würfel)* dice, die

würfeln (v) to play dice

Würfelspiel (n) dice game, game of dice

Wut (f) anger, fury, rage

Wutanfall (m) fit of rage; tantrum, temper tantrum

wütend (adj) furious, to be mad

Z

Zahlung (f) payment

zahnen (v) to teethe; **Periode des Zahnens** teething stage

Zahnfee (f) tooth fairy

Zankapfel (m) bone of contention

zärtlich (adj) affectionate

Zeichenblock (m) drawing block

zeichnen (v) to draw

Zeichnung (f) drawing

Zeigefinger (m) index finger

Zeit, die eine Erzieherin mit dem Kind verbringt contact time

Zensur (f) > Note

zentrale Zielsetzung (f) core aims and objectives

zerrüttete Familienverhältnisse broken home; **zerrüttete Ehe** broken marriage

Zerstörungswut (f) vandalism

Zeugnis (n) certificate, school report

Zeugungsunfähigkeit (f) male infertility

Ziegenpeter (m) mumps

Ziel (n) aim

zielgerichtete Intervention (f) focused intervention
Zielgruppe (f) target group
Zielsetzung (f) objective; **Hauptziel** main objective
Zirkulärreaktion (f) circular reaction
Zivildienst (m) (D) (*Abk coll* **Zivi**) compulsory non-military national service; ~ **Leistender** person on compulsory non-military national service
Zone der aktuellen Entwicklung zone of actual development
Zone der nächsten Entwicklung zone of proximal development
Zorn (m) anger
zornig (adj) angry
Zufall (m) contingency
Zufallsbeobachtung (f) random observation
Zufluchtsort (m) *(fig)* haven
Zufriedenheit (f) contentment, satisfaction
zuführen (v) *(Nahrung)* to feed
Zugangstest (m) admission test
Zugangsvoraussetzung (f) entry requirement
Zugehörigkeit (f) belonging, attachment; **der Begriff der** ~ the concept of attachment; **ein Gefühl der** ~ a sense of belonging
Zuhause (n) home; **aus einem kaputten ~ kommen** to come from a broken home
Zulassungsbedingungen (f,pl) conditions of admission
Zulassungsbeschränkung (f) restriction on admission
Zulassungszahl (f) intake
Zunahme (f) increase
Zuneigung (f) affection (**zu** for, towards)
Zungenbrecher (m) tongue twister, jaw-breaker
zurückgeblieben (adj) retarded, backward, **geistig ~** mentally retarded
zurückweisen (v) to reject
Zusammenarbeit mit Eltern working together with parents
zusammenbleiben (v) to keep together, to stay together
Zusammenfassung (f) summary, résumé, *(schriftlich)* précis
zusammenflicken (v) to patch together, to patch up
zusammengehörendes Verhalten (n) linked behaviour

Zusammenkunft (f) reunion
zusammenwachsen (v) to grow together
Zusatz- *(in Zusammensetzungen) (im Sinne von Ergänzung:)* supplementary; *(im Sinne von Assistenz:)* auxiliary
Zusatzangebot (n) supplementary service
Zusatzausbildung (f) supplementary training
Zusatzleistung zum Gehalt (n) fringe benefit
Zuschuss (m) allowance
zustande bringen (v) to achieve
zuständig (adj) responsible, to be in charge; **wer ist hier zuständig?** who's in charge here?
Zuständigkeitsbereich (m) area of responsibility
zustimmen (v) *(einwilligen)* to consent, *(einer Meinung)* to agree, *(billigen)* to approve
zuteilen (v) *(z.B. Finanzmittel)* to allocate, *(jemandem eine Rolle ~)* to assign a role to somebody
Zuverlässigkeit (f) reliability
Zuwanderer, Zuwanderin (m,f) migrant
Zuwendung (f) *(finanziell)* benefit, contribution, support; *(emotional)* love and care
Zuwendungsempfänger(in) (m,f) recipient of a grant
Zwang (m) *(Notwendigkeit)* compulsion; *(Gewalt)* force; *(Druck)* pressure; **gesellschaftliche Zwänge** social constraints
Zwangsvorstellung (f) obsession
Zweideutigkeit (f) ambiguity
zweisprachig (adj) bilingual; **zweisprachige Erziehung** bilingual education
Zweisprachigkeit (f) bilingualism
Zweiter Bildungsweg (m) evening school
zweiter Vorname (m) middle name, second forename
Zweitsprache (f) second language
Zweitspracherwerb (m) second language learning / acquisition
zwiespältig (adj) ambivalent, ambiguous
Zwiespältigkeit (f) ambivalence
Zwilling (m) twin; **eineiige Zwillinge** identical twins; **zweieiige Zwillinge** fraternal twins

Zwischenbericht (m) interim report
zwischenmenschlicher Kontakt (m) interpersonal contact
Zwischenprüfung (f) interim examination

Der positive Blick auf das Kind

Bildungsprozesse von Kindern beobachtet im ersten Early Excellence Centre in Berlin
Eine Videobeobachtung von Franziska Wilke

Dieses Video zeigt Ausschnitte aus der pädagogischen Arbeit des „Kinder- und Familienzentrums Schillerstraße", einer Einrichtung des Pestalozzi-Fröbel-Hauses in Berlin. Es verfolgt anhand dreier Kinder, wie gezielte Beobachtungen eingesetzt werden können, um die individuelle Förderung von Kindern zu verbessern und die Arbeit der Erzieherinnen professioneller und transparenter zu gestalten. Damit wird eine positive Zusammenarbeit mit den Eltern ermöglicht, indem zum Beispiel Entwicklungsgespräche mit ihnen auf der Grundlage dieser Beobachtungen geführt werden können. Pädagogische Schlüsselbegriffe, die dabei erläutert werden, sind „Wohlbefinden", „Engagiertheit" und „Verhaltensmuster".

**Franziska Wilke: Der positive Blick auf das Kind.
Eine Videobeobachtung. PFH-Beiträge zur pädagogischen Arbeit,
Band 8, 30 min., 2005,
VHS: ISBN 978-3-9809179-7-1; DVD: ISBN 978-3-938620-01-4,
Preis 19,50**

Kinderbeobachtung in Kitas
Erfahrungen und Methoden im ersten Early Excellence Centre in Berlin

Eines der aufregendsten neuen pädagogischen Modelle der Tagesbetreuung für Kinder ist sicher das Konzept der englischen Early Excellence Centres, wobei hier wiederum das Pen Green Centre for Under Fives and their Families in Corby, Northamptonshire, besonders hervorsticht. Unter dem Dach von Early Excellence Centres finden sich Angebote frühkindlicher Bildung und Betreuung in Verbindung mit neuen Formen der Zusammenarbeit mit Eltern und Angeboten der Erwachsenenbildung.
Seit fünf Jahren gibt es in Berlin das erste deutsche Early Excellence Centre, das Kinder- und Familienzentrum Schillerstraße des Pestalozzi-Fröbel-Hauses. Im intensiven Austausch mit den Kolleg/innen in Corby wird in einem Modellversuch dieses Konzept erprobt und wissenschaftlich begleitet.

Sabine Hebenstreit-Müller, Barbara Kühnel (Hg.): Kinderbeobachtung in Kitas Erfahrungen und Methoden im ersten Early Excellence Centre in Berlin; PFH-Beiträge zur pädagogischen Arbeit, Band 6. 112 Seiten, zahlreiche farbige Abbildungen, ISBN 978-3-9809179-5-7, Preis 17,90 €

Growing Together at the Pen Green Centre
Ein Video aus dem „Pen Green Centre for Under Fives and their Families" in Corby

Dieses 37-Minuten-Video dokumentiert die Arbeit von Eltern-Kind-Gruppen in diesem Familienzentrum in Mittelengland. Das Konzept der „Early Excellence Centres" lässt sich an diesem Beispiel gut studieren, besonders die Themengebiete „Beobachtung" und „Arbeit mit Eltern" als auch „Wohlbefinden". Es handelt sich um ein Lehrvideo im englischen Original mit deutschen Untertiteln und eingeblendeter Zeitcodierung. Dazu gehört ein Textheft mit der kompletten deutschen Übersetzung, den eingeblendeten Texttafeln auf Deutsch und auf Englisch, eine Darstellung der Gruppen auf Englisch sowie eine Literaturliste.

The Pen Green Centre Team: Growing Together at the Pen Green Centre, Video (VHS) 37 min, mit Materialheft (40 S.), ISBN 978-3-9809179-0-2; Preis 25,00 Euro

Das Growing Together Übungsvideo
aus dem Pen Green Centre for Under Fives and their Families in Corby

Dieses Video ist die Ergänzung zu „Growing Together at the Pen Green Centre". Das Übungsvideo enthält 45 Minuten Beobachtungen von Kindern zu den Themen Wohlbefinden, Engagiertheit, Verhaltensmuster (schemas) pädagogische Strategien sowie holding / containment / attachment. Dazu gehört ein Materialheft mit 40 Seiten Erläuterungen zu diesen Begriffen sowie Anleitungen zum Umgang mit den Beobachtungen und den beigefügten Übungsbögen.

The Pen Green Centre Team: Das GrowingTogether Übungsvideo. Hg. der deutschen Ausgabe: Sabine Hebenstreit-Müller, Barbara Kühnel, 45 Minuten, mit Materialheft und Übungsanleitungen, VHS: ISBN 978-3-9809179-8-8; DVD: ISBN 978-3-938620-00-7, je 25,00 Euro

Integrative Familienarbeit in Kitas

Individuelle Förderung von Kindern und Zusammenarbeit mit Eltern

Eltern sind die ersten Erzieher ihrer Kinder und sie müssen in dieser Rolle von Erzieher/innen ernst- und angenommen werden. Durch eine enge Zusammenarbeit zwischen Erzieher/innen und Eltern kann das Kind in seinen Entwicklungs- und Bildungsschritten individuell unterstützt werden.
Wie eine solche Einbeziehung der Eltern in die Bildungsprozesse ihrer Kinder aussehen kann, welche Bedeutung dabei der Beobachtung der Kinder und der Dokumentation davon zukommt und auf welche konzeptionellen und theoretischen Überlegungen eine integrative Familienarbeit aufbaut, das wird in diesem Band dargestellt und erläutert.
Wir wollen damit einen Beitrag zur Diskussion um Fragen der Zusammenarbeit mit Eltern leisten, der zugleich auch praktische Anregungen gibt. Dies gelingt am besten, wenn man Einblicke in die konkrete Praxis „aus erster Hand" erhält. Eine Reihe von Beiträgen wurde deshalb von den Praktiker/innen selbst erstellt.

Sabine Hebenstreit-Müller, Barbara Kühnel (Hg.): Integrative Familienarbeit in Kitas Individuelle Förderung von Kindern und Zusammenarbeit mit Eltern, Beiträge zur pädagogischen Arbeit des Pestalozzi-Fröbel-Hauses, Band 9, 180 Seiten, zahlreiche farbige Abbildungen, ISBN 978-3-938620-02-1, 17,90 Euro

Als Erzieherpraktikantin in Europa
Sieben Berichte aus fünf Ländern

Am Pestalozzi-Fröbel-Haus in Berlin können Studierende im Rahmen ihrer Erzieher/innen-Ausbildung ein sechsmonatiges Praktikum im europäischen Ausland durchführen. Nach ihrer Rückkehr aus dem Ausland müssen sie einen ausführlichen Erfahrungsbericht unter einer bestimmten Themenstellung schreiben. In diesem Band finden Sie sieben solcher Erfahrungsberichte, ungekürzt, unwesentlich bearbeitet. Es geht (natürlich) um zweisprachige Erziehung in der Altersgruppe bis 6 Jahre in Frankreich und Spanien, um bestimmte Bildungsanforderungen in Frankreich und England, um die Arbeit mit Jugendlichen und jungen Erwachsenen in Fremdunterbringung in Schottland und der Schweiz - und darum, was man tut, wenn man mit völlig anderen Erziehungsvorstellungen konfrontiert wird, z.B. in Irland.

Barbara Schmitt-Wenkebach, Heidrun Schmidt (Hg.): Als Erzieherpraktikantin in Europa; Sieben Berichte aus fünf Ländern, PFH-Beiträge Band 7, 160 S., ISBN 978-3-9809179-6-4; 12,90 Euro

Dreisprachiges Wörterbuch der Pädagogik Deutsch-Türkisch-Englisch
Für die pädagogische Ausbildung und Praxis

Von Serap Sikcan, Koordinatorin des bundesweiten Projekts Kinderwelten zur vorurteilsbewussten Bildung und Erziehung in Kitas, und Wolfgang Dohrmann

In drei Teilen mit der Anordnung Deutsch-Türkisch-Englisch/Türkisch-Deutsch-Englisch sowie Englisch-Deutsch-Türkisch enthält dieses Wörterbuch rund 10.000 Stichwörter und Wendungen.

„...Brücken brauchen auch ArchitektInnen und IngenieurInnen, dazu Werkzeug und Material, damit Kommunikation und in der Folge Verständigung entstehen kann. Genau dies bietet das vorliegende dreisprachige Wörterbuch der Pädagogik. Zentrale Begriffe und damit auch Themen für das Zusammenleben mit Kindern und Familien aus verschiedenen Kulturen und für die pädagogische Arbeit in Kindertageseinrichtungen werden hier identifiziert und in drei Sprachen Deutsch, Türkisch und Englisch dargestellt.... Serap Sékcan hat als Ko-Autorin auch neue Inhalte und Themen der vorurteilsbewussten Bildung und Erziehung in die Architektur des Wörterbuches eingebracht."

Dr. Christa Preissing, Internationale Akademie (INA gGmbH) an der Freien Universität Berlin

Sikcan, Dohrmann: Wörterbuch der Pädagogik - Pedagoji Sözlügü - Dictionary of Education, 16x15 cm, 420 Seiten
ISBN 978-3-938620-03-8, 14,90 Euro

„Wolfgang Dohrmann unternimmt mit seinem ‚Wörterbuch der Pädagogik, Englisch-Deutsch' den sehr anerkennenswerten Versuch, angehenden Erzieherinnen und Erziehern, Studierenden der Erziehungswissenschaft wie auch engagierten Praktikern den Einstieg in die englischsprachige pädagogische Fachterminologie zu erleichtern. Das Wörterbuch enthält nicht nur spezielle pädagogische Fachbegriffe, sondern auch viele Begriffe aus dem allgemeinen Wortschatz, die im Bereich pädagogischen Handelns häufig vorkommen. Es handelt sich um ein Wörterbuch aus der Praxis für die Praxis. Dem Wörterbuch ist zu wünschen, dass es von Auflage zu Auflage weiter wächst und eine möglichst große Verbreitung findet."
- **Prof. Dr. Wolfgang Tietze, Arbeitsbereich Kleinkindpädagogik, Freie Universität Berlin**

„Das Wörterbuch der Pädagogik (Dictionary of Education) schließt eine Lücke in einem sonst so umfassenden Angebot an Sprachführern. Es soll als Wörterbuch für die erzieherische Ausbildung und Praxis... verstanden werden und kommt diesem Anspruch vollkommen nach...Doch auch für diejenigen Erzieherinnen, die *Europa* bereits als gesellschaftliche Perspektive angenommen haben und einen Auslandsaufenthalt (vielleicht ein Praktikum) erwägen, wird das Wörterbuch ein unentbehrlicher Reisebegleiter sein. Und schließlich darf eine Anwendung nicht vergessen werden: Mit solchem Arbeitsmaterial macht der Englischunterricht in der Erzieherausbildung endlich Sinn."
- **Dr. Roger Prott (klein & groß, 12/2003)**

„Der Mehrsprachigkeit in Einrichtungen der Kinder- und Jugendhilfe kommt in den nächsten Jahren eine immer größere Bedeutung zu. Erzieherinnen, Erzieher, Sozialpädagogen, Sozialpädagoginnen müssen sich dieser Herausforderung stellen. ... Das vorliegende Buch bietet die Möglichkeit, in den Fachschulen stärker als bisher pädagogische Materialien aus dem Ausland fachlich zu bearbeiten und somit eine anregende Diskussion über Konzepte und Entwicklungen im Ausland zu verstehen."
- **Norbert Hocke, GEW, Leiter des Organisationsbereiches Jugendhilfe und Sozialarbeit**

„I'd just like to say how very useful, actually invaluable, we find your dictionary and we'll doubtless be ordering some more next year on behalf of our new students."
- **Dr Lesley Johnson, Ketteler-La-Roche Schule, Oberursel**